Women in the Later Years: Health, Social, and Cultural Perspectives

Women
in the Later Years:
Health, Social,
and Cultural
Perspectives

Lois Grau, PhD, RN
Editor

in collaboration with
Ida Susser, PhD

The Haworth Press
New York • London

Women in the Later Years: Health, Social, and Cultural Perspectives has also been published as *Women & Health*, Volume 14, Numbers 3/4 1988.

The Haworth Press, Inc., 10 Alice Street, Binghamton, NY 13904-1580
EUROSPAN/Haworth, 3 Henrietta Street, London WC2E 8LU England

Library of Congress Cataloging-in-Publication Data

Women in the later years.

    Published also as Women & health, v. 14, no. 3/4.
    Includes bibliographical references.
    1. Aged women – United States – Social conditions. 2. Aged women – Health and hygiene – United States. 3. Aged women – Cross-cultural studies. I. Grau, Lois. II. Susser, Ida.
HQ1064.U5W6   1989   305.4   88-35826
ISBN 0-86656-888-3

We wish to acknowledge the important contributions of the Brookdale Research Institute on Aging of the Third Age Center, Fordham University, which were critical in making this special issue possible. Particular thanks goes to the Institute's Director, Marjorie H. Cantor, University Professor and Brookdale Distinguished Scholar; the Brookdale Doctoral Fellows, Eileen Chichin and Tina Mendis; and the Institute Secretary, Madeline Nugent.

ABOUT THE EDITOR

Lois Grau, RN, PhD, is the Director of the Nerken Center for Geriatric Research, a unit of the Jewish Institute for Geriatric Care located in New Hyde Park, New York. She was formerly the Associate Director of the Brookdale Research Institute on Aging of the Third Age Center, Fordham University. Dr. Grau, a teacher, researcher, and writer in the field of gerontology and the delivery of long-term care within the U.S., has also conducted research in Great Britain.

Women in the Later Years: Health, Social, and Cultural Perspectives

CONTENTS

Introduction

The past twenty or so years have seen the emergence, explosive growth, and general acceptance of specialized policy, practice and research in aging. References to our "aging society" or to the "demographic shift" of the population are commonplace, familiar to lay persons as well as to gerontologists. Despite the recognition of the aging of human populations, a great deal is yet to be learned about the later years of life and the articulation of older persons within societal structures, both now and in the future.

This special volume attempts to touch upon a number of current issues and concerns within gerontology. The overarching focus is on older women rather than the elderly as a whole. This is because, in large measure, aging is a women's issue. Women live longer than men, but also tend to be poorer and less healthy than men who survive into old age. Women's social roles and relationships in old age also differ from those of men. While the majority of elderly men are married or remarried at the time of their deaths, most older women are widows. Other important events which signify stages in a woman's life also may be different from the events which demarcate life stages for men. These differences cumulate over the lifecourse influencing how old age is perceived and lived. Moreover, societal changes which have affected women's relationships to their families and to the marketplace will alter the face of aging for future cohorts of older women.

This collection of articles reviews the process of aging for women from four different perspectives: intergenerational relations and public policy, health and well-being, social support, and ethnic and cross cultural perspectives. These themes were chosen because they reflect areas which have only recently been empirically investigated and which have important health and social policy implications.

The first section on intergenerational relationships and public

1

policy attempts to bring together the related notions of intergenerational exchanges as they occur within society at large and within individual family units. Faulkner and Micchelli overview the relationship between current public policy and women's roles as family caregivers. Their critique underscores the need for family-centered policies which address the economic and social needs of women whose lives are circumscribed by their responsibilities for the care of frail parents or spouses. Catchen focuses on the controversies surrounding the concept of intergenerational equity. He argues convincingly that the issue is not the young versus the old, but rather social class divisions which cut across age groups and determine the need for public programs and services. The section concludes with a paper by Cantor and Hirshborn which deals with the intriguing and only partially explored issue of why families care for each other across generations. They provide a conceptual framework for the investigation of the various cultural and emotional factors which motivate intergenerational exchanges and support.

The second section on health and well-being includes overviews of important physical and mental health concerns of older women, addresses health service delivery issues, and reports the finding of empirical studies which focus on specific health problems. The section begins with the Older Women's League report on the health of midlife and older women. The report gives an overview of women's most important health problems and the failure of the public and private sectors to provide adequate health resources and services. This is followed by Grau's paper on mental health problems of older women and gaps in mental health services targeted to the elderly. The issue of service delivery is then directed at the provision of nonprofessional homecare to the frail elderly. Chichin describes the role and job-related problems and satisfactions of women who care for the elderly as homecare workers. Little is known about this group of workers despite their critical importance in supplementing family care for the frail elderly who continue to reside in the community. We then move to one of the most important health concerns of women — osteoporosis. Roberto reports the findings of a study which investigated stress and adaptation patterns among women suffering from this disfiguring and disabling condition. The last paper, by Magaziner and Cadigan, is concerned with the utilization of health and community services by older women who live alone and compares their utilization patterns with women who live with adult children.

One of the most important concerns of older women is the maintenance of family ties and friendships throughout old age, which is the next section of this special volume. Although a great deal of attention has been given to social supports and health among the general population, relatively little is known about family and friendship relations among older women. This section includes Lewittes' consideration of a number of theories and perspectives on friendship and social support for women. Her discussion is highlighted by the findings of two studies of friendship among socially involved older women. This paper is complemented by Lubben's investigation of relationships between social support, health status, and widowhood on psychological well-being among low income elderly women. The paper challenges the assumption that family relations are more important for well-being than involvement with friends. Last is Reinhardt and Fisher's study of friendship and morale, which investigates the relative importance of daughters and friends for the morale of older widows and underscores the importance of mother/daughter relationships.

The last section includes a number of perspectives on ethnicity and culture as it influences the experience of growing old. Padgett's paper explores the quadruple jeopardy experienced by older minority women as well as the adaptive strengths and resources minority women utilize in developing strategies for survival. We then move from a consideration of race/ethnicity to the status of older women in nonindustrial societies. Foner highlights the power accorded to older women by virtue of their age and the consequences of this power on the lives of younger women. She points to how, in each society, the distribution of resources, marriage patterns and rules of inheritance shape relations between generations of women. The life of older Puerto Rican women is illustrated by Sánchez-Ayéndez's ethnographic study which underscores the importance of culture in shaping social roles and relationships within and outside of the family. The last paper, by Heisel, is of particular interest for its critical review of stereotypes which suggest that families can and do provide care to the elderly in Third World countries. She argues that aging is a hidden, unacknowledged problem in many poor countries where families lack the resources to adequately care for their members, regardless of age.

Lois Grau, PhD, RN

The Aging, the Aged, and the Very Old:
Women the Policy Makers Forgot

Audrey Olsen Faulkner
Margaret Micchelli

SUMMARY. The nation's policy on aging has not adequately addressed the disjuncture between the compelling increase in the number of aged and the changing family and social roles of women. There is a continuum of mid-life, aged and very old women engaged in inter-generational exchange of care, who have unmet needs both as care givers and care receivers. Shortcomings in public policy arrangements are discussed, along with proposals for a national policy on aging that focuses on the family as a caring unit.

INTRODUCTION

Changes in the demographics of aging, and the changes in the status of women have been rapid and dramatic in recent decades. The population 65 and over has grown from 22.4 million in 1975, to 26.8 million in 1982. Estimates are that by the year 2000, 35 million Americans, or more than thirteen percent, will be over age

Audrey Olsen Faulkner is Professor, School of Social Work, and Margaret Micchelli is a doctoral student, School of Social Work, Rutgers, The State University of New Jersey, New Brunswick, NJ 08903.

65 (Lowy, 1985). The fastest growing subgroup of this older population is made up of those over 75; this is also the group for whom the probability of chronic health problems and functional impairment is greatest.

More than three million women between the ages of 35 and 54 returned to the labor market during the 1970s; and the number of women over 50 who are in paid employment is increasing (Porcino, 1983). In 1982, 52.6 percent of women in metropolitan areas, and 49.8 percent of rural women were in the paid labor force (Morris, 1986).

The nation's policy on aging has not adequately adapted to the longer life and attendant frailty of the aged, to women's changing role in the family and the society, or to the relationship between the two. There is an increasing disjuncture between the policy on aging and the needs of mid-life aging women, aged women, and very old women.

Policies aimed at providing benefits to the elderly affected women in larger numbers than men, for the world of the old is increasingly female (Haug, 1985). In 1981 the average national life expectancy for women was 77.9 years, and for men it was 70.3 years, a difference of 7 1/2 years (Hammond, 1986). While rates of growth and life expectancies of American minority groups differ somewhat from the general averages, the direction of change is the same (McNeely and Colen, 1983).

The Family Is the Locus of Care for the Aged

The family has always been considered the basic unit for delivering care and nurturance to the society's members. The nuclear family, consisting of mother, father and minor children has been the American ideal for many decades, but only one out of seven households in the United States now conforms to this model. However, even though family members may live in separate households, the accumulated evidence suggests the continuity of intergenerational ties and assistance (Sussman, 1965). The concept of a "modified extended family" is used to describe this type of family arrangement (Cohler, 1983).

The greater longevity of females, along with the increase in divorce and the addition of paid employment to the homemaking labor of women, have further changed the structure of the family. It is not now uncommon for a family to consist of one generation that includes a young woman, her spouse and young children (or a young woman with children but no spouse present); a mid-life woman who is divorced or widowed, or is caring for an ailing husband, and third and fourth generation women who have outlived spouses and sons. One or more of these women may be employed for pay outside the home. That this family does not live under one roof may affect the details of daily interaction, but it does not alter the identification of the members as belonging to a single family, or eliminate the rights and obligations that accompany family membership. Its members sustain intergenerational ties through the exchange of emotional and instrumental support involving services, gifts, time, money, advice, caregiving and emotional support (Foner, 1986).

Although family forms have changed, and there have been role shifts for women to paid work outside the home, the family's central function of providing care and support for its older members has not changed.

Women Are the Primary Caregivers to the Aged

Neither has there been a noticeable shift in primary responsibility for the family's caregiving function. It rests with the women of the family, who are most often at the heart of the intergenerational exchange between the older and the younger members (Brody, 1981, 1985). Elderly women provide care for ill or disabled spouses, even though they may be limited by their own aging processes and health problems (Snyder and Keefe, 1985). When a woman is unable to provide assistance to her elderly spouse or she herself needs care, it is usually the middle aged or young-old daughter or daughter-in-law who assumes responsibility for caregiving (Shanas, 1979). In fact, empirical evidence points to gender as the most important and consistent predictor of caregiving to elders (Houser, Berkman and Bardsley, 1985).

Several studies point to the importance of acknowledging racial and cultural differences in both family structures and caretaking behavior (Mutran, 1985; Hanson, Sauer and Seelbach, 1983). While socioeconomic status and value differences may account for variations in the amount of caregiving, it is still the woman in most cases who is the primary caregiver.

Women's Caregiving Responsibilities —
the Aging Continuum

At each stage of the life cycle, women fulfill a variety of roles. Some of the major roles and responsibilities of the stages from mid-life on, and their implications for caregiving/care receiving follow. The literature has focused on the "sandwich generation" (Miller, 1981) and in particular, the "woman in the middle" (Brody, 1981). These mid-life aging women, aged 40 to 60, are coping with multiple and sometimes competing responsibilities for both the younger and the older generation, being in the middle of a generational line of women that may extend four or five generations. One study found a "crisis accumulation" in women 40 to 50 years of age.

> [women] very often were confronted with the role of a mother, mother-in-law or even grandmother on the one hand, and with the role of daughter or daughter-in-law of aged parents who need help and care, on the other hand. (Lehr, 1984)

Young-old women, age 60 to 75, face many of the same issues. Many who have formerly experienced the "empty nest" may find that they have renewed responsibilities toward younger generations due to changing economic circumstances. Adult children may move into the home of aging parents or require their assistance with child care. The responsibilities of their grandparent role may be expanded. They may be providing the services for an aging spouse that prevents his institutionalization. In a study of 753 noninstitutionalized older people, Stoller (1982) found that elderly men were more likely than women to name their spouse as a source of help during a period of disability. Foner (1986) reports that older men depend on marriage for emotional support more than older women do.

At the same time, they may be actively engaged in care of their parents. Lang and Brody (1983) found that those women over 50 years of age had more responsibilities for parent care than those in their 40s. This suggests that women who are dealing with their own aging process and developmental tasks, such as their or their spouse's retirement planning, are also actively involved with their parents' aging process. Schmidt (1980) refers to this as the "parallel aging of interlocking generations."

Finally, there is the situation of the old-old woman, 75 or more. Her grandparent and great-grandparent roles may continue, although multiple losses of family and friends are likely. Reduced physical functioning is an increased probability. In spite of the fact that there are many vigorous old women, and functional dependency is not unexpected. Blenker (1969) discussed the "normal dependencies of old age," including economic, physical, mental and social dependency, stressing that these were neither unusual or pathological at this late phase of the life cycle. When these dependencies occur, women family members are expected to provide care; however, twenty-five percent of women 70 or over have no living children, and over sixty percent of them are widowed, divorced or single (Lewis, 1985). This group of women often has devoted considerable time to caregiving, but has outlived those who might have cared for them.

It is evident that there is a continuum of mid-life aging women, young-old women, and old-old women who provide the major share of caregiving within families, and who also require such help themselves.

This summary overview of the multiple roles and responsibilities of aging women raises several issues. One is the reciprocal responsibility for family members, both in the younger and older generations. Women must negotiate the balance between autonomy and interdependence at each phase of the life cycle. Furthermore, as women age, there is the likelihood that interdependence will be replaced with dependency, and diminished capacity and opportunity for reciprocity. Another issue is whether the feasible limits of caregiving have contracted as women's work roles have expanded beyond the home and family. There is the issue of the appropriate and reasonable division of responsibility for caregiving tasks and services between the women of the family and the society. Finally, but beyond the scope of this paper, there is the individual responsibility of each woman for her own well being.

Are There Limits on Caregiving for the Aged in the Family?

As previously noted, Blenkner (1969) regarded the dependencies of old age as normal. She conceptualized filial maturity as a developmental stage characterized by adult childrens' care of aged parents. However, the life stage of caregiving for an older family member may occur at the chronological age of 40, 50 or 65, or even older. Also, a woman's response to this new role is influenced by the specific combination of factors in her own life — marriage, children, work, finances, etc. Brody (1985) challenges the notion that filial maturity (or the acceptance of caretaking responsibilities) is exclusively a function of psychological maturity or resolution. She argues that caregiving for the aged in the family may be, instead, a normative life experience for women given the current demographics of aging.

There is a broad range of response by women to family caregiving need. The motivating factors behind the willingness to give help are varied (Hess and Waring, 1978). Some adult children view it as an obligation to return the care given to them by their parents. Others view it as "credits" earned that will be returned to them by their own children should they need assistance in their old age. In some instances, it is an internalized cultural or religious value (Kingson, Hirshorn and Cornman, 1986).

Conversely, there are reasons why a family member would be reluctant to make the compromises involved in caregiving. Perhaps an earlier conflict with the parent has been revived and this creates an obstacle to giving care freely. There may be attitude differences that are a source of strain in the relationship. As previously mentioned, the real-life competing responsibilities of the middle-age child may be impossible to reconcile with the parent's current needs. For example, a 45-year-old woman with a responsible professional position travels a great deal in her work. How much is she expected to give up in order to care for her parents? What is the appropriate or normative standard under these circumstances?

There is a limited societal response to the needs of aging and old family members, male or female, who need care. When assistance is needed, the usual pattern is for families, primarily daughters of daughters-in-law, to give most of the help until the breaking point is reached and institutionalization becomes inevitable (Kingson, Hirshorn and Cornman, 1986). If the young-old woman is giving care to a dependent spouse or to an old-old parent, there again is little social support to prevent her from compromising her own physical or emotional health through the strain of caregiving (Cantor, 1983). However, there is no normative standard about what degree of filial responsibility is appropriate to what degree of parental dependency, or how much care women should be expected to give to the older members of the family and under what circumstances. When families do all that they can until the situation becomes intolerable, it is the three groups of mature women — midlife, young-old and old-old, who suffer the most under the arrangement. If this burden is to be lessened, implicit norms about women's caregiving roles will need scrutiny.

Demographic Trends That May Affect Caregiving and Receiving

As the number of elderly rises, a crises in caregiving is predictable. There will be more elderly needing care, and too few family caregivers to provide it. Women are the primary caregivers from mid-life on; they are also the major proportion of those needing care. The older a women is, the more likely she is to be without younger women who are obligated by family bond to care for her. This situation may become even more pronounced for future cohorts of the old. These are some of the trends that can be expected to affect caregiving and the availability of family caregivers:

1. The current trend toward increasingly adequate economic resources in old age may be reversed for substantial numbers of women, as their economic responsibilities for themselves and their children increases. The growing concentration of poverty in households headed by women (Dinerman, 1986) portends an even more difficult struggle for women to balance their work role and their family caregiving role. Two groups of women are especially vul-

nerable: (1) very young women, unmarried, whose assumption of the single parental role is more an artifact of youth and ignorance about the probability of impregnation and the costs and consequences of parenthood than a deliberately chosen state; (2) mid-life women, once married, who are caretakers of children, and who have chosen to exit from marriages that had more problems than strengths, or whose husbands have chosen other pursuits, other wives and newer families, abandoning responsibility for the old. Difficulty in earning a living for self and family, and finding time and strength for caregiving to either the younger or older generation, can be anticipated. As these women age, their health needs may be greater, reflecting the poorer health care their low incomes have purchased throughout their younger years. Their need for care, then, may be greater, while their economic resources for their own care will be scanty.

2. Reconstituted families resulting from divorce-remarriage, are increasing. In these families, there are complex and undefined reciprocal relationships between the in-laws and the child-parent-grandparent generations. Whereas it is assumed that a mid-life woman may have caregiving responsibilities for her mother and her husband's mother, in a re-constituted family she may, in addition, be needed to care for her step-mother and her husbands's step-mother.

3. Women are having fewer children, having them later, and are assuming, either by choice or necessity, more economic responsibility for them. This results in these mothers being less available to provide care to elders in the family now and in the near future. It also foretells fewer prospective caregivers when these women become old and frail themselves.

Shortcomings in Public Policy Arrangements

The Effects of Public Policy on Aging
Are Not Gender-Neutral

Public policy on aging is assumed to be gender-neutral. In actuality, however, treating women and men equally acts to the disadvantage of women, who carry an unequal share of the caregiving.

1. Current Medicaid policies require that a couple spend down almost all of its resources for whichever spouse needs nursing home care before Medicaid will assume nursing home costs. The effect of this policy is to impoverish the remaining spouse. Since men tend to be older than their wives, and therefore experience the frailty of old age in advance of their wives, this often means that services for the husband, both in the home and later in an institution, will be paid from the couple's resources, leaving the wife to live out her years in want. Since women, as a class, outlive men, as a class, the Medicaid policy has a differential negative impact on them. Some elderly wives, in order to survive, must resort to legal separations and a suit against their institutionalized spouse for maintenance (NASW, 1987).

2. Public policy places more emphasis upon services that replace the family than on services that support the family. Moroney (1976) points out that ideally policies should support the family when it needs support and substitute for it when it does not exist or is incapable of meeting its members' needs. However, there is a strong American heritage of favoring a residual, rather than an institutional approach (Wilinsky and Lebeaux, 1958) to the provision of social services. The residual philosophical stance is that only when the family has used up its total resources is the public provision of services defensible. The institutional approach advocates the provision of adequate and equitable social arrangements to support the family in its social and economic tasks, thereby avoiding family breakdown.

The paucity of publicly financed and available supportive services to assist the families of older people living in the community has the effect of creating a requirement for a "spend down" on the physical and emotional energy of the caregiver (in addition to the economic spend down), before public services can come into the picture. There is often an unspoken assumption that female caregivers will manage without support until their emotional exhaustion or stress produced physical illness creates a crisis in caregiving, to which the community will finally make a crisis response.

The threat of overexpenditure of self hangs most heavily over female caregivers. There is less likelihood that this same spend down expectation will be applied to males; their taking on the care-giving role is generally seen as novel and outside of usual role demands. Usually men are primary caregivers only in those cases when, by default, there are no women in the family to assume the role (Horowitz, 1985).

3. Public policy favors the delivery of services in institutional settings rather than in the homes of the aged. The old and their families overwhelmingly favor home care, and most families do not make a decision to institutionalize an older member until all family and community resources have been exhausted. In spite of this strong consumer preference, services that conserve the emotional and physical energy of the caretaker while contributing to the well being of the person needing care, are in short supply for any but affluent families. Homemaker service, home health care, adult day care, companion services and respite care are inadequately financed under Medicaid, and provided to the aged in their homes with stringent eligibility and use restrictions. National health policy skews public expenditures toward long-term nursing home care and short-term acute hospital care (Kaye, 1985). This imbalance between public expenditure for in-home services and those that are institutionally based creates two hardships for families. First, family caretakers have inadequate or no assistance available to them for keeping their older members in the community. Second, they and the older family member are faced with the painful decision to seek a nursing home placement, whether or not that is the most appropriate solution. This imbalance between home delivered services and institutionally delivered services contributes materially to the physical and emotional burden of caregivers. There is, of course, personal satisfaction to be derived from being a loving and competent caregiver (Simon, 1986), but while this may help to mediate the burden, it cannot eliminate the jeopardy.

Policies Have Not Incorporated Changes
That Reflect the Mass Entry of Women
into the Paid Labor Force

As primary caregivers to the young as well as the old, and as primary or co-breadwinners for the family, women may find the competing demands inside and outside the home a source of intense stress. Consider the case of a woman who has young children and who works outside the home. Her own mother needs continual supervision of activities of daily living. What are the options? She can (1) contribute financially if she is able, to supplement paid help; (2) provide the care herself; (3) bring the parent into her home; or, (4) share some aspects of the care with other siblings if they are available. Her real options are few, and her difficult choices for the distribution of her time and effort are themselves a source of stress, apart from the caregiving labor that is required of her.

Policies About Services for the Aged
Are Not Directed Toward Them
as Family Members but as Individuals

The defined beneficiaries of services for the aged are individuals, not family units. This may result in recognition of the individual aged person's need, without concomitant recognition of the needs of the caregiver (Kamerman and Kahn, 1978). Since caregivers are drawn primarily from women's ranks, this failure to consider the family as the unit for service impacts inequitably upon women.

Some Proposals for Reform
in National Aging Policy

Public social welfare policy is notably intransigent, even in the face of documented experience and predictable crisis, as historical review of proposals for welfare reform will attest. The current social mood tends toward still another redefinition of individuals and families as having more responsibility, and the society having less, for meeting the needs associated with aging and being old. Under these circumstances, women from the mid-life generation on may soon find themselves and the women they care for even more imperiled. Aging is a woman's issue (Faulkner, 1980; Russell, 1987) and it is urgent that professional women, especially those in the caring professions, promote an agenda for social change.

Policy, while recognizing the heterogeneity of the aging and aged population, should be gender responsive. Policies would take account of the special situation of women as the majority occupants of the ranks of the old, while not ignoring the situation of men. This may mean, for example, that women need to be considered as separate economic units in the family or household so that the spend down provisions for medical care of spouses do not operate in ways that impoverish them. Where funds are available, contributions should be made to the care of the spouse, but the marriage assets should be distributed between the parties in such a way that the remaining spouse need not give up the autonomy and dignity that accompany financial independence.

It may be time to consider whether marital status should guide eligibility requirements and the distribution of benefits to older persons. Care giving, receiving, and exchanging relationships, rather than legal marital ties, might figure in such determination. It may be a caring unit, rather than a marriage unit, that is appropriate for the receipt of assistance when financial or personal energy resources are not sufficient to support the needs of any one of the generations in the family.

New norms for the appropriate sharing of reward and burden between the sexes, the generations and the public/private sector are needed. Women are unlikely to give up the emphasis on caregiving which has been a traditional female sphere; however, changes in the life situation of women, and the longer lives of the elderly, presage a caregiving crunch that will demand attention. The present day expectations for self sufficiency of the caregiving women in the family are becoming increasingly unrealistic in view of smaller family sizes, the paid labor force participation of women, and increased longevity and resultant greater fragility of many elders.

Policies need to be cohort responsive. Cohort analysis of the younger age groups and the context in which they can be expected to grow old is the best predictor of future need (Riley, 1985). A more proactive approach to policy making would reflect anticipated demographic shifts in economics, health and education, as well as changes in life expectancy and family configurations. Such an analysis, for example, would take account of the possibility that the increased number of female household heads who are poor may lead in the future to a large group of impoverished older women, thereby reversing the present trend to relatively more economic affluence that is now in process for people presently old.

Today's young women are tomorrow's older women. A policy that supports and fosters the interdependence of the generations would diffuse and discredit the present argument that benefits being provided to the old by the society are at the expense of the young, and are consuming resources that rightfully belong to younger generations. Women know that their welfare cannot be separated from that of other women, young and old.

Services are needed, along with good access, to support female caregivers at a point early enough in the course of a long-term caring episode to prevent the stress that is now the burden of many of those women who care for the older generations.

This nation has never reached adequate consensus to support a family policy aimed at the welfare of children. Its policy for care for the aging and the old is fragmented and unresponsive to the special situation of women as caregivers and care receivers. It may be that the crisis in the welfare of children, and the near crisis in the welfare of the old, can point us in the direction of a national family policy that would treat the needs of all members of the family, including children and the aged, as inter-related. A policy addressing the welfare of all the generations in the family could deal with the needs of all members, including mid-life, aging, and old women, more equitably and effectively.

REFERENCES

Blenkner, M. (1969). The normal dependencies of aging. In R. Kalish (Ed.), The dependencies of old people (pp. 27-38). Ann Arbor, MI: Institute for Gerontology.

Brody,, E. M. (1985). Parent care as a normative family stress. *Gerontologist*, *25*, 19-29.

Brody, E. M. (1981). "Women in the middle" and family help to older people. *Gerontologist, 21*, 471-480.

Candor, M. H. (1983). Strain among caregivers: a study of experience in the U.S. *Gerontologist, 23*, 597-604.

Cohler, B. (1983). Autonomy and interdependence in the family of adulthood: a psychological perspective. *Gerontologist, 23*, 33-39.

Dinerman, M. (1986). The woman trap: women and poverty. In N. Van Den

Bergh & Lynn B. Cooper (Eds.), Feminist visions for social work (pp. 229-249). Silver Spring, MD: National Association of Social Workers.

Faulkner, A. (1980). Aging and Old Age: The Last Sexist Rip-Off. In E. Norman & A. Mancuso (Eds.), Women's issues and social work practice (pp. 57-89). Itasca, Il: F. E. Peacock Publishers, Inc.

Foner, A. (1986). Aging and old age. Englewood Cliffs, NJ: Prentice-Hall.

Hammond, D. B. (1986). Health care for older women: curing the disease. In M.J. Bell (Ed.), Women as elders: images, visions, and issues (pp. 59-69). New York: The Haworth Press, Inc.

Hanson, S. L., Sauer, W. J., & Seelbach, W. C. (1983). Racial and cohort variations in filial responsibility norms. *Gerontologist, 23*, 626-631.

Haug, M. R., Ford, A. B., & Sheafor, M. (1985). The physical and mental health of aged women. New York: Springer Publishing Co.

Hess, B. & Waring, J. M. (1978). Parent and child in later life: rethinking the relationship. In R. Lerner & G. Spanier (Eds.), Child influences on marital and family interaction (pp. 241-273). New York: Academic Press.

Horowitz, A. (1985). Sons and daughters as caregivers to older parents: differences in role performance and consequences. *Gerontologist, 25*, 612-617.

Houser, B. B., Berkman, S. L., & Bardsley, P. (1985). Sex and birth order differences in filial behavior. *Sex Roles, 13* 641-651.

Kamerman, S. B. & Kahn, A. J. (1978). Family policy: government and families in fourteen countries. New York: Columbia University Press.

Kaye, L. W. (1985). Homecare. In A. Monk (Ed.), Handbook of gerontological services (pp. 408-432).

Kingson, E. R., Hirshorn, B. A., & Cornman, J. M. (1986). Ties that bind: the interdependence of generations. Washington, DC: Seven Locks Press.

Lang, A. M. & Brody, E. M. (1983). Characteristics of middle-aged daughters and help to their elderly mothers. *Journal of Marriage and the Family, 45*, 193-201.

Lehr, U. (1984). The role of women in the family generation context. In V. Garms-Homelova, E. M. Hoerning & D. Schaeffer (Eds.), Intergenerational relationships (pp. 125-132). Lewiston, NY: C. J. Hogrefe.

Lewis, M. (1985). Older women and health: an overview. *Women & Health, 10*, 1-16.

Lowy, L. (1985). Social work with the aging. New York: Longman Inc.

McNeely, R. L. & Colen, J. L. (1983). Aging in Minority Groups. Beverly Hills, CA: Sage Publications.

Miller, D. A. (1981). The "sandwich" generation: adult children of the aging. *Social Work, 26*, 419-423.

Moroney, R. M. (1976). The family and the state: considerations for social policy. New York: Longman Group Limited.

Morris, L. C. (1986). The changing and unchanging status of rural women in the workplace. *Affilia: Journal of Women and Social Work, 1*, 20-29.

Mutran, E. (1985). Intergenerational family support among blacks and whites:

response to culture or to socioeconomic differences. *Journal of Gerontology, 40*, 382-389.

NASW NEWSLETTER (1987). Silver Spring, MD: National Association of Social Workers.

Porcino, J. (1983). Growing Older, Getting Better. Reading, MA: Addison-Wesley Publishing Company.

Riley, M. (1985). The changing older woman: a cohort perspective. In Haug, M. R., Ford, A. B. & Sheafor, M. (Eds.), The Physical and Mental Health of Aged Women (pp. 3-15). New York: Springer Publishing Co.

Russell, C. (1987). Aging as a feminist issue. *Women's Studies International Forum, 10*, 125-132.

Schmidt, M. G. (1980). Failing parents, aging children. *Journal of Gerontological Social Work, 2*, 259-268.

Shanas, E. (1979). The family as a social support system in old age. *Gerontologist, 19*, 169-174.

Simon, B. L. (1986). Never-married women as caregivers to elderly parents: some costs and benefits. *Affilia: Journal of Women and Social Work, 1*, 29-42.

Snyder, B. & Keefe, K. (1985). The unmet needs of family caregivers for frail and disabled adults. *Social Work in Health Care, 10*, 1-14.

Stroller, E. P. (1982). Sources of support for the elderly during illness. *Health and Social Work, 1*, 111-122.

Sussman, M. B. (1965). The family life of older people. In R. H. Binstock & E. Shanas (Eds.), Handbook of Aging and the Social Sciences (pp. 62-92). New York: Van Nostrand Reinhold.

Wilensky, H. L. & Lebeaux, C. N. (1958). Industrial society and social welfare. New York: Russell Sage Foundation.

Generational Equity:
Issues of Gender and Race

Harvey Catchen

SUMMARY. Recent attempts to portray the relative affluence of the current generation of older Americans as causing economic hardship for younger generations are examined in this paper. This argument, commonly referred to as the "generational equity" thesis, ignores the basic issues of gender and race. We argue that: the elderly are more sharply stratified into rich and poor than younger groups, the official poverty level used by the federal government underestimates the number of poor older persons living in poverty, and that older women and minorities have disturbingly high rates of poverty. Reducing current federal benefit levels to the elderly would do little to alleviate the problems experienced by younger generations, and would cause severe hardship for many older people. Women and minorities would be especially hard hit by such reductions since they are more likely to be poor than white males.

In recent years there has been a dramatic shift in the way that the elderly are depicted in both the academic and popular literature. In the 1960s and early 1970s most writers spoke of the widespread poverty and isolation of old age. This image of the elderly was an important element in building political momentum which resulted in the enactment of Medicare and Social Security amendments which increased benefit levels. Recently, a new image of the aged has appeared in the literature. They are seen as relatively affluent, not paying their fair share of taxes, and as recipients of a disproportionately high percentage of all federal benefits. This new view of older Americans began to emerge in the last years of the Carter Administration when the country was faced with high unemploy-

Harvey Catchen is affiliated with Department of Community Health and Biological Sciences, SUNY/College, Old Westbury, NY 11568.

ment, mounting inflation, and a growing crisis in the Social Security system (Binstock, 1983).

This phenomenon of a "backlash" against the gains made by older Americans in the public policy arena in the last two decades can itself have significant policy consequences. Bergman (1986) has suggested that the hidden agenda of these critics is the dismantling of the entire Social Security System. The academic and interest group advocates of this new image of the elderly argue for a shift in the allocation of federal resources away from programs for the elderly. It is therefore important to carefully analyze the arguments presented, and the data about the socio-economic status of the aged population relative to younger segments of the population. This paper builds upon earlier works which have addressed these issues (Minkler, 1987; Binstock, 1983; Kingston et al., 1986; and *On the Other Side of Easy Street*, 1987). I shall argue that those who depict the elderly as relatively affluent ignore social class as a major variable which increases in significance as people age, and miss the fact that a large group of the elderly, primarily women, continue to live in extreme poverty.

The next section of this paper summarizes the arguments of writers who articulate this new view of older Americans, commonly referred to as the "generational equity" thesis. Then we look at the current economic status of the elderly. Data is presented to support the following arguments:

- The elderly are more sharply stratified into rich and poor than are younger groups.
- The official poverty level used by the government underestimates the number of elderly living in poverty.
- Older women and ethnic minorities have disturbingly high rates of poverty.

THE GENERATIONAL EQUITY THESIS

Perhaps the most systematic attempt to reverse the image of the elderly in society can be found in the writings of the demographer, Samuel Preston. His work first appeared in *Demography* (1984A) and in a slightly revised form received much wider circulation in *Scientific American* (1984B). Preston begins his argument by observing that in recent decades there has been a sharp drop in fertility rates in the American population. The number of children has been declining, while the number of elderly has increased dramatically. Classical demographic theory would predict that children would now have more favorable life chances while the condition of older people would deteriorate since many would have to compete for scarce resources. Preston, however, argues, ". . . that exactly the opposite trends have occurred in the relatively well-being of our two groups of age dependents . . . conditions have deteriorated for children and improved dramatically for the elderly . . ." (1984A). To support his thesis Preston presents data to show that government spending for children has been cut back while spending for the elderly is increasing. This has been reflected in declining school performance, an increasing number of single parent families, and higher suicide rates among children. In contrast, the mortality rate among the elderly has been declining, the percentage living under the federal poverty level has decreased dramatically, suicide rates have declined, and decreased labor force participation has occurred among older adults. Preston assumes that older persons are now doing so well that they no longer need to work. Although Preston ends his *Scientific American* article by cautioning that he does not want, ". . . to paint the elderly as the villains of the piece. I am primarily concerned about the fate of children. . . ." The message is clear: federal spending is a zero sum game. The more we selfishly invest in our elderly population, the less there will be available to support the needs of children. In the conclusion to his *Demography* article Preston warns that if we truly care about future generations we will have to invest more on the young! Only if we act selfishly (we all hope to get old) will we continue to invest so extensively in the requirements of older Americans (1984A).

There are two major problems with Preston's analysis. Reductions in federal spending for children which Preston documents, such as aid to dependent children, social service block grants, child health, and Headstart, are programs designed to serve poor children and their families. These benefits are funded from general tax revenues. The principal programs that serve the elderly, Social Security and Medicare, are both funded through a separate payroll tax. Savings generated by cutbacks in these benefits could not be used to fund programs that serve the poor. The primary beneficiary of reductions in the Social Security payroll tax would be large corporations which must match employee contributions to the Social Security trust fund.

The major general tax revenue program which serves the elderly is Medicaid. Designed originally to pay for the health care needs of the poor, 38 percent of all Medicaid dollars went to meet the health care needs of older Americans in 1985 (Fast Facts and Figures about Social Security, 1987). Most of these funds went to cover the cost of long-term care services. Since almost all aged persons currently receiving such care are extremely ill, and reside in nursing homes, it is hard to see how this benefit could be realistically curtailed. Recent cutbacks in spending for the poor are not a new historical phenomena. Historically, aid to the poor has always been the first type of service to be reduced in times of fiscal austerity. When Preston talks about lower academic standards in schools, the increase of single parent families, and of rising suicide rate among teenagers, he is documenting broad historical trends. While it may be accurate to say that massive federal spending could ameliorate some of these problems, the government has never contemplated such a massive reallocation of federal funds. Nowhere in his work does Preston call for such a redistribution of funds to address the worsening condition of children in our society.

Recently, a new national organization, Americans for Generational Equity (AGE), has received wide media attention and has become the primary advocate of the generational equity thesis. Most of the board of directors of AGE are top corporate managers, and representatives of conservative organizations such as the American Enterprise Institute and the Heritage Foundation. In contrast to Preston who argues that the children are being neglected in order to serve the needs of the elderly, AGE is primarily concerned with the economic burdens such federal support presents to the baby boom generation. Like Preston's poor children, baby boomers are seen as suffering so the current generation of older adults can live a life of affluence.

In his opening statement to the first AGE conference, Senator Durenberger began by observing that the current generation of young American families have been finding it increasingly difficult to achieve the level of economic prosperity of their parents. In the 1950s the average American male experienced a 188 percent gain in income as he passed from age 25 to 35. During the 1960's the average gain in income made by this age group was 128 percent. In the 1970's the gain in income made by the average American male passing from age 25 to 35 slowed to only 16 percent. At the same time, Americans experienced a tremendous increase in inflation. This rise in inflation hit young Americans hardest when they wanted to buy a home. In 1949 the cost of mortgage payments on a median priced home for the average 30-year-old was 14 percent of his income. By 1984 the mortgage payment on a similar home was now 44 percent of the average 30-year-old's income (Durenberger, 1986).

Philip Longman (1987), AGE's research director, points to a number of other disturbing economic and social realities experienced by the baby boom generation. Most distressing is a series of two tier union contracts negotiated in many industries. In such contracts, newly hired younger workers are paid significantly less than older workers. Other disturbing economic indicators include: the tremendous increase in foreign imports, a mounting federal debt, and an increasing reliance on foreign investors to support this federal debt. Other signs of the difficulties experienced by the baby boom generation include the rising divorce rate, the increase of single parent families, and the rise in the number of children born out of wedlock. Such statistics suggest that the baby boom generation is in for a difficult time in the twenty-first century. Since the baby boom generation is having fewer children and will live longer than previous generations, Longman argues, they will become the first generation of seniors to contribute more to Social Security than they will receive in benefits.

Longman estimates that today's elderly will receive at least three times as much in benefits as they have paid into the system. He is also concerned about the relative number of older as compared to younger members of society. Longman cites current projections by the Social Security administration which show that starting in 2020 when the first baby boomers will reach retirement age, there will be so few workers that they will be forced to pay Social Security taxes comparable to or higher than Federal Income Taxes (Longman, 1985). In addition, legislature compromises enacted in 1981 insured that current benefit levels for Social Security recipients were preserved, at the expense of future generations. Retired individuals now have to pay taxes on half their Social Security benefits if their income exceeds $25,000 per year. Longman (1984) points out that even if inflation is low for the next few decades, $25,000 will be a very modest income by the time the baby generation retires. Starting in 2003 the eligibility age to receive Social Security benefits will be increased two months each year for six years. By 2009 the eligibility age will be sixty-six. A second round of increases in the eligibility age will begin in 2020. By the year 2027, the retirement eligibility age to receive Social Security will be sixty-seven (Rich and Baum, 1984). Since the possibility of suffering physical incapacity, mental impairment or death increases with age, the loss of two years of retirement income will have a profound negative impact on many baby boomers when they retire. Consider that individuals who die at age 77 will have lost 20 percent of their retirement life span if they retire after the year 2027.

The constant theme that appears in the works of generational equity writers is that we are mortgaging the economic future of our society so that the current generation of older Americans can lead a life of luxury. While all of the statistics presented above do paint a disturbing picture of the economic future of our society, reducing federal benefits to the elderly would do very little to halt these long-range economic trends. Addressing these issues directly would involve contemplating radical changes in the American life style and the structure of American industry. It is far easier to find a convenient scapegoat (Binstock, 1983) such as the elderly and identify them as the cause of current problems. The future health of the Social Security System is directly linked to the health of the U.S. economy in the next century. Since it is impossible to predict the impact of the use of computers, robotics, and other technological innovations on economic life, predicting the future health of the economy over long periods of time is impossible at the present time.

THE ECONOMIC STATUS OF THE ELDERLY

Older Americans currently live longer than ever before and have achieved a higher standard of living than any generation of older people. In 1900, life expectancy at birth was 47 years for men and 49 years for women. In 1985, it was 71.5 years for men and 78.8

years for women. Approximately 80 percent of the population can expect to reach age 65 and half of those 65 years old can expect to live past 80 (Kingston et al., 1986). These dramatic gains in the number of people living to old age are unprecedented in the history of the human race. The introduction of federally financed economic, medical and social welfare programs that serve older Americans has resulted in a dramatic change in the quality of life experienced by older adults.

In 1984, the median family income of families with household heads aged 65 and older was $18,118 or about two-thirds of the median income of families with household heads aged 25 to 64 ($28,972). The median income of the single elderly ($7,286) was about half that of the non-elderly single populations ($15,028) (Developments in Aging, 1986). However, fewer older people in the U.S. live below the federal poverty level than ever before in history (Etheridge, 1984).

In general older people have lower incomes than younger age groups. A number of life changes occur as people age which contribute to the reduced income of the elderly. The most important of these changes are: retirement, death of a spouse and declining health (Developments in Aging, 1986). When individuals retire they lose earnings and become dependent upon Social Security, pensions, assets accumulated over their work lives, or government programs designed to help the poor. Although Social Security benefits have risen dramatically in the past decade, they are still not sufficient to allow people to maintain their pre-retirement lifestyle unless supplemented by other sources of income. A recent Louis Harris poll indicates that most older Americans rely on Social Security as their only source of income (Elder, 1987). The death of a spouse normally results in a decrease in family income since that individual's Social Security check stops with his or her death. Since Social Security is the primary source of income for a majority of older persons, the reduction often results in a significant decrease in income. This is especially the case if it is the husband who dies first. His pension, if he has one, usually stops with his death. The widow must manage on her Social Security check, which is usually much less than what her husband received. Thus, widowhood can often lead to pauperization for older women and is a significant factor contributing to the high poverty rate of older women (to be discussed below). Changes in the health status of older persons also result in pauperization. Most of the health and social services that infirm older persons must utilize, such as home health care or nursing homes, are very expensive. These services are, for most persons not reimbursable under Medicare. The costs involved, which are astronomical, can easily exhaust assets accumulated over a lifetime of work in a few short years. Many older persons who managed to maintain a middle class life style all their lives find themselves forced to "spend down" to the Medicaid eligibility level in order to receive the medical and supportive services they require. A recent study conducted by the Select Committee on Aging of the House of Representatives found that 70 percent of the elderly living alone, nationwide, spend down their income to the federal poverty level within 13 weeks of entering a nursing home (1987). A study conducted in Massachusetts reported similar findings (Torres-Gil, 1986). The economic security that Social Security and pensions provide for the elderly is no guarantee that a major health catastrophy will not pauperize them at any time. The vulnerability that the elderly feel has been documented in recent studies (Uehara et al., 1986; Cook and Kramek, 1986). These studies found that older persons were more likely to perceive themselves as having fewer options in the advent of hardship than younger adults.

Social Class and the Elderly

Class differences within the older population are frequently overlooked by researchers. Unfortunately, the Census Bureau does not regularly report comparisons by age of the share of income going to each fifth of the population. The most recent such study (Radner, 1982) using unadjusted microdata for 1972 reported a direct relationship between age and increasing inequality. Moreover, the elderly were even more sharply stratified into rich and poor than younger age groups.

As people age, there appears to be a tendency for income to concentrate in the top 20 percent of the population. Among family units (families or unrelated individuals) ages 25 to 34, the top fifth of all families had 37.4 percent of all income. For family units 65 and older, the corresponding figure was 53 percent. Since census income statistics are largely based upon self-reported questionnaires there is a tendency for private pension, interest income, dividends, rents and royalties to be under-reported (Crystal, 1986). Thus, the differences cited above underestimate the gap between rich and poor (Radner, 1982).

There is also some evidence to suggest that the gap between rich and poor has increased in recent years. Moon (1986), using income estimates projected by the Urban Institute's household income micro simulation model, found that between 1980 and 1984, after tax family income adjusted for inflation rose an average of 4 percent for all families. Families were divided into five equal groups ranked in terms of disposable incomes from lowest to highest. The bottom two quintiles (40 percent of all families) had declining incomes while the income of the top quintile rose by an average of $3,525. Incomes among the remaining two quintiles (the third and fourth highest) remained basically unchanged during that time period.

Poverty Among the Elderly

The most frequently cited statistic used to support the argument that the elderly are no longer a disadvantaged group is the official federal poverty index. In 1959, 35 percent of persons 65 and older, and 22.4 percent of the general population had incomes below the federal poverty level. By 1984, the corresponding figures were 12.4 percent of the elderly as compared to 14.4 percent of the total population (Characteristics of the Population Below the Poverty Level, 1984). Drawing upon these figures the President's Council of Economic Advisors announced that the elderly were no longer a disadvantaged group. They concluded that the real poverty rate for older Americans was only 4 percent, if the value of Medicare and other in-kind benefits were taken into account (Annual Report, 1985). Minkler (1986) has observed that such logic would lead one to conclude that an elderly woman with an income of $3,000 per year would no longer be poor if she were hit by a truck and received $4,000 in medical treatment covered by Medicare.

The official poverty level developed in the early 1960s was based upon a 1955 survey of food consumption by the Department of Agriculture. That study found that families spent approximately one-third of their income on food. The official poverty level was set at three times the cost of enough food to feed each member of the family unit to insure that they received all essential vitamins and minerals. Poverty levels were set by calculating the cost of a mini- mally adequate diet for households of varying sizes and then multi- plying by three. These levels have been adjusted over the years to reflect the changing cost of purchasing foods that make up the "Economy Food Plan" (Characteristics of the Population below the Federal Poverty Level, 1984). The index ignores the cost of hous- ing, the health status of family members, rural/urban differences and other important factors which have a significant impact on the economic status of households (Cook and Kramek, 1986). The most glaring flaw in the index is its treatment of the elderly. Ana- lysts working out the original economy food plans assumed that an adequate diet for a typical healthy older person would be less costly since their nutritional requirements are lower than those of younger people. Using this assumption, they calculated the poverty level threshold at a lower income level for older as compared to younger persons. The authors of the index assumed that since the cost of food for the elderly was lower, all their other basic costs would also be lower (*The Other Side of Easy Street*, 1987). While it is true that housing costs for older persons are frequently lower, their out-of- pocket health care costs tend to be significantly higher than those of younger persons (Kosterlitz, 1986).

The discriminatory standard used by the federal government results in the poverty threshold being 8.5 percent higher for younger single persons and 11.2 percent higher for younger couples. In 1985, the official poverty line for a single adult aged 64 or younger was $5,593. The corresponding level for a person 65 or older was $5,156. The gap between older and younger persons is even greater for couples. In 1985, the poverty level for a couple age 64 or youn- ger was $7,231, while for couples 65 and older it was $6,503. Ac- cording to a recent estimate by the Villers Foundation staff, if the same standard were applied to both young and old to determine poverty levels, the poverty rate for the elderly would jump from 12.6 percent to as high as 15.2 percent. The Villers Foundation

Report concludes that the official poverty definition of poverty, ". . . is both deficient and discriminatory. It seriously understates the extent of poverty among the elderly" (On the other Side of Easy Street, 1987).

A number of legislative changes increased Social Security payments to the aged in the 1970s. The most important of these were the 1972 amendments to the Social Security Act. Starting in 1975, Social Security payments were automatically indexed to the consumer price index. In addition, Congress passed a 20 percent across-the-board rise in benefits for all current Social Security recipients. As a result, average monthly benefits increased 140 percent between 1970 and 1980 (Burt and Pittman, 1985). However, even this increase was inadequate. Cook and Kramek (1986) compared the 1983 poverty rate of the elderly to all mature adults over the age of 24. While 14.1 percent of the elderly fell below the Federal poverty level (using the official poverty level), only 10 percent of persons 45 to 64, and 11.9 percent of persons 25 to 44 were so classified. The elderly were only less likely to be poor when compared to children, young persons entering the job market, and students. Cook and Kramek (1986) also point out that if one uses a slightly more generous definition of poverty (125 percent of the official Federal rate) 20 percent of all persons in families lived below this level in 1983. This statistic was highest for the elderly — 22.4 percent followed by adults aged 25-44 with 16 percent, and those aged 45-64 with 13 percent. Hence, the increase in Social Security benefits served only to lift many of the elderly to income levels slightly above the federal poverty line.

The Poor Elderly: Women and Minorities

Money income of the elderly comes primarily from four sources: (1) Social Security and other federal retirement programs; (2) private pensions; (3) earnings; and (4) assets. The poor elderly receive all or almost all of their income from Social Security or other federal retirement programs.

If we look at poverty rates for subgroups of the population across age groups, several factors emerge. Poverty levels are consistently higher for single as compared to married persons and for minority group members in all age groups. Poverty rates are highest for children under 18 and decrease until age 64. The lowest poverty rates for all races are in the 45 to 64 age groups. Poverty increases after age 65 with retirement. A similar pattern exists when we compare males and females. At every age single women have higher poverty rates than families (Characteristics of the Population Below the Federal Poverty Level, 1984). Thus, the poor old, with some exceptions, are the poor young at a later stage in the life cycle. The aged poor are mostly people who tended to have low income jobs and sporadic work histories when they were young.

The low income elderly are disproportionately women and minorities. Table One shows poverty rates for these groups for the years 1959 and 1985.

Table One indicates that there has been a dramatic reduction in the poverty rate for white males during the past three decades falling from 39.7 percent in 1959 to 11 percent in 1985. During this time period the rates for minorities and women declined less significantly and remained alarmingly high — 31 percent for blacks and 24 percent for Hispanic elderly in 1985. In 1959 roughly one out of every three elderly men and women had incomes below the federal poverty level. In 1985 women (15.6 percent) were twice as likely as men (8.4 percent) to live in poverty. During the past thirty years the relative gap between poor whites and minorities has increased rather than declined. In 1959 blacks were twice as likely to be poor as whites, by 1983 they were three times as likely. The primary reason why poverty rates for women and minorities have not declined as rapidly as those for white males is a function of the job histories of these groups. Since women and minorities tend to have lower paying jobs and to have more sporadic work histories, they benefited less from changes in the Social Security laws than did white males (Burt and Pittman, 1985).

The elderly who are most likely to be poor represent the fastest growing sectors of the aged population. In 1980, 12 percent of the older population was nonwhite. By the year 2025, this figure will increase to 15 percent and by the year 2050 to 18 percent, almost one in five of older Americans.

TABLE 1. Sources: 1959 data U.S. Bureau of Census statistical Abstracts of the United States, 1984 (Washington, DC, U.S. Governments Printing Office, 1985) Table 781. 1985 Data *On the Other Side of Easy Street*, the Villers Foundation, Washington, DC 1987.

1985 (Percent of Elderly U.S. Population)

	1959	1985
All Elderly	35.2	12.6
White	33.1	11.0
Black	62.5	31.5
Hispanic	*N.A.	23.9
Women	36.6	15.6
Men	34.7	8.4

*N.A. = Not Available

Sources   1959 data U.S. Bureau of Census statistical Abstracts of the United States, 1984 (Washington, D.C., U.S. Governments Printing Office, 1985) Table 781. 1985 Data On the Other Side of Easy Street, The Villers Foundation, Washington D.C. 1987.

Elderly Women

Currently there are 17 million women 65 years of age and older. Older women are more likely than older men to be poor, widowed, divorced, to have worked in low paying jobs, to lack access to affordable health care, and to be providers themselves of health care to other frail elderly individuals (Estes et al., 1984).

In 1985 the poverty rate for elderly women living alone, was 26.8 percent. This figure increased to 54.5 percent for older black women living alone. Elderly black women have the highest poverty rate in the nation today (*On the Other Side of Easy Street*, 1987).

The primary cause of the economic problems experienced by women are the inequalities in the labor force and the resulting lower wages paid to women. Other contributory factors include the rising divorce rate, the increase in the number of single parent families, and the fact that women live longer than men (Estes et al., 1984).

Although there has been a tremendous increase in the number of working women in recent years, they continue to occupy low paying jobs with few or no job-related benefits. Approximately three-quarters of all working women above the age of 45 work in traditional areas of female employment; clerical, sales, and service jobs. When women retire they tend to receive lower Social Security payments than men. In 1985 the average benefit received by women was $399 compared to an average of $521 for men. Only 20 percent of all retired women, but 43 percent of retired men received a private pension in 1984. The number of female headed households has increased in recent years. Since women usually earn less than men, single parent families frequently have incomes close to the poverty level. In 1978, the median income of female headed single parent families was $8,540, or less than half the median income of all families (Estes et al., 1984). Women depend upon employment and/or marital status for health insurance coverage. Almost half (40 percent) of all divorced women and approximately one-quarter (27 percent) of all widows not in the labor force have no private health insurance.

The frail elderly (85 years and older) are the fastest growing section of the elderly population. They tend to be poorer than the young old. In 1985 the poverty rate for this age group was 18.7 percent or almost twice as high as the total elderly population (11 percent). Current projections are that by the year 2000 approximately two-thirds of the frail old will be women (Estes et al., 1984).

CONCLUSION

In this paper we have examined the arguments of writers who present a new view of the social contract in American society. Authors such as Preston and Longman have sought to portray the improved social and economic condition of this generation of older Americans as contributing to the poverty of children and the perceived economic deprivation of the baby boom generation. Preston has argued that there is a direct relationship between increased resource allocation for the elderly in recent years, and decreased spending for children. I have suggested that this is a spurious argument since programs designed to help these two age dependent groups are funded from different revenue sources. Social Security and Medicare, the principle programs providing benefits to the elderly, are both financed by a separate payroll tax. Programs that serve children are funded from general tax revenues. Reducing funding for programs serving older persons would cause severe hardship among the aged, and would have little impact on the quality of life of children. Preston is quite correct to be concerned about the future consequences of the continued failure to provide for the needs of children. Most of the reductions in funding for children he documents, occurred because the children served were poor. Legislators unfortunately, have historically found the poor an easy budget cutting target in times of fiscal austerity. It is significant that the children's Defense Fund, the major lobbying group for poor children, does not call for a reduction in federal spending for older Americans. Rather it identifies the recent increases in spending for the military, and huge tax subsidies for corporations as the primary causes of the current budget crisis (A Children's Defense Budget, 1987).

Longman is concerned about the current and future economic

viability of the baby boom generation. Baby boomers, he argues, are making economic sacrifices so senior citizens can enjoy a life of affluence. He is also concerned about the future viability of the Social Security system. While the baby boom generation is finding it harder than their parents did to own a house or maintain a middle class life style, it is hard to see how reductions in Social Security payroll taxes would have a significant impact on their current economic status. The economic viability of the baby boom generation has much more to do with macroeconomic processes and trends as does the ability of the Social Security system to provide benefits to future generations of the elderly.

Perhaps the most important result of the generational equity debate is that it has focused attention on the amount of poverty that continues to exist within the aged population. Older Americans experienced a dramatic increase in income in the past two decades. However, many elderly continue to be poor. Older women and minorities are two to five times as likely as white males to live under the federal poverty level.

Poverty among both the young and the old is a critical social problem. Addressing this problem would involve a massive fiscal commitment on the part of the Federal government, one which is said to be unthinkable in the current era of fiscal constraint. Yet, the unthinkable might become a national priority if the future social and economic costs of current policies were understood. The critical issue of modern society is not generational but racial and sexual economic equity. Poverty in America is largely a question of gender and race. To conjure up a struggle between the poor young and the poor old is to imagine a struggle between mothers and daughters, between grandparents and their grandchildren. For the poor old are often the poor young at another point in the life cycle.

REFERENCES

Aging in America (1984). U.S. Senate Special Committee on Aging in Conjunction with the American Association of Retired People, Washington, D.C.

Annual Report of the President's Council of Economic Advisors (1985). U.S. Government Printing Office, Washington, D.C.

Bergman, G. (1986). AGE: An organization of, by and for whom? Gray Panther Network: Age and Youth in Action, Summer: 3

Binstock, R. (1983). The aged as scapegoat, The Gerontologist, 23:136-143.

Burt, M.R. & Pittman, K.J. (1985). Testing the Social Safety Net, The Urban Institute Press, Washington, D.C.

A Children's Defense Budget FY 1988 (1987). The Children's Defense Fund, Washington, D.C.

Characteristics of the Population below the Poverty Level: 1983, Consumer Income Series P-60, No. 152, U.S. Department of Commerce, Bureau of the Census: Washington, D.C.

Cook, F.L. & Kramek, L.M. (1986). Measuring Economic Hardship Among Older Americans, The Gerontologist, 26, 1:38-47.

Crystal, S. (1986). Measuring Income and Inequality Among the Elderly, The Gerontologist, 21, 1:56-59.

Developments in Aging: 1984 (1985). A Report of the Special Committee on Aging, United States Senate, U.S. Government Printing Office, Washington, D.C.

Durenberger, D. (1986). 2020 Vision: Planning Together for the Future, Remarks Presented at the First Americans for Generational Equity Conference (Mimeo).

Elder, J. (1987). Portrait of the elderly: Still independent despite limitations, The New York Times, January 15:cl.

Etheredge, L. (1984). An Aging Society and The Federal Deficit, Milbank Memorial Fund Quarterly, 62(4):521-543.

Estes, C.L., Gerard L. & Clarke, A. (1984). Women and the Economics of Aging, International Journal of Health Services, 14, 1:55-67.

Fast Facts and Figures about Social Security, 1987 (1987).Social Security Bulletin, 50(5) May.

Kosterlitz, J. (1986). Protecting the Elderly, National Journal, 25:1254-1258.

Kingston, E.R., Hirshann, B.A. & Cornman, J.M. (1986). Ties that Bind: The Interdependence of Generations, Seven Locks Press, Washington, D.C.

Longman, P. (1987). Born to Pay the New Politics of Aging in America, Houghton Mifflin Co: Boston.

Longman, P. (1985). Justice Between Generations, The Atlantic Monthly, 255:73-81.

Long-Term Care and Personal Impoverishment: Seven in Ten Elderly Living Alone are at Risk (1987). A Report Presented by The Chairman of the Select Committee on Aging, House of Representatives Committee Publication No. 100-631, W.S. Government Printing Office, Washington, D.C.

Minkler, M. (1986). 'Generational equity' the new victim blaming: an emerging public policy issue, International Journal of Health Services, 16, 4:539-551.

Moon, M. (1986). Impact of the Reagan Years on the Distribution of Income of the Elderly, The Gerontologist, 26, 1:32-37.

On the Other Side of Easy Street (1987). The Villers Foundation, Washington, D.C.

Preston, S. (1984). Children and the Elderly: Divergent Paths for America's Dependents, Demography, 21, 4:435-457.
Preston, S. (1984). Children and the Elderly in the U.S., Scientific American, 251, 6, 44-49.
Radner, D.B. (1982). Distribution of Family Income: Improved Estimates, Social Security Bulletin, 45, 7:13-26.
Rich, B.M. & Baum, M. (1984). The Aging: A Guide to Public Policy, University of Pittsburgh Press: Pittsburgh, PA.
The Challenge of an Aging Society Planning for the Baby Boom Generation's Retirement: A Statistical Abstract (1987). Americans for Generational Equity: Washington, D.C. (Mimeo)
Torres-Gil, F. (Ed.) (1986). Hispanics in an Aging Society, Carnegie Corporation of New York: New York.
Uehara, E.S., Geron, S. & Beeman, S.K. (1986). The Elderly Poor in the Reagan Era, The Gerontologist, 26, 1:48-55.
Update Report (1987). What they're Saying about Americans for Generational Equity and Intergenerational Issues, Americans for Generational Equity: Washington, D.C. (Mimeo).

Intergenerational Transfers Within the Family Context — Motivating Factors and Their Implications for Caregiving

Marjorie H. Cantor
Barbara Hirshorn

SUMMARY. The interdependence of generations, in both psycho-social and economic terms, has raised critical issues about the nature and role of reciprocity between adult children and their parents. This paper focuses on adult children as caregivers for their elderly parents and provides a conceptual paradigm for intergenerational familial exchanges. The paper builds on empirical studies of family care by investigating the factors that motivate the provision of support and assistance across generations.

The recent reports of the Gerontological Society — *Ties that Bind* and *The Common Stake: The Interdependence of Generations* take as their point of departure the proposition that in modern society no generation is separate unto itself. In fact, a recognition of the interdependence of generations is a prerequisite for constructive policy deliberations. Such interdependence, as noted in the reports, is inherent in both public transfer programs such as Social Security, and in private transfers of assistance provided within the familial or kinship network. This paper examines more closely some aspects of intergenerational transfers within the family context, with particular

Marjorie H. Cantor is Brookdale Professor of Gerontology, Director, Brookdale Research Institute, Third Age Center, Fordham University, New York, NY 10023.

Barbara Hirshorn is affiliated with the Institute of Gerontology, Wayne State University, Detroit, MI 48201.

emphasis on the factors that motivate people of different generations to assist one another. Through high-lighting the importance of motivation in the caregiving process, we hope to sharpen some of the policy, research and practice implications that emanate from the interrelatedness of generations in their role as caregivers.

Although American cultural norms emphasize independence and self-sufficiency, there are certain times in the life course, most notably during childhood and old age, when society looks more kindly on dependency and the assumption of a caring posture towards individuals in need of assistance. The notion of caregiving associated with these periods frequently involves the extraordinary and sustained assistance required for the socialization of youngsters and the care of the very frail older adult.

The role of family in the nurturance of children has been well documented in the past 50 years. More recently as an increasing proportion of the population is living longer, researchers have turned to a careful analysis of the role of family in sustaining the elderly. Starting with the early research of Shanas et al. (1968), Sussman (1977), and Rosenmyer (1977), and the subsequent work of Brody (1977, 1978), Bengston (1979, 1981), the United States Government General Accounting Office (1977) and our own study in New York City (1975a,b; 1979a,b; 1980, 1981a), it has become clear that family members are the main caregivers of the elderly. Further studies have documented the nature of the informal helping networks and the assistance provided in the case of older people of diverse ethnic, gender and class backgrounds (Bengston 1979, 1981, Hill 1972, 1978; Cantor 1979c; Guttman 1979). Even more recently attention has shifted to an examination of the impact of caregiving responsibility on the family life of caregivers and to legislative and programmatic suggestions for minimizing the stress and strain inherent in extraordinary caregiving situations (Horowitz and Dobrof 1982; Brody 1978, 1981; Cantor 1981b, 1982; Poulcheck and Noelken 1982; Zarit 1980).

Other papers in this collection provide overviews of research on familial transfers. Here we address two issues. First, in order to better understand the caregiving process we will attempt to integrate the various aspects of caregiving into an overall framework or potential model. Then we will explore more fully one portion of this paradigm by addressing the question: What are some of the factors that motivate intergenerational assistance — that in effect provide the glue that binds the generations together? By broadening our inquiry to encompass motivation as well as behavior of caregivers we hope to contribute to a better understanding of the total picture of intra-familial exchanges over the life course. The caregiving framework suggested is, we believe, applicable to caregiving at any point on the life cycle, but as gerontologists we will confine our attention to private transfers occurring within the family in support of older people.

When caregiving is considered in breadth, including both the usual short term assistance provided by members of all generations to each other (gifts, socializing, assistance during illness) and the extensive involvement of family members who must deal with substantial frailty or disability, several elements of interest emerge.

First, and fundamental to caregiving is the need for assistance. In the case of the elderly this is usually expressed in terms of disability, level of functional ability to carry out the tasks of daily living, and need for emotional sustenance. The need may occur as a result of an illness episode, or may be a symptom of progressive frailty. It can be overtly expressed by the person in need of care, or become apparent to family members interacting with the older person. The need is the background against which the caregiving process and our model is enacted.

Second, and interacting with need, are the basic motivating factors influencing whether or not family members respond to need, This domain encompasses the "why" of caregiving. Included in it are those factors intrinsic to the family — the values, attitudes, idiosyncratic history of the particular family, and the psyche of individual family members which trigger the response. Clearly involved are family dynamics which operate in different ways given different family constellations, different family histories, and varying ethnic, class and cultural contexts.

Next there is the domain encompassing societal and personal factors which mediate the initial familial responses and condition how family members will respond. Significant in this domain are the availability of societal responses in the form of entitlements and formal service; the ability of the older person to purchase services if not eligible for public services, and the availability and capacity of family members to respond to need for assistance. With respect to potential family caregivers, such things as age, sex, health, work status, and geographic location are factors which intervene and shape the nature of familial responses.

And finally there is the response domain encompassing the nature of the care provided, the circumstances under which assistance is given by whom, and the impact of caregiving on family members. From a strictly modeling standpoint, this is clearly the dependent or criterion variable.

Gerontological research on caregiving, to date, has in the main concerned itself with the response domain as it relates to the nature of the need for assistance. Only rarely do we find studies clearly delineating the role of societal resources, including both the availability and utilization of formal services. And perhaps most neglected in the research on caregiving to date has been an examination of the qualitative aspects of the caregiving relationship—most particularly the motivating factors involved in caregiving and how they interact with the other domains to affect the level of assistance provided.

What are some of these motivating forces? The following enumeration recognizes that they are still conceptually imprecise, and at times overlapping in definition and content. Furthermore, persons from different disciplines give different names to the things that bind generations together. Nevertheless, the literature on caregiving repeatedly suggests consideration of some subset or composite of the following factors to explain why family members, all over the world, care for the elderly, often at considerable personal sacrifice.

At the most elemental level, and preceding any social contract between family members, are the psychological attachments which bond husband and wives and parents and children to each other. Notions of love, hate, affection, intimacy, nurturance, and the positive and negative aspects of dependency are included in this concept of psychological bonding. A sometimes overlooked aspect of ego development is a person's definition of self as reflected in those with whom one is intimate. The caregiving process enables adult children to appreciate both the difficulty and necessity of adjusting to diminished autonomy and thereby helps to expand their understanding of self.

Clearly related to, and perhaps overlapping with the notion of psychological bonding, is the concept of family solidarity as explored by family sociologists (Bengtson 1981; Troll and Bengtson 1979). Intergenerational solidarity, according to Bengtson et al. (1985) has several elements including associational solidarity the extent and nature of interaction between family members; affectual solidarity encompassing the degree of positive sentiment (i.e., warmth, closeness, emotional gratification) present in the family; and, consensual solidarity — the degree to which there is agreement or conflict among family members regarding values and opinions. To what extent do family members see things the same way; that is, have compatible views of the world even if they differ with respect to objective characteristics such as education, class, and age?

We hypothesize that families who evidence high levels of solidarity are more likely to positively respond to the needs of older family members. Important contributions to family solidarity are family rituals, gatherings and opportunities for informal socialization, as well as the more tangible record of instrumental assistance provided within the family context.

In considering family norms and how they influence behavior, one attitudinal subset seems particularly germane to caregiving behavior: attitudes towards filial and familial responsibility and the appropriate role of individuals, family and society in caring for elderly and other dependent persons.

A third group of motivating factors interacting with and influencing the normative consensus within particular families are the broader societal norms regarding such things as appropriate relationships between generations. Included in this are the moral, ethical and religious values regarding family and the place of children within society. In some societies, such as China, these norms of responsibility and respect for the elderly are strongly enunciated and even written into the constitution of the country. In the United States, despite elimination of filial responsibility under law, the notion that children have an obligation to assist parents and other older persons is a widely accepted and internalized value among all generations. Elaine Brody's research on three generations of women is particularly illuminating in this respect (Brody 1981). Certainly the biblical command to honor thy mother and father has had a long imprint regardless of adherence to organized religion as such. However, the impact of norms and the effect of normative solidarity upon caregiving behavior needs considerably more exploration. Particularly relevant in this respect is the growing literature regarding the impact of race and ethnicity on expectations and values relating to filial and familial responsibility. (See Leahy 1983; Guttman 1979; Hill 1978; Rogler and Cooney 1984; James et al. 1984; Bengtson and Burton 1981 for illuminating research regarding Italian, Eastern European, Black, Hispanic, Irish and Mexican American values regarding family responsibility and intergenerational exchanges.)

Interestingly, the pragmatic test of the concept of filial responsibility, and its importance as a major motivator of intergenerational caregiving, is relatively new. Prior to recent changes in the age structure of our population, few persons lived to old age and few families were called upon to provide extensive care. Futhermore, in agricultural societies the means of production were in the hands of older family members, rendering intergenerational relationships more a matter of economic survival and inheritance than filial responsibility as such. Today, however, the situation has changed. Social Security provides most older people with a base of financial independence so that the degree to which children are involved in and responsible for the care of parents rests more on conscious decision than necessity or law. As a result, as Schorr (1980) notes, the value of filial responsibility has grown in importance as a motivating factor in intergenerational caregiving.

Another frequently cited factor in explaining intergenerational exchanges is the concept of reciprocity and the operation of exchange theory as a theoretical construct for understanding assistance between generations. Sussman (1986) notes that "filial responsibilities" provide boundaries and conditions for interaction based on a profit/cost, reward/punishment model, while Black and Bengtson (1973) talk in terms of a "developmental stake" equation. Thus, the concept of reciprocity is not time specific but encompasses serial interactions over the life cycle. Horowitz and Shindleman (1983) conceptualize reciprocity in the case of the elderly as stemming from the credits earned by the older person for past help given to the caregiver. Implicit in such reciprocity is the fact that the adult child caregiver, in turn, expects similar assistance from succeeding generations if beset with chronic and debilitating illness.

The notion of reciprocity as an on-going process from birth to death is particularly important in the case of the elderly. Although exact reciprocity between children and parents is impossible, most studies indicate that, except in circumstances of severe disability, assistance between generations flows in two directions (Cantor 1975a,b; 1979a,b; 1980; 1981; Bengtson 1979; Brody 1981; Horowitz and Dobrof, 1982). And recent research involving younger, more affluent elderly, even suggests that such elderly may actually give more than they receive in return (Cantor and Brook 1986).

Another important proposition of exchange theory is distributive justice. Individuals who help more should be rewarded more in return. It is here that issues of inheritance, as the economists say "the bequest motivation," intersects with the concept of reciprocity.

On the subject of the importance of inheritance there is a paucity of data and some difference of opinion among the few researchers who have explored this motivating factor. Clearly for most families, inheritance no longer plays the role it did in preindustrial society, as a mechanism for passing down through the generations economic support — the means for survival. However, inheritance has not lost all importance, particularly as a psychological factor. Sussman, in a 1970 study of inheritance patterns among 659 randomly selected families, found that allocations made according to notions of distributive justice were clearly accepted by family members. Testators willed their estates to designated children or other individuals according to the needs of children, their emotional ties to the testate, and the services exchanged among family members over the years. Sibling members of the middle generation were found to accept the giving of a greater part of the inheritance to those who helped the most.

On the other hand, there is some indication that some parents purposely stress "equality of inheritance" through providing equal shares in order to avoid threatening sibling solidarity.

Furthermore, Bengtson and Treas (1980) suggest that currently inheritance is important to many, mainly for its symbolic value. According to this perspective, family heirlooms and other items of symbolic value are seen as the chief resources passed from generation to generation. Attention to aging kin springs not from fear of disinheritance, but from sentiments such as affection, guilt, gratitude or a wish for parental approval so that inheritance is mainly important as an embodiment and expression of these emotional ties.

Although the extent of assets in most situations may not be large, anyone who has worked with older people knows the importance to the elderly of having something to leave to grandchildren, even if only items of sentimental as opposed to monetary value.

Clearly one cannot totally dismiss the issue of inheritance and it is likely that it plays a role in some circumstances. However, more research is needed to determine its current importance in the caregiving process, both in financial and symbolic terms.

And finally we cannot overlook the importance of the continuity of generations as a motivating factor in child-parent relationships. Caregiving involves the passing on of the wisdom, mores, and values of the family, whatever is uniquely distinguishing from generation to generation. The adult child who cares for an older sick parent is not only repaying his or her personal debt to the older generation, but is illustrating in a graphic way what is expected from his/her own children in turn. Thus, caregiving affirms a more expanded notion of family life involving joys, obligations and rewards far beyond the mere passing of genetic inheritance. If one cannot care for loved ones in need how can one expect to be cared for in turn?

What does all this mean in terms of research practice and public policy pertaining to older people and the caregiving process? It is unlikely that any one of these motivating factors, or even these factors as a group, can explain all the variance in the nature or amount of assistance provided by children. One study, for example, examining the effect of affection and past history of assistance on current caregiving, suggests these are significant variables related to level of assistance (Horowitz and Shindleman 1983). Other researchers emphasize the importance of the nature and level of need (i.e., physical and mental health and economic status) as major factors conditioning filial response (Cantor 1979a; Zarit et al. 1980).

But what role does the availability or absence of societal resources and entitlements play in determining how children respond? Clearly there is a need to dynamically relate all the various domains of the caregiving paradigm to each other, and to the caregiving response. Utilizing multi-variate models such as pathanalysis, and controlling for class, race and cohort, would enable us to move beyond description to an understanding of the relative role of a variety of factors in explaining given levels of familial assistance. Such research and model building can expand our understanding of the process of caregiving and enhance the effectiveness of proposed interventions to sustain the caregiving role of family with respect to dependent members of all ages.

But clearly it is not necessary to wait for future research before considering the impact of the motivating factors just discussed on current practice and policy deliberations. For persons working directly with older people and their families an understanding of family dynamics is essential. Practitioners by their actions can strengthen or undermine family solidarity, patterns of reciprocity and psychological bonding. Appreciation of familial norms and how they relate to broader societal values will enhance our understanding of why some families are willing to consider institutionalization while others resist all interventions from the formal service system.

Perhaps most important is sensitivity to the notion that current caregiving efforts on the part of family members do not occur in a vacuum. There is a family history, both of reciprocal exchanges and expectations over the life course and these conditions influence responses. Social workers and other practitioners can help families reflect on this history, can offer assistance in the resolution of outstanding conflicts, and can consciously make an effort to strengthen family fabric. Thus, in most situations, the family, rather than the older person, is the appropriate client and focus of attention. Unfortunately, current reimbursement practices and excessive caseloads often impede rather than enhance such a holistic approach on the part of practitioners.

In considering policy and legislative initiatives, we must continue to ask what is the meaning of the initiatives for the family and the common stake of all generations. Interestingly enough, a Presidential Interdepartmental Working Group on the Family recommended the institution of a "family fairness statement" for all relevant legislation or regulations similar to the currently required environmental impact statements (*New York Times*, November 14, 1986). Certainly such an approach would, at a minimum, suggest a reconsideration of eligibility requirements for many entitlement programs. Most glaring is the current SSI regulation reducing SSI allowances in the case of older persons moving in with their family. In the same vein, what is the impact on family solidarity and intergenerational reciprocity of our current Medicaid spend-down and divestment policies? To what extent is familial responsibility strained by the alleged premature release of hospitalized patients into the community under Medicares' Prospective Payment System?

Furthermore, we need to make policymakers aware that intergenerational transfers are not only public in nature, but involve a variety of types of private transfers within the family system. Enlightened public policy must at a minimum facilitate such transfers through taxation policy and programmatic assistance. Recent demographic trends point to increasing demands on the family for caregiving. At the same time, women are increasingly entering the labor market. Unless we are careful, we may find ourselves placing excessive burdens on family systems without providing needed supports.

Finally, recognizing the important role of families, this country needs, at a minimum, a pro-family policy that is more than rhetoric. Basic to such a policy development is recognition of the role played by private intergenerational family transfers and the motivating factors which act to bind the generations together across the life course.

REFERENCES

Bengston, V. L. (1985). Generations, cohorts and relations between age groups. In R. Binstock and E. Shanas (eds.). *The Handbook of Aging and the Social Sciences Second Edition*. NY: Van Nostrand Reinhold Co.

Bengtson, V., Burton, L. and Mangen, D. (1981). Family support systems and attribution of responsibility, contrasts among elderly Blacks, Mexican-Americans and whites. Paper presented at 34th Annual Meeting of the Gerontological Society, Toronto.

Bengtson, V. and Treas, J. (1980). The changing family context of mental health and aging. In J. Birren and B. Sloan (eds.). *Handbook of Mental Health and Aging*, Englewood Cliffs, NJ: Prentice Hall, pp. 400-428.

Bengtson, V. (1979). Ethnicity and aging: Problems and issues in current social science inquiry. In D. Gelfand and A. Kutzik (eds.). *Ethnicity and Aging*, NY: Springer, pp. 9-31.

Black, K. D. and Bengston, V. L. (1973). Solidarity across generations: Elderly parents and their middle aged children. Paper presented at the Annual Meeting of the Gerontological Society.

Brody, E. M. (1981). Women in the middle and family help to older people. *Gerontologist*, 21: 471-480.

Brody, E. M. (1978). The aging of the family. *Annals of the American Academy of Political and Social Science*, 438: 13-27.

Brody, E. M. (1977). *Long-Term Care of Older People*. NY: Human Sciences Press.

Cantor, M. and Brook, K. (1986). *Growing Old in Suburbia: The Experience of the Jewish Elderly of Mt. Vernon.* NY: The Brookdale Research Institute, Third Age Center, Fordham University.

Cantor, M. (1982). Caring for the frail elderly—Impact on family, friends and neighbors. In *Financial Incentives for Informal Caregiving—Direction from Recent Research.* NY: Community Council of Greater New York.

Cantor, M. (1981a). The extent and intensity of the informal support system among New York's inner city elderly. In *Strengthening Informal Supports for the Aging*, NY: Community Service Society.

Cantor, M. (1981b). Factors associated with strain among family, friends and neighbors caring for the frail elderly. Paper presented at 34th Annual Scientific Meeting. Gerontological Society, Toronto.

Cantor, M. (1980). The informal support system: Its relevance in the lives of the elderly. In E. Borgotta and N. McCluskey (eds.). *Aging and Society*, Beverly Hills: Sage.

Cantor, M. (1979a). Neighbors and friends: An overlooked resource in the informal support system. *Research on Aging*, Vol. 1.

Cantor, M. (1979b). Life space and social support. In T. O. Byerts, S. C. Howell, and L. A. Pastalan (eds.). *Environmental Context of Aging: Life Styles, Environmental Quality and Living Arrangements*, pp. 33-61.

Cantor, M. (1979c). The informal support system of New York's inner city elderly: Is *Ethnicity and Aging*. NY: Springer.

Cantor, M. (1976). The configuration and intensity of the informal support system in a New York City elderly population. Paper presented at the 29th Annual Meeting, Gerontological Society, NY.

Cantor, M. (1975a). Life space and the social support system of the inner city elderly of New York. *Gerontologist*, 15: 23-27.

Cantor, M. H. (1975b). The formal and informal social support system of older

New Yorkers. Paper presented at the 10th International Congress of Gerontology, Jerusalem, Israel.

Guttman, D. (ed.) (1979). *Informal and Formal Support Systems and Their Effects on the Lives of the Elderly in Selected Ethnic Groups.* Washington, DC: School of Social Service, Catholic University of America.

Hill, R. B. (1978). Excerpts from the Black elderly. In M. Seltzer, S. Corbett and R. Atchley (eds.). *Social Problems of the Aging: Readings*, Belmont, CA: Wadsworth, pp. 273-277.

Hill, R. B. (1972). *The Strength of Black Families*. NY: Emerson Hall.

Horowitz, A. and Shindelman, L. (1983). Reciprocity and affection: Past influences on current caregiving. *Journal of Gerontological Social Work*, 5: 5-20.

Horowitz, A. and Dobrof, R. (1982). *The Role of Families in Providing Long-Term Care to the Frail and Chronically Ill Elderly Living in the Community. Final Report*. Submitted to the Health Care Financing Administration, Grant #18-P-97541/2-02, NY: Brookdale Center on Aging of Hunter College.

James, A., James, W. and Smith, H. (1984). Reciprocity as a coping strategy of the elderly: A rural Irish perspective. *The Gerontologist*, 24: 483-488.

Leahy, J. (1983). Interdependence and aging. In J. Sokolovski (ed.). *Growing Old in Different Societies*. Belmont, CA: Wadsworth Publishing Co.

Morgan, J. N. (1984). The role of time in the measurement of transfers and well-being. In M. Moon (ed.). *Economic Transfers in the United States*. Chicago, IL: The University of Chicago Press.

New York Times, Friday, November 14, 1986 — U.S. Report asserts administration halted liberal anti-family agenda.

Ovin, W. (1983). Personal and family adjustment in later life. *Journal of Marriage and the Family*, 45: (1).

Poulshock, W. and Noelker, L. (1982). *The Effects on Families of Caring for Impaired Elderly in Residence*, Cleveland, OH: The Benjamin Rose Institute.

Rogler, L. and Cooney, R. (1984). Puerto Rican families in New York City: Intergenerational Processes, Maplewood, NJ: Waterfront Press.

Rosenmayr, L. (1977). The family — a source of hope for the elderly. In E. Shanas and M. Sussman (eds.). *Family, Bureaucracy and the Elderly.* Durham, NC: Duke University Press.

Schorr, A., (1980). Thy father and thy mother — A second look at filial responsibility and family policy, Washington, DC: *Social Security Publication No. 13-11953*, pp. 1-62.

Shanas, E. and Townsend, P. (1968). *Old People in Three Industrial Societies*. NY: Atherton Press. (Reprinted Arno Press, 1980.)

Shanas, E. and G. Streib (eds.) (1965). *Social Structures and the Family: Generational Relations*. Englewood Cliffs, NJ: Prentice-Hall.

Sokolovsky, J. (1983). *Growing Old in Different Societies: Cross-cultural Perspectives.* Belmont, CA: Wadsworth Inc.

Sussman, M. B. (1986). The family life of older people. In R. Binstock and E. Shanas (eds.). *The Handbook of Aging and the Social Sciences Second Edition.* NY: Van Nostrand Reinhold Co.

Sussman, M. B. (1979). *Family, Bureaucracy and the Elderly,* Durham, NC: Duke University Press.

Sussman, M. B., Cates, J. N. and Smith, O. T. (1970). *The Family and Inheritance.* NY: Russell Sage Foundation.

Troll, L. and Bengtson, V. (1979). Generations in the family. In W. R. Burr et al. (eds.). *Contemporary Theories About the Family, Vol. 1,* New York: Free Press.

United States General Accounting Office (1977). *Home Health: The Need for a National Policy to Provide for the Elderly.* Washington, DC: Report #HRD78-19.

Zarit, S. H., Reever, K. E. and Bach-Peterson, J. (1980). Relatives of the impaired elderly: Correlates of feeling of burden. *Gerontologist,* 20: 649-655.

HEALTH AND WELL-BEING

The Picture of Health
for Midlife and Older Women
in America

Older Women's League

SUMMARY. This report overviews the major health problems of middle aged and older women and health care access issues. The relationship of labor force involvement to health status and insurance benefits is considered. Other payment sources such as Medicaid and Medicare are critiqued for their failure to finance needed prevention and other services.

INTRODUCTION

Longevity has increased tremendously during the 20th century in the United States due to remarkable advances in modern medicine and public health. In 1900, the life expectancy of a newborn was 48

This report was originally published by the Older Women's League, May, 1987, Lou Glasse, President.

A number of contributors to this report were participants in a group project of Women In Leadership, a public affairs training program conducted by the Coro Foundation and sponsored by the Junior League of Washington. These contributors were Diana Berardocco, Barbara Buhl, Suzanne Higgins, Barbara Rohde, and JoAnn Thoms.

Other contributors were: Elizabeth Conway, Janet Jenson, Fran Leonard, Lisa Lederer, Alice Quinlan, Judy Smith, and Evangeline Swift. Edited by Alice Quinlan.

years for females; today it is 78. The life expectancy for male new-borns increased 25 years during the same period.

Largely because of these advances, health and illness patterns have changed dramatically. At the turn of the century, infectious diseases such as smallpox, diphtheria and tuberculosis were leading causes of death. Today, those diseases have been largely wiped out as a cause of death in the United States. Instead, women over 45 die from heart disease, cancer, strokes, diabetes and emphysema — noninfectious diseases that are much more likely to have chronic and debilitating effects.

While American women live longer today, they do not necessarily have longer periods of good health. In several national surveys, Americans who report their health to be fair or poor are disproportionately low-income, uninsured, Black, out of the labor force, and female.

TABLE 1

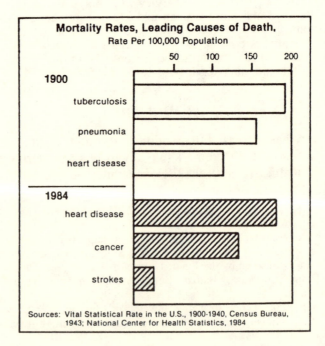

Mortality Rates, Leading Causes of Death,
Rate Per 100,000 Population

Sources: Vital Statistical Rate in the U.S., 1900-1940, Census Bureau, 1943; National Center for Health Statistics, 1984

In fact, women can expect increased and longer periods of chronic health problems. These changes in longevity and mortality have a major impact on how America ages — and serious public policy implications.

To be responsive to the needs of the public, health care delivery and payment systems must keep pace with these changes. To a considerable extent, they have not.

Medicare was set up in 1965 to assure that older Americans had access to basic medical care. But just a quarter of a century later, Medicare already has huge gaps in coverage for older women because it does not adequately address the needs associated with chronic health problems.

Midlife women, too, often fall through the cracks between private and public insurance coverage. At a time in their lives when prevention is paramount, women in their forties and fifties often must empty their pockets to pay for routine preventive procedures.

These inadequacies caused significant problems for a sizable segment of our society. There are 23 million American women aged 45 to 64 and another 17 million aged 65 or older. More women are employed than ever before, but they remain concentrated in low paying jobs. The median income of midlife women is approximately one-third that of midlife men; the average income for a women over 65 is less than $6,500. Thus, the resources available to older women are woefully inadequate to fill gaps in health care coverage.

The picture of health of our nation's midlife and older women is an evolving picture that is constantly altered by breakthroughs in research and technology, changing population demographics, and developments in public and private insurance availability. To be responsible, health care delivery and payment systems must keep pace with these changes. A health care policy transfusion is long overdue.

WOMEN'S HEALTH PROBLEMS

Women tend to have more chronic diseases and disabilities than men, partly because of their greater longevity. Some health problems are faced by both men and women, and in similar proportions;

others are unique to women. Still others are age-related, and more likely to appear among women, who make up the majority of the aged population.

Cancer

As a cause of death, cancer is #1 among women 35-54, #2 among women 55-74 and #3 among women over age 75. With the exception of cancers related to smoking, the differences in death rates from cancers common to both sexes is small, although there are variations within types of cancer. But cancers specific to females are devastating.

Breast cancer is the leading cause of death among American women. One in every eleven women in the United States will develop this disease in her lifetime. Currently, the only significant possibility for further improving survival rates is early detection and treatment. Survival from breast cancer has not improved since 1973. Five-year survival rates are considerably higher for white women (75%) than for Black women (63%).

Regular breast self-examination and mammography are the most effective and proven means of early detection. Studies suggest that the combined use of less radical surgery and radiation is as effective as the more radical surgery used in the past. More research is needed to confirm this and to resolve issues of toxicity, side-effects, and psychological implications of the various courses of treatment.

The risk of reproductive tract cancers increases with age. Among the most common are endometrial, cervical, and ovarian cancers. Cancer of the endometrium (uterine lining) is the most common reproductive tract cancer. This disease occurs primarily in menopausal and post-menopausal women, and is associated with hypertension, obesity, and long-term estrogen replacement therapy.

Each year, 10,000 American women die of uterine cervical cancer; nearly half of them are over 60. The cure rate for cancers of the cervix is now 85%. This is largely attributed to widespread availability of the Papanicoleau (Pap) smear, a quick and safe screening method that has led to increased diagnosis of pre-malignant or early cancerous conditions of the cervix.

Tragically, women over 60 are least likely to have annual Pap

TABLE 2

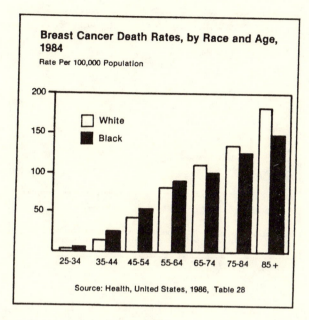

Breast Cancer Death Rates, by Race and Age, 1984

Rate Per 100,000 Population

Source: Health, United States, 1986, Table 28

TABLE 3

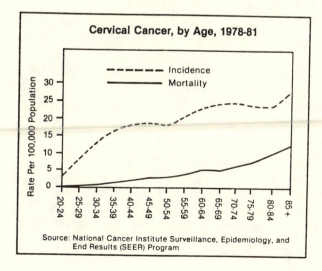

Cervical Cancer, by Age, 1978-81

Source: National Cancer Institute Surveillance, Epidemiology, and End Results (SEER) Program

TABLE 4

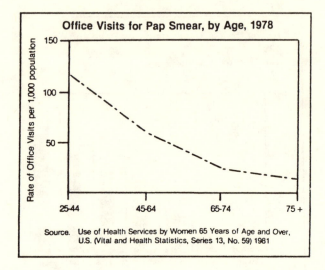

Office Visits for Pap Smear, by Age, 1978

Source. Use of Health Services by Women 65 Years of Age and Over, U.S. (Vital and Health Statistics, Series 13, No. 59) 1981

smears, or to have ever had this screening. Lack of a prior Pap smear is the most common reason for the non-detection of invasive cervical cancer. Medicare and most private health plans do not pay for such preventive tests and screenings.

While far less common than cervical cancer, ovarian cancer has a significantly higher death rate, due to the lack of mass screening technique for early detection. Once discovered, ovarian cancers require removal of the tumor and aggressive chemotherapy. This treatment now results in a two-year survival rate of 70% (up from 30% less than five years ago). Serum markers now being tested may allow future mass screening and earlier diagnosis through blood tests.

By far the fastest growing cancer among women is lung cancer. Although the incidence of lung cancer among men is far higher, rates for women have been rising since the 1960s, reflecting the increase in female smoking that began in the 1930s. For several years, experts have predicted that lung cancer will surpass breast cancer as the leading cause of death among women, but this has not yet happened.

Cardiovascular Disease

Heart disease is the leading cause of death for women over 65. Black women are at greater risk than white women, except the very old. Death rates for diseases of the heart have been declining steadily since the 1960s, due partly to progress in prevention, especially smoking cessation, control of high blood pressure and reduction of serum cholesterol. Overall, women have only about half the coronary heart disease of men, but they have no survival advantage once the disease becomes overt. In fact, women who have heart attacks are more likely to die from them than men in nearly every age group.

About two in five persons over 65 have high blood pressure. Hypertension increases with age, is twice as prevalent among Blacks as whites, and generally affects men more than women. But older Black women have the highest rates of hypertension of any group.

High blood pressure is the most common cause of increased risk to heart disease and vascular disease. Both sexes benefit from reducing blood pressure to prevent future cardiovascular disease. There is no detectable cause of the disorder in more than 90% of those who have it. Women who use oral contraceptives have a greater tendency to have strokes at an early age than women not taking the pill.

Osteoporosis

Osteoporosis, a condition marked by thinning of the bones after age 35, affects half of women over age 45, and fully nine in ten women over 75. Osteoporosis is implicated in many bone fractures, which are a leading cause of hospitalization among older women.

Sex differences in bone loss are dramatic. Between 40 and 50, men lose less than 1% of bone mass yearly. But women's loss is twice that rate, and following menopause may be four times the rate of men. Men have 30% more bone mass than women, and Blacks 10% more than whites. High risk groups thus include slender white women.

TABLE 5

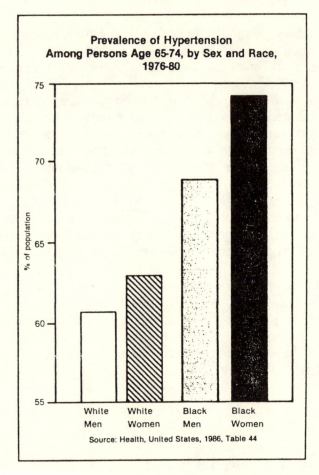

Prevalence of Hypertension Among Persons Age 65-74, by Sex and Race, 1976-80

Source: Health, United States, 1986, Table 44

Dementia

Alzheimer's disease accounts for about 75% of dementia among the elderly. It is a crippling organic brain disorder, manifested in intellectual deterioration, loss of recent memory, and behavioral and personality changes. Its victims are somewhat more likely to be female, possibly a function of women's greater longevity. As a degenerative condition, Alzheimer's has a very high "secondary victimization" rate, taking an excessive toll on family caregivers, most of whom are women.

HEALTH AND WOMEN IN THE WORKPLACE

Women have entered the workplace in dramatic numbers in recent decades, with significant implications for health status and health access. About half of all women between 45 and 65 were in the paid labor force in 1986. For midlife women, employment brings current income, the opportunity to earn Social Security and pension credits for retirement and — of key importance to millions — health insurance.

About 85% of all private health care coverage in the U.S. is group coverage through employment. But millions of full-time workers are uninsured. More than half of them work in the retail trade or service sector, three-fourths of uninsured workers earn less than $10,000 annually. Because women are more likely to be low-wage earners employed in the service sector and in small businesses, or in part-time jobs with no employee benefits, women predominate among the employed uninsured.

For midlife women, coverage is related both to employment and marital status. Married women are more likely to have coverage than widows or divorced women, whether in or out of the labor force.

Misconceptions about employed women's health status persist, despite data that show little difference between men and women. Studies suggest that the number of sick days women use is not significantly different from men, and that women are more likely to use non-work days to manage health problems. Other studies show that employed women have more days of restricted activity and lose on average just one half-day more per year than male counterparts. Such differences are minimal when allowances are made for women's reproductive role, and may also be due to their family caregiving responsibilities rather than their own health problems.

Hospital utilization rates for midlife women and men are virtually identical. After age 65, men are more likely to be hospitalized than women, although women on average stay slightly longer. Employer belief that the cost of providing health coverage for midlife women workers will be greater is not based on fact.

Employed women report fewer chronic health problems, days of incapacity, and health-related limitations on their activities than women not in the paid labor force. Both groups report about the same number of physician visits. Employed women have lower hospitalization rates, but the differences narrow after age 45. Women in "higher status" jobs, especially those over 40, report better health than women in jobs with "lower status".

Work-related health problems vary with occupation. Among midlife workers, there is not much difference in work days spent in bed (bed disability days) each year, 4.0 days for white collar and blue collar workers, and 5.5 days for service workers.

Nearly three out of four midlife women in the labor force are in clerical, other administrative, service, professional or managerial jobs. Workplace hazards in these occupations include: prolonged standing/sitting/restricted movement; poor lighting; inadequate ventilation; noise; and stress. Many chronic conditions may result: foot/leg/back/neck pain; varicose veins; muscle strain; metacarpal tunnel syndrome; visual problems; fatigue; and other stress-related health problems.

Environmental health effects often take a long time to become evident and are very difficult to trace to a single cause. Unless occupationally-related health conditions are acute, they are not usually attributed to the workplace that induced or contributed to them.

In the past, workplace and health studies have focused on traditionally male occupations. More recently, research efforts have examined occupational hazards unique to women or in predominately female occupations, often studying the health consequences on pregnancy and childbirth. Few studies have examined the effects of work on health or women over 45.

HEALTH CARE COVERAGE FOR WOMEN

Women pay for health care through private insurance, public insurance, and out of their own pockets. But age 65 is the continental divide. Before age 65, most women pay for their health care through private insurance; after age 65, most pay through Medicare and private supplement, out-of-pocket, and Medicaid.

Most women between the ages of 40 and 65 have employer-provided group health insurance, either through their own or their husband's employment. But more than 35 million Americans under age 65 have no health insurance coverage from any source. Nearly five million of them are women over 40, and their dependent children account for many more of the uninsured.

Fewer women than men have group health insurance. In 1984, almost a million more women than men had no health insurance; 14% of midlife women were uninsured compared with 11% of midlife men. Between 1980 and 1984, the number of uninsured midlife women increased by about 200,000. The risk of being uninsured increases with age, decreases with family income, and varies with marital and employment status.

Women who have group health insurance through their spouse's employment can lose coverage when marital or work status changes. A federal law enacted in 1986 provides transitional coverage, but is not retroactive. Midlife women who are widowed, divorced, or separated are almost twice as likely to be uninsured as married women.

Lack of health insurance is also related to income. In 1984, more than one in three midlife women below the poverty level had no health insurance, while only one in twenty with income of at least 3 times the poverty level was uninsured.

High-risk individuals have difficulty getting health insurance. Without group coverage, thousands of midlife women who have been diagnosed with cancer, diabetes, or other "preexisting" health conditions cannot obtain private individual health insurance at any price.

Lack of health insurance significantly reduces the amount of health care women purchase. It also increases the percentage of income they must pay out-of-pocket for medical expenses. In 1980, uninsured midlife women spent only one-third as much on medical care as women with insurance, although there is no evidence that their medical needs were any less. Eighty percent of their medical expenses came directly out-of-pocket, compared to only 27% of the

TABLE 6

General Inflation and Medical Costs, 1977-86

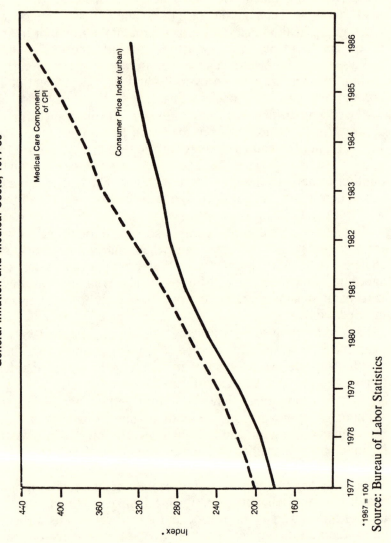

Medical Care Component of CPI

Consumer Price Index (urban)

*1967 = 100

Source: Bureau of Labor Statistics

64

medical expenses of those with insurance. In addition, health care costs have been rising faster than general inflation for the past ten years.

Even for those with insurance, many of the preventive services women need are not covered. In 1985, only 13% of all workers were covered by private health insurance that included a routine physical.

Medicaid does not fill in the gaps for most midlife women. Jointly funded by federal and state governments, Medicaid pays for a broad range of health care, including physician, hospital, and nursing home expenses. But Medicaid is required to cover only two groups of low-income persons: those who qualify for Aid to Families with Dependent Children (AFDC) or Supplemental Security Income (SSI). If a woman does not have children under age 18 or is not over 65, blind or disabled, she cannot qualify for Medicaid no matter how low her income is. Typically, to qualify for Medicaid, an applicant must have less than $1,800 in assets and $340 per month in income. Many midlife women without private insurance are too young for Medicare and unable to get Medicaid because they have grown children or are not quite poor enough.

Nearly all (94%) women age 65 and over are covered by Medicare, which pays for about half the health expenditures of the elderly. But consumers still bear a large portion of the costs of their health care. Out-of-pocket payments represent the second largest source of payment, after Medicare, and were an estimated $1,575 per person in 1984.

Medicare's emphasis on "acute care" hospitalization and physician services penalizes older women. Because many of their chronic health care needs are not covered, older women must pay a greater percentage of their income on medical expenses. It is estimated that in 1986 Medicare paid for 49% of the total health care expenditures of unmarried men over age 65, 44% of the total health care expenditures of married couples over 65, but only 33% of the total health expenditures of unmarried older women.

Unmarried women age 65 and over spent a greater percentage of their income on health care (16.3%), than did either unmarried older men (12.2%) or older married couples (8.9%). This is due both to women's lower median incomes and to their greater likelihood of having health needs that Medicare does not pay for.

Services not covered by Medicare include: preventive health screenings and examinations (for example, Pap smears and mammograms); eyeglasses; hearing care; dental services; all outpatient prescription drugs; and all long-term or chronic nursing home care. Many of these services, particularly prescription drugs and long-term care, are used extensively by older women.

LONG TERM CARE

Women are the primary users of long term care because they have more chronic health problems and live longer than men. "Long term care" includes in-home services, adult day care, and care in resident facilities, convalescent homes, intermediate care and skilled nursing facilities.

The majority of the elderly are not in nursing homes. Contrary to popular belief, only 5% of the elderly are institutionalized at any given time; 20% may require nursing home care sometime during their lifetime. The chance of institutionalization increases with age. Only 2% of persons between 65 and 74 are nursing home residents, compared with 22% of those over age 85.

The need for long term care services varies substantially by gender and age. Women reside in nursing homes at about twice the rate of men. But they also outnumber older men, especially in the oldest age categories where nursing home use is greatest. Among the 1.2 million elderly residents of nursing homes, about 900,000 — almost 75% — are women.

In 1985, about $35 billion, or 8% of national health care expenditures, was spent for nursing home care. This is three times the amount spent a decade ago, and sixteen times what was spent in 1965 when Medicare and Medicaid were established. At the same time, current public and private expenditures for home health care and other community-based long term care are only a small fraction of the amount now spent on nursing homes.

Medicare does NOT pay for long-term chronic care. Unfortunately, millions of elderly persons and their young family members incorrectly believe that it does. In fact, only if skilled nursing care

TABLE 7

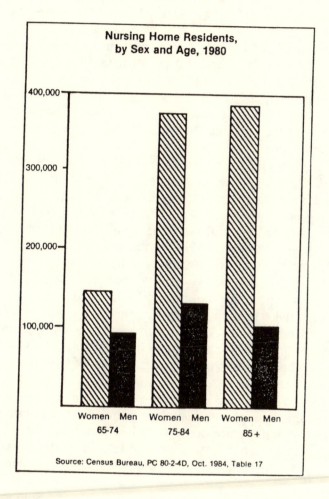

**Nursing Home Residents,
by Sex and Age, 1980**

Source: Census Bureau, PC 80-2-4D, Oct. 1984, Table 17

is needed after discharge from a hospital will Medicare pay for 20 days of nursing home care and assist with the cost of 80 additional days. In 1985, less than 1% of Medicare expenditures was spent on nursing home care.

The average cost of one year in a nursing home is approximately $22,000. This is more than the median income of elderly couples (about $18,000) and several times the median income of older women ($6,313). Most older women cannot pay for their own long term care and are often impoverished if their spouses need such care.

About half of the country's total nursing home bill is paid by residents and their families. But personal savings are quickly expended. One study estimated that two out of three elderly would exhaust their financial resources within the first year of a nursing home stay. Consequently, Medicaid, a program designed to fund health care for the poor, has become the predominant public payer of long term care.

Many women face the financial nightmare of "spousal impoverishment." Once a spouse becomes eligible for Medicaid, much of the couple's monthly income may be considered available to pay the nursing home bill. The non-institutionalized spouse may then keep only a small "spousal maintenance allowance" for living expenses. Women are more likely than men to be pauperized in this way both because they are less likely to have incomes in their own name and because they tend to outlive their husbands.

Millions of elderly, most of them women, need home-based care. In 1982, about 4.6 million non-institutionalized persons over age 65 were considered disabled; they needed assistance with personal care (such as bathing, dressing, eating) or with other daily activities (such as meal preparation or shopping). About 65% of these elderly persons are women.

Coverage of home care is extremely limited under both Medicare and Medicaid. Few private insurance policies cover at-home care, either, although more are doing so. Most home-based care is provided by unpaid caregivers, primarily female relatives. They receive no pay, no benefits, and little relief from this demanding work.

The average age of caregivers of the elderly is 57. But more than one in three is over age 65, indicating that the informal care system is composed in part of the "young-old" caring for the "old-old." About one-third of family caregivers are employed, but many reduce their hours or quit work altogether in order to meet caregiving responsibilities. The average woman today can expect to spend as many years caring for a dependent parent as she does in caring for a dependent child.

TABLE 8

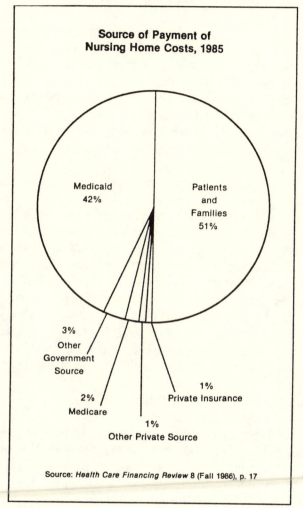

Source of Payment of
Nursing Home Costs, 1985

Medicaid
42%

Patients
and
Families
51%

3%
Other
Government
Source

2%
Medicare

1%
Other Private Source

1%
Private Insurance

Source: *Health Care Financing Review* 8 (Fall 1986), p. 17

By the year 2010, average female life expectancy is projected to increase to 86.1 years, and the number of women over age 85 will more than double. Now and in the future, the cost and availability of long term care and the lack of public and private financing alternatives are a critical concern of women.

GENDER DIFFERENCES IN HEALTH CARE

Since medicine reflects society, it is hardly surprising that sexism manifests itself in health care. Medical personnel, and doctors in particular, bring preconceptions to their interaction with patients that can work against midlife and older women. Too often women are omitted from research on aging and on diseases that affect both genders. Research on health problems that affect mostly women may be underfunded. Until recently, women in health occupations were predominately nurses. Only now are more women becoming doctors.

Research on sexism in health care delivery has resulted in evidence that health care providers treat women differently from men. Several studies conclude that physicians give women less thorough diagnostic evaluation than men with similar complaints, are more likely to give women prescriptions as part of office visits, and provide less explanation in response to questions from women than from men. Sex bias is one explanation for these differences.

There is evidence of gender differences in physician attitudes. One study of physicians showed that 65% felt women's complaints were influenced by emotional factors, 25% felt women were more likely than men to make excessive demands, and 21% thought women's complaints were more likely than men's to be psychosomatic.

Advocates have long claimed that women are more likely to undergo unnecessary surgery, such as hysterectomies. The most recent study of hysterectomy in the U.S. is inconclusive, however, partly because there is no agreement about the definition of "necessary." The research could confirm the preoperative diagnosis in only half of all hysterectomies; the diagnostic pathological examination showed no abnormalities in one in five cases.

Sexism in research is common, often by simply omitting women from the study. Important knowledge of aging-over-time is based on longitudinal studies that excluded women. The Baltimore Longitudinal Study of Aging, the leading long-term research study of the nature and experience of aging in the United States, ran for 20 years before finally adding women in 1978.

Many health research projects are conducted on men only. This is based on the justification that women's hormonal cycles make controlled conditions difficult. But findings based on research on men may then be inappropriately applied to women. Studies show that women with high blood pressure have fewer strokes and heart attacks than men with high blood pressure; yet treatment for both is based on the male model.

Research on prescription drugs also usually involves only males. The reason is to prevent possible reproductive hazards to female subjects in the study. But such drugs as anti-arthritics, tested on young men for a year or less, are then prescribed to older women for many years, with little research on appropriate dosage for women and without any research on the long-term effects on older women.

The increase of women at all levels of medical practice and research will likely change some of these practices and research protocols. Nineteen eighty-seven marks the first time that more female freshman college students say they are planning to become physicians than nurses. Twenty years ago, among female college students, prospective nurses outnumbered prospective physicians three to one.

CONCLUSION

Health care is a pressing and often overwhelming concern for older women. Women today live longer than ever before, and Americans can justifiably be proud of the strides made in increasing life expectancy. But the quality of the lives we prolong must also be considered. Women are not experiencing increased periods of good health. In fact, they can expect increased and longer periods of chronic health problems.

In short, our health care system is not adequately addressing the needs of midlife and older women. Neither medical research, health care delivery systems nor payment systems have kept pace with women's changing needs. The goal of this report is to examine what is really happening to women, so that priorities can be reordered and goals established that will lead to change. With Congress considering several crucial aspects of health care delivery and payment systems, the time is ripe to comprehensively assess health care for midlife and older women.

REFERENCES

Introduction: Census Bureau, *Vital Statistical Rates in the U.S., 1900-1940* (1943); S. Chapman, et. al., "Life Expectancy and Health Status of the Aged," *Social Security Bulletin* 49 (Oct. 1986), 24-48; Robert Wood Johnson Foundation, *Special Report* (No. 1, 1983); L. Harris for Commonwealth Fund Commission, *Problems Facing Elderly Americans Living Alone* (1987); L. Harris for National Council on the Aging, *Aging in the 80's: America in Transition* (1981); Public Health Service, *Health, United States, 1986* (1986); L. Verbrugge, "Longer Life but Worsening Health? Trends in Health and Mortality of Middle-Aged and Older Persons," in *Health and Society* 62 (No. 3, 1984), 475-519.

Women's Health Problems: American Cancer Society, *Cancer Facts & Figures-1987* (1987); Boston Women's Health Book Collective, *The New Our Bodies, Ourselves* (1984); College of American Pathologists, "Uterine Cervical Cancer" public service spot (1986); L. Krakoff, "Hypertension in Women," in *Health Needs of Women as They Age* (1985); J. Mandelblatt et. al., "Gynecological Care of Elderly Women," in *Journal of the American Medical Association* 256 (Jul. 18, 1986), 367-371; National Cancer Institute, "Surveillance, Epidemiology and End Results (SEER) Program"; National Center for Health Statistics, *Use of Health Services by Women 65 Years of Age and Over* (Series 13, No. 59, 1981), and *Patterns of Ambulatory Care in Obstetrics and Gynecology* (Series 13, No. 76, 1984); National Institute of Arthritis, Information Office and "Scientific Workshop: Research Directions in Osteoporosis," (1987); Public Health Service, *Health, United States, 1986,* and *Smoking and Health: A National Status Report* (1987); L. Verbrugge, "A Health Profile of Older Women with Comparison to Older Men," In *Research on Aging* 6 (Sept. 1984), 291-322.

Women and Health in the Workplace: M. Berk, "Women and Divorce: Health Insurance Coverage, Utilization, and Health Care Expenditures," in *American Journal of Public Health* 74 (Nov. 1984), 1276-1278; Boston Women's Health Book Collective, *The*

New Our Bodies, Ourselves, (1984); Bureau of Labor Statistics, *Employment and Earnings* (Aug. 1986); Census Bureau, *Disability, Functional Limitation and Health Insurance Coverage: 1984-85* (p-70, No. 8, 1986); S. Chapman et. al., "Life Expectancy and Health Status of the Aged," in *Social Security Bulletin* 49 (Oct. 1986), 24-48; D. Chollet, Employee Benefit Research Institute, *Uninsured in the United States: The Nonelderly Population without Health Insurance* (Mar. 1987); C. Muller, "Health and Health Care of Employed Women and Homemakers," in *Women and Health* 11 (Spring 1986); Public Health Service, *Health, United States, 1986;* D. Rice and A. Cugliani, "Health Status of American Women." in *Women and Health* 5 (Spring 1980); Women's Bureau, U.S. Dept. of Labor, *Women and Office Automation: Issues for the Decade Ahead* (1985); K. Yordy, "Health Statistics Make a Difference," in *Proceedings of the 1985 Public Health Conference on Records and Statistics,* National Center for Health Statistics (1985).

Coverage: *General Accounting Office, Health Insurance: Comparison of Coverage for Federal and Private Sector Employees* (Dec. 1986); Health Care Financing Administration, *Health Care Financing Program Statistics: Medicare and Medicaid Data Book, 1984* (June 1986); ICF Incorporated, *Medicaid's Role in Financing the Health Care of Older Women,* Prepared for the American Association of Retired Persons (Dec. 1986); F. Leonard, *Health Care Financing and Midlife Women: A Sick System,* Older Women's League (1986); Older Women's League, "Group Health Insurance Continuation: A New Law May Help You . . . ," (Oct. 1986); K. Schwartz and M. Moon, *The Health Insurance Status of Midlife Women: The Problem and Options for Alleviating It,* Urban Institute, Prepared for the American Association of Retired Persons (Dec. 1986).

Long Term Care: Census Bureau, *Persons in Institutions and Other Group Quarters* (PC80-2-4D, Oct. 1984); General Accounting Office, *An Aging Society: Meeting the Needs of the Elderly While Responding the Rising Federal Costs* (Sept. 1986); K. Liu et. al., "Home Care Expenses for the Disabled Elderly," in *Health Care Financing Review* 7 (Winter 1985), 51-58; National Center for Health Statistics, *Nursing Home Characteristics* (Advance Data, No. 131, Mar. 27, 1987); Select Committee on Aging, House of Representatives, *Exploding the Myths: Caregiving in America* (Com. Pub. No. 99-611, Jan. 1987); D. Waldo, "National Health Expenditures, 1985," in *Health Care Financing Review* 8 (Fall 1986), 1-21.

Gender Differences: K. J. Armitage et. al., "Responses of Physicians to Medical Complaints in Men and Women," in *Journal of the American Medical Association* 241 (1979), 2186-2187; B. Bernstein and R. Kane, "Physicians' Attitudes Toward Female Patients," in *Medical Care* 19 (June 1981); K. Irwin et. al., "Hysterectomy Among Women of Reproductive Age, United States, Update for 1981-1982," in *Centers for Disease Control Surveillance Summaries: MMWR* 35 (No. 1SS, 1986); N. Lee, et. al., "Confirmation of the Preoperative Diagnosis for Hysterectomy," in *American Journal of Obstetrics and Gynecology* 150 (No. 3, Oct. 1984), 283-287; L. Verbrugge and R. Steiner, "Prescribing Drugs to Men and Women," in *Health Psychology* 4(1985), 79-98; J. Wallen et. al., "Physician Stereotypes about Female Health and Illness," in *Women and Health* 4 (No. 2, 1979).

Mental Health and Older Women

Lois Grau

SUMMARY. Currently it is estimated that up to 25 percent of the elderly manifest symptoms of mental disorder. The recognition of the seriousness of the problem has lead to a growing body of research in the field of geriatric mental health. This paper presents an overview of early gerontological studies of life satisfaction and morale of older persons and of the two most prevalent mental health problems of the aged, depression and dementia. Mental health service delivery and utilization issues are also considered.

INTRODUCTION

Recent years have seen the growth in specialty practice and research in what has come to be known and broadly defined as "geriatric mental health." This is the result of the recognition that older people are, in many ways, different from their younger counterparts. And it is these differences—biological, social, economic, and psychological—that shape the research and practice interests of those concerned with the mental health needs and problems of older persons.

Just as there are differences between younger and older persons, there are also gender differences among the elderly which influence their risk and experience of mental health ill or disorder. However, with the exception of studies of gender related life change events such as retirement or widowhood, little attention has been directed at the role gender plays in the mental health of older persons.

This paper briefly overviews two facets of mental health. The first is concerned with relatively early gerontological studies which

Lois Grau is Director, Nerken Center for Geriatric Research of the Jewish Institute for Geriatric Care, New Hyde Park, NY 11042.

examined the concepts of life satisfaction and morale and their correlates. The third focuses on mental disorder, specifically depression and dementia, among older persons. Lastly, we briefly consider mental health service resources and their utilization by older
persons.

MENTAL HEALTH AND OLDER PERSONS

Specialized research on the epidemiology and treatment of mental disorders among the elderly is a relatively recent phenomenon.
Earlier studies, which fall under the general rubric of mental health,
were undertaken by gerontologists interested in older persons' levels of life satisfaction and morale. This general construct, which
rarely comes into play in the mental health literature of younger
populations, reflects the long-standing emphasis in gerontology on
various domains of quality of life. In the 1960s and 1970s, the
elderly were often portrayed as disenfranchized citizens, abandoned
by their families and society. Hence, studies were motivated by the
relevance of life satisfaction findings for public policy, as well as
by theoretical interest in factors associated with subjective well-
being.

Although the findings of these studies are not clear-cut, the majority find or suggest that physical health is the most important correlate of life satisfaction (Cutler, 1972; Palmore & Kivett, 1977;
Thompson, 1973). That health is positively associated with morale
and life satisfaction is not surprising in view of the fact that most
illnesses of older people are chronic and disabling in kind, resulting
in a loss of independence and fear of continual decline and death.

Employment, income, housing arrangements, and marital status
have also been studied for their relationship to life satisfaction, but
their results are somewhat ambiguous. Most studies of retirement
find that nonretired persons are more satisfied with their lives than
retirees (Edwards & Klemmack, 1973; Harris, 1975). However,
some studies indicate that socio-economic status is as important as
employment status in accounting for life satisfaction; that is, when
socio-economic status is controlled in the analysis the influence of
employment disappears except among those in the lowest income
groups (Chatfield, 1977). Also, the reasons for retirement, rather

than retirement itself, may account for lower satisfaction. A study by Thompson (1973) concluded that retired persons had lower morale because they also experienced poorer health, were functionally impaired, poorer, and older than those who were still employed.

Although most studies of life satisfaction fail to show differences between men and women, some areas, such as retirement, have not been adequately investigated. For example, little is known about the mental health consequences of retirement for women. As increasing numbers of women enter the labor force, retirement will become as important a life change event for women as it is for men today. Whether retirement is perceived as a release or a loss may be influenced by the extent to which employment was voluntary or an economic necessity and the degree of career commitment and involvement.

A major policy issue has been the role age segregated housing plays in the well-being of older persons. Age segregated living arrangements, such as public housing projects, "retirement villages," and age segregated "life care" communities, operate on the assumption that older people prefer to live among their own kind. However, this assumption has not been consistently supported. Some studies have found that persons in an age-segregated environment had high morale (Carp, 1967; Teaff et al., 1978), while others found the opposite (Poorkaj, 1967; Redick & Taub, 1980). Older people vary in their preference for type and composition of housing stock as they vary in other areas of life. Moreover, age composition is but one aspect of a living situation, and it may be less important than other factors such as physical location, affordability, and proximity to children and friends. Nor is it possible to generalize among different types of age segregated arrangements. Residence in a luxury retirement community, with the requisite golf course and pool, is a far cry from survival in an inner city public housing project.

An issue which has not been given sufficient attention is the role marital status plays in satisfaction with life and various types of housing arrangements. For example, couples living in retirement communities typically "age in" over time, increasing the likelihood that the female partner will become a widow. Little is known about whether and how widows are retained within or edged out of the social fabric of such communities.

Life satisfaction research set the ground work for identifying risk factors for low morale and dissatisfaction with life. While important, this body of work has been criticized for its lack of conceptual models and the failure to use mainstream social science theories to direct research on the dynamics of subject well-being (Sauer and Warland, 1982).

DEPRESSION AND DEMENTIA

More recent studies are epidemiological in kind and focus on specific organic brain and psychiatric disorders. Such investigations draw on data collection techniques (screening and diagnostic interviews) patterned after criteria specified in the Diagnostic and Statistical Manual (Version 111) of the American Psychiatric Association and use designs similar to those employed in studies of the general population.

Data from studies of the general population consistently suggest that approximately 10 percent of all persons residing in the community require some type of mental health care. This rate is exceeded among the elderly (Redick & Taub, 1980; Romaniuk, McAuley & Arling, 1983). A review of relevant studies by Finkel (1981) concludes that between 15 percent and 25 percent of older persons display significant symptoms of mental illness. The two most prevalent disorders among the elderly are depression and dementia.

Depression

Roughly 13 percent of elderly in the community evidence symptoms of depression (Gurland, Dean & Cross, 1980) and estimates suggest that between 21 and 54 percent of all elderly psychiatric patients are depressed (Peak, 1973; Redick & Taub, 1980; Vickers, 1976). Unfortunately, gender differences in the prevalence and manifestation of depression are only rarely addressed by geropsychiatrists. When they are, it is generally in reference to high rates of suicide among elderly men.

The determination of the prevalence of depression is also complicated by the use of different definitions and methods of assessment. Gurland (1976) notes that when cases are defined by psychiatrists, milder, so called neurotic depressions, have their greatest incidence between the ages of 35 and 45, while psychotic depressions manifest themselves for the first time most frequently among those between the ages of 55 and 65. After that age depressions become infrequent. On the other hand, when depression is assessed on the basis of survey instruments in community studies, the highest prevalence has been found among persons average 65. But, even community studies vary in their findings from prevalence rates of 34 percent (Gianturco & Busse, 1978; Gurland & Toner, 1982) to less than 2 percent because of the use of different assessment instruments and scoring procedures. A recent community study by Blazer, Hughes and George (1987) attempted to address this problem by assessing various sub-types of depressive disorder. They found that 8 percent of elderly persons living in the community suffered from various forms of severe or moderate depression. Nearly 19 percent had less severe dysphoric symptomatology. They point out that there are relatively large numbers of older persons in the community who suffer from clinically significant depressive symptoms who do not meet the criteria for a major depressive episode or dysthymia.

Assessment of Depression

As defined by the DSM III of the American Psychiatric Association (1980), depression is characterized by a persistently dysphoric or sad mood with loss of pleasure in usual pastimes. Epstein (1976) found that older depressed patients were more likely than younger depressed persons to experience apathy, listlessness, and self-deprecation. Worry, feelings of uselessness, sadness, pessimism, fatigue, inability to sleep and volitional difficulties also tend to be somewhat more common among older than among younger patients (Blazer, 1982).

Another important difference is the tendency of the depressed elderly to express their symptoms in somatic rather than psychological terms (Auso-Gutierrez, 1983; Blumenthal, 1975 & 1980; Card & Judge, 1974; Goldstein, 1979; Pfeiffer & Busse, 1973) and to deny the existence of dysphoria or sadness, the linchpin of DSM III criteria. Common somatic complaints include constipation, insomnia, anorexia and fatigue (Pfeiffer, 1970). Despite the denial of psychological symptoms, these individuals are as likely as those with psychological complaints to respond to treatment.

The phenomenon of somatization of depression among older persons has lead some geropsychiatrists (Fogel & Fretwell, 1985) to suggest that a new sub-type of geriatric depression be included in the DSM III classification system because somatization often results in inappropriate health service utilization (Waxman, Carner & Blum, 1983) diagnostic uncertainties (Salzman & Shader, 1979) and mis-diagnosis by primary care physicians (Fogel & Fretwell, 1985; Levin, 1965).

However, work in cross-cultural psychiatric epidemiology indicates that somatization has been found to be the most prevalent symptomatic expression of depression among adults in most non-Western countries (Kleinman & Kleinman, 1985; Marsella, 1980). Also, adults in developed countries who are of lower socioeconomic class, who reside in rural areas, or who maintain traditional religious or ethnic lifestyles are more likely to somatize than their more affluent counterparts (Kleinman & Good, 1985). These data underscore the importance membership in a particular cohort, socio-economic and ethnic group may have on the ways in which mental disorders are manifested.

Another difficulty in assessment is the close association between physical and mental disorders in the latter years of life. Verwoerdt (1981) contends that the magnitude of the depressive response is associated with the severity, rate of progression, and duration of the illness. Conditions likely to lead to depressive reactions include cardiovascular disease and cancer as well as vision and hearing losses. Persons with Parkinson's disease are also vulnerable, although it is not known whether this is a reaction to disability or biochemically related to the disease process itself (Assnis, 1977). Endocrine disorders also place the individual at risk. Hypothyroidism is particularly notable with an 80 percent incidence of depression (Addington and Fry, 1986). Lastly, certain medications can aggravate pre-existing depression or trigger depressive-like symptoms such as sedation, apathy, and lethargy. They include digitalis, antihypertensives, anti-Parkinson's, and anti-cancer drugs (Blazer, 1982).

The assessment of depression is complex and difficult because its manifestations may mimic those of physical illness and dementia while, at the same time, it may co-exist with these disorders. Crucial to assessment is the recognition of the potential for the co-existence of and interaction between social, physical, psychological and organic brain problems.

Dementia

Estimates of the prevalence of dementia among U.S. elderly range from over 2 percent to nearly 7 percent (Cross & Gurland, n.d.). Epidemiological studies in Europe have similar findings with prevalence rates varying from 1 percent to 8 percent. The range in figures is due to differences in the type of assessment instruments used and the populations studied. For example, some studies do not include persons in institutions such as nursing homes. Because over 50 percent of nursing home residents and two-thirds of patients in state and county mental hospitals have a diagnosis of "senility" or "chronic organic brain syndrome" (Meyer, 1977; Milazzo-Sayre, 1978), their inclusion or deletion in samples is important.

The risk of dementia increases with age. About 1 percent of those between the ages of 65 and 74 suffer from dementia. This figure increases to 7 percent for those between age 75 and 85, and to 25 percent for persons over age 85. If these age-specific rates remain unchanged, the growth in the number of older persons will result in a fourfold increase in cases of dementia by the year 2040 (Cross & Gurland, n.d.).

Alzheimer's Disease and Related Disorders account for roughly 50 percent of all dementias among the elderly, followed by multi-infarct dementia which is estimated to represent between 13 percent and 50 percent of cases of dementia.

Assessment of Dementia

The DSM-111 (American Psychiatric Assn., 1980) describes Alzheimer's disease as consisting of three components: (1) memory and other cognitive impairment; (2) functional and structural impairment of the brain; and (3) behavioral manifestations that affect the ability for self-care, interpersonal relationships, and life in the community. As yet there are no diagnostic tests specific to Alzheimer's Disease and related dementias. The existence of the disease can only be definitively determined on the basis of autopsy or biopsy of large numbers of neurofibrillary tangles and senile plaques in the cerebral cortex of clinically demented individuals (USDHHS, 1984). Hence, clinical diagnosis is based on the elimination of other known causes of cognitive impairment based on client history, physical assessment, neurological and psychiatric evaluations, mental status examinations and psychometric tests, as well as by laboratory studies and computerized axial tomography (CT).

Early symptoms of Alzheimer's disease include short term memory loss, such as forgetting familiar names or where objects were placed. However, the clinical interview may fail to reveal objective evidence of memory impairment. As the disease progresses, the client encounters problems with retaining information and recalling recent events. Nor is the individual able to recall the context of forgotten events so that cues which normally trigger recall fail to work. Memory loss is accompanied by a decline in the performance of routine activities, accompanied by social withdrawal, loss of initiative, impaired judgment and inappropriate social responses.

As the disease progresses, the client is no longer able to live without assistance in activities such as bathing and dressing, although toileting and eating often remain intact. The latter stage of the disease is characterized by a lack of awareness of time and place, the inability to recognize family members and friends, and personality and emotional changes which can include delusional, paranoid, and obsessive behavior, and agitation. Finally, the client loses most communication skills, is incontinent, and requires total assistance in personal care.

Possibly the two most difficult problems associated with the assessment of Alzheimer's disease is distinguishing between this type of dementia and normal benign senescence, and distinguishing Alzheimer's disease from other types of dementia and pseudodementias.

Diagnosis is particularly difficult during the early stage of the disease because symptoms of memory loss may mimic the benign loss associated with normal senescent forgetfulness (USDHHS, 1984). The publicity accorded to Alzheimer's disease and its progressive tragic course, have created fear in many elderly that they have, or will, become its victims. As a result, focus may be placed on situations of short term memory failure exaggerating its severity and frequency of occurrence. Assessment of the onset, type, context, and frequency of memory loss can aid in diagnosis. The memory loss associated with Alzheimer's disease tends to be gradual in onset and progression and the individual has difficulty with recalling forgotten events, even with prompting. The use of psychometric tests coupled with clinical evidence of cognitive impairment, may be instructive, but not indicative of the presence of organic brain disease.

Another critical issue is distinguishing Alzheimer's disease and related disorders from other organic dementias and from pseudodementia. Multi-infarct or arteriosclerotic dementia is the result of small strokes which cumulatively lead to progressive dementia. Whereas the symptoms of Alzheimer's Disease tend to have a gradual onset and generally progress slowly, arteriosclerotic dementia is characterized by a more abrupt onset, sudden deterioration with stable intervals between, emotional lability, and evidence of arteriosclerotic disease. The distinction between Alzheimer's disease and multi-infarct dementia is important because the causes of the latter are similar to those for major strokes (hypertension, high blood cholesterol, obesity, smoking, etc.) and may be amenable to preventive measures.

Global cognitive impairment may be the result of self-limiting or treatable disorders such as depressive pseudodementia, and acute confusional states or delerium (Kral, 1962). The term pseudodementia has been applied to elderly persons who complain both of depression and of memory and other cognitive problems. It has been estimated by Post (1962) that between 7 percent and 19 percent of dementias are, in fact, pseudodementias. However, he points out that it is difficult to determine whether memory deficits are concomitants of depression, or if depression occurs as an accompaniment to memory loss in the early stages of organic dementia. This problem is complicated by the fact that psychomotor slowing or agitation, labile affect, decreased libido, constipation and paranoid ideation may be features common to both depression and organic brain syndrome (Zung & Green, 1972). However, other symptoms appear to differ between the two disorders. Symptoms of depression tend to occur with a clearly defined onset and without progressive deterioration, while patients with dementia are characterized by an insidious onset with progressive failure at work and in routine activities. In addition, there is some evidence that depressed patients usually perform better on memory tests than those who are demented; however, depressed patients complain more than their demented counterparts about memory problems (Miller, 1980).

Problems of differential diagnosis between organic brain dementia and other non-organic problems are attested to by the fact that somewhere between 10 percent and 20 percent of cases diagnosed as dementia represent other, treatable conditions such as hyperthyroidism, depression, or untoward drug reactions (Gurland et al., 1980). This problem is crucial because mis-diagnosis can lead to unnecessary despair and anguish for the client and his or her family. Additionally, the irreversible and progressive nature of dementia can result in labeling clients as "untreatable" when, in fact, treatment may result in cure or improvement.

THE DELIVERY OF MENTAL HEALTH SERVICES

Probably the most significant and shocking aspect of service delivery is that the mentally frail, with few exceptions, are cared for by non-mental health workers. The reasons for this are complex. First, is the issue of access. Economic barriers to care are set up as a result of limited payment by Medicare for outpatient mental health services, the relatively small proportion of older persons who carry private health care insurance and the high costs of mental health treatment. Second, there is a shortage of mental health providers available to older persons. Mental health providers, including psychiatric mental health nurses, tend to cluster in areas where the vast majority of the population is comprised of young and middle-aged adults. In the U.S. there are more counties in the country without any licensed mental health providers than there are with providers. And lastly, the elderly themselves often tend to be reluctant to seek mental health care. For many, psychiatric illness is understood only in terms of madness. The stigma of mental illness places mental health care outside of psychological reach.

What then are the consequences of these problems for service utilization? Although approximately 25 percent of the community living elderly suffer from symptoms of mental disorder, only .6 percent to 2.7 percent of patients treated by private mental health practitioners are older adults (Harrington et al., 1986). And, while the elderly comprise over 11 percent of the population, only 6 percent of the clients of community mental health centers are 65 years of age or older (Joe, Meltzer & Yu, 1985). Racial and ethnic elderly fare even worse. The community mental health movement of the 1960s and 1970s failed to adequately assess their needs, and treatment programs were not designed to deal with their problems. As a result, the minority elderly continue to be significantly underrepresented in the utilization of mental health services.

As noted in other papers in this volume, the foremost caretaker of the elderly is the family. This informal system of care is often augmented by formal care and services, many of which are community-based programs targeted to older persons. It is only when the resources of these informal and formal systems are inadequate to meet the care needs of the frail elderly are they likely to be placed in institutions.

Formal Community-Based Services

The availability of community-based geriatric services varies from one geographic region to the next. Unlike the Western European countries, the United States does not have a national policy or system of care for the aged. Because of this, community care resources vary, depending on state and local legislation, level of economic resources, and the extent and type of philanthropic or voluntary organizations and services. Hence, what may be true for one city or part of the country is not necessarily true of another.

Despite these differences, there are national trends in service delivery. One of the most important is in the development of day care centers for the elderly. In 1980 there were fewer than 600 such programs in the country. Today there is an unknown but vastly higher number, and their growth continues. Some programs are medical in kind; that is, they provide health assessment, rehabilitation, and other health related services. Relatively few target their services to the mentally frail elderly. The majority of centers draw on a social model of care. These emphasize group activities and outings, but may also offer programs such as reality orientation. Access to day care may be limited by cost. Some programs are funded by public monies and charge limited or no fees, but others are private and may charge more than many families can afford.

Another form of community-based care is case management. Case management functions vary, but their major role is to tie together packages of services to meet the individual needs of clients. Case management has been the core of a number of federal demonstration projects which provide Medicare or Medicaid waivers enabling clients to have access to services that are otherwise not reimbursed by public dollars.

Respite care, which provides temporary relief of caregiving responsibilities to families, is a growing but still limited service within this country. Some nursing homes offer inpatient respite services. Beds are set aside for short term stays of a few days to two weeks to enable family caregivers to vacation or be temporarily relieved of caretaking responsibilities. Community agencies and private entrepreneurs are beginning to offer a range of various types of in-home "sitting" services for the same purpose. With rare exceptions, respite care is private, not reimbursed by Medicaid, Medicare or other government programs.

A major source of home care for the mentally frail elderly living in the community are non-professional homecare workers. Homecare workers are comprised of a variety of sub-groups — home health aides, home attendants, personal care workers, etc. — based on level of training and funding source (Medicaid, Medicare, or private pay). Although different in title, they have in common low wages and minimal training, despite the high level of responsibility they assume on the job. This situation has resulted in public scandals (not unlike the nursing home scandals of the 1970s) of cases of elder abuse and neglect by homecare workers. The actual incidence of such cases is unknown, but it appears to be relatively small. However, the potential for abuse and neglect remains large. Homecare workers may operate with little or no supervision, and attempts at quality assurance techniques are in their infancy.

Community-based nursing care is available to older persons under the Medicare program. However, clients must qualify as needing "skilled" and "intermittent" care under the order of a physician. Because the Medicare program is geared toward acute care needs the provision of covered homecare services is limited. Nursing care can also be obtained for a fee from the private sector, but costs are high and generally not covered by public programs or private insurance.

Institutional Care

Today, the nursing home is the foremost source of institutional care for the elderly with psychiatric and organic brain illnesses. It is estimated that between 50 and 66 percent of all nursing home residents suffer from depression or some type of organic brain disorder. The evolution of the nursing home into a mental health institution is the result of a number of factors, including the enormous growth in the private nursing home industry since the 1950s, the rapid rise in the number of elderly and concomitant increase in the prevalence of dementia; and, the failure of public policy to finance and regulate institutions designed to care for the elderly mentally ill.

Nursing homes are neither financed, regulated or staffed as mental health institutions. As a result, most facilities do not have professional personnel trained in psychiatry or mental health, let alone in geriatric psychiatry. Although some institutions use psychiatrists on a consultant basis, such persons may or may not have the training and experience necessary to deal appropriately with the complex diagnostic and treatment issues that are presented by the elderly suffering from multiple physical and mental disorders.

CONCLUSION

The mental health needs of older women are increasingly being recognized. However, inadequate attention has been paid to gender differences in the epidemiology and treatment of mental disorders. The fact that women comprise the majority of older persons does not negate the need to address gender issues. For example, while widowhood is objectively the same life change event for men as for women, its consequences are often different. Typically widowed men remarry, while widowed women do not. The result is that they often must contend with the range of psychosocial stressors associated with widowhood. Also, because women live longer then men they must deal with aging and often declining health without the support of a spouse.

The under-utilization of mental services by both older men and women is a critical problem and one that is likely to increase in the face of cost containment measures. Despite evidence that disorders such as depression are as treatable among the old as the young, most mental health workers continue to target their services to younger populations. Although the problems of service delivery and utilization are complex, involving both social and economic issues, consideration must be given to the role sexism and ageism play in the failure of society to adequately respond to the mental health needs of older women.

REFERENCES CITED

Addington, J. and Fry, P.S. (1986). Directions for clinical-psychosocial assessment of depression in the elderly. In T.L. Brink (ed.) *Clinical Gerontology: A Guide to Assessment and Intervention*. New York: The Haworth Press, Inc.

American Psychiatric Association (1980). *Diagnostic and Statistical Manual of Mental Disorders, 3rd Edition*. Washington, D.C.: A.P.A.

Assnis, G. (1977). Parkinson's disease, depression and ECT: A review and case study. *American Journal of Psychiatry*, 134:191-199.

Auso-Gutierrez, L. (1983). Late life depression — clinical and therapeutic aspects. In Davis, J.M. and Mass, J.W. (eds.) *The Affective Disorders*. Washington, D.C.: The American Psychiatric Press.

Blazer, D.G. (1982). *Depression in Late Life*. St. Louis: C.V. Mosby.

Blazer, D.G., Hughes, D.C., and George, L.K. (1987). The epidemiology of depression in an elderly community population. *The Gerontologist*, 27:3.

Blumenthal, M.D. (1975). Measuring depressive symptomatology in a general population. *Archives of General Psychiatry*, 32:971-978.

Blumenthal, M.D. (1980). Depressive illness in old age: Getting behind the mask. *Geriatrics* (April) 34-43.

Card, F.I. and Judge, T.C. (1974). *Assessment of the Elderly Patient*. London: Pitman Medical.

Carp, F. (1967). The impact of environment on old people. *The Gerontologist*, 7:106-108.

Chatfield, W. (1977). Economic and sociological factors influencing life satisfaction of the aged. *Journal of Gerontology*, 32:393-399.

Cross, P.S. and Gurland, B.J. (n.d). *The Epidemiology of Dementing Disorders.* A report on work performed for and submitted to the United States Congress, Office of Technology Assessment, Washington, D.C.

Cross, P., Gurland, B., and Mann, A. (1983). Long-term institutional care of demented elderly people in New York City and London. *Bulletin of the New York Academy of Medicine*. 59:267-275.

Cutler, S. (1972). The availability of personal transportation, residential location, and life satisfaction among the aged. *Journal of Gerontology*, 27:383-389.

Edwards, J. and Klemmack, D. (1973). Correlates of life satisfaction: A re-examination. *Journal of Gerontology*, 28:497-502.

Epstein, L.J. (1976). Depression in the elderly. *Journal of Gerontology*, 31:271-282.

Finkel, S. (ed.) (1981). *Task Force on the 1981 White House Conference on Aging of the American Psychiatric Association*. Washington, D.C.: APA Press.

Fogel, B.S. and Fretwell, M. (1985). Reclassification of depression in the medically ill elderly. *Journal of the American Geriatrics Society*. 33:446-448.

Gianturco, D.T. and Busse, E.W. (1978). Psychiatric problems encountered during a long-term study of normal aging volunteers. In A.D. Isaacs and F. Post (eds.) *Studies in Geriatric Psychiatry*. New York: John Wiley.

Goldstein, S.E. (1979). Depression in the elderly. *Journal of the American Geriatrics Society*, 27:38-42.

Gurland, B.J. (1976). The comparative frequency of depression in various adult age groups. *Journal of Gerontology*, 31:283-292.

Gurland, B., Dean, L., Cross, P., and Golden, R. (1980). The epidemiology of depression and dementia in the elderly: The use of multiple indicators of these conditions. In J. Cole and J.E. Barrett (eds.) *Psychopathology in the Aged*. New York: Raven.

Gurland, B. and Toner, J.A. (1982). Depression in the elderly: A review of recently published studies. In Eisdorfer, C. (ed.) *Annual Review of Geriatrics and Gerontology, vol. 3*. New York: Springer Publishing Co., 228-265.

Harrington, C., Estes, C., Lee, P., and Newcomer, R. (1986). Effects of state Medicaid policies on the aged. *The Gerontologist*, 26:437-443.

Harris, L. and Associates (1975). *The Myth and Reality of Aging in America*. Washington: National Council on Aging.

Joe, T.C., Meltzer, J., and Yu,, P. (1985). Arbitrary access to care: The case for reforming Medicaid. *Health Affairs*, 4: 59-74.

Kleinman, A. and Good, B. (eds.) (1985). *Culture and Depression*. Berkeley: University of California Press.

Kleinman, A. and Kleinman, J. (1985). Somatization: The interconnections in Chinese society among culture, depressive experiences, and meanings of pain.

In A. Kleinman and B. Good (eds.) *Culture and Depression*. Berkeley: University of California Press.

Kral, V.A. (1962). Senescent forgetfulness: Benign and malignant, *Canadian Medical Association Journal*, 86:257-260.

Levin, S. (1965). Depression in the aged. In M.A. Berezin and S.H. Cath (eds.) *Geriatric Psychiatry: Grief, Loss and Emotional Disorders in the Aging Process*. New York: International Universities Press, Inc., 203-245.

Marsella, A.J. (1980). Depressive experience and disorder across cultures. In H. Triandis and J. Draguns (eds.) *Handbook of Cross-Cultural Psychology, Vol. 6: Psychopathology*. Boston: Auyn and Bacon, Inc., 237-289.

Meyer, N. (1977). Diagnostic distribution of admissions to impatient services of State and County mental hospitals, United States, 1975. *Mental Health Statistical Notes 138*, United States National Institute of Mental Health.

Milazzo-Sayre, L. (1978). Changes in the age, sex, and diagnostic composition of resident populations of State and County mental hospitals, United States, 1965-1973. *Mental Health Statistical Note No. 146*, United States National Institute of Mental Health.

Miller, E. (1980). Cognitive assessment of the older adult. In J.E. Birren and R.B. Sloane (eds.) *Handbook of Mental Health and Aging* (pp. 520-536). Englewood Cliffs, N.J.: Prentice Hall.

Palmore, E.B. and Kivett, V. (1977). Change in life satisfaction: A longitudinal study of persons aged 46-70. *Journal of Gerontology*, 32:311-316.

Peak, D. (1973). Psychiatric problems of the elderly seen in an outpatient clinic. In E. Pfeiffer (ed.) *Alternatives to Institutional Care for Older Americans: Practice and Planning*. Durham, N.C.: Duke University, Center for the Study of Aging and Human Development.

Pfeiffer, E. (1970). *Multidimensional Functional Assessment: The Oars Methodology*. Durham, N.C.: Duke University, Center for the Study of Aging and Human Development.

Pfeiffer, E. and Busse, E.W. (1973). Affective disorders. In E.W. Busse and E. Pfeiffer (eds.) *Mental Illness in Later Life*. Washington: American Psychiatric Association.

Poorkaj, H. (1967). *Social psychological factors and "successful aging"*. Doctoral dissertation. University of Southern California, Dissertation Abstracts International, 28(1A), (No. 306).

Post, F. (1962). *The Significance of Affective Symptoms in Old Age*. Maudsley Monograph 10. London: Oxford University Press.

Redick, R,W. and Taube, C.A. (1980). Demography and mental health care of the aged. In J.E. Birren, R.E. Birren and R.B. Sloan (eds.) *Handbook of Mental Health and Aging*. Englewood Cliffs, N.J.: Prentice Hall.

Romaniuk, M., McAuley, W., and Arling, G. (1983). An examination of the prevalence of mental disorder among the elderly in the community. *Journal of Abnormal Psychology*, 92:458-467.

Salzman, C. and Shader, R.I. (1979). Clinical evaluation of depression in the elderly. In A. Roskin and L. Jarvik (eds.) *Psychiatric Symptoms and Cognitive Loss in the Elderly.* Washington, D.C.: Hemisphere Publishing Corp.

Sauer, W.J. and Warland, R. (1982). Morale and life satisfaction. In D.J. Mangen and W.A. Peterson (eds.) *Research Instruments in Social Gerontology: Clinical and Social Psychology, Vol 1.* Minneapolis, Minn.: University of Minnesota Press.

Teaff, J., Lawton, M., Nahemow, L., and Carolson, D. (1978). Impact of age integration on the well-being of elderly tenants in public housing. *Journal of Gerontology,* 33:126-133.

Thompson, G. (1973). Work versus leisure roles: An investigation of morale among employed and retired men. *Journal of Gerontology,* 18:339-344.

U.S.D.H.H.S. (1984). Alzheimers Disease: *Report of the Secretary's Task Force on Alzheimers Disease.* Chapter 3. Washington, D.C.: U.S. Government Printing Office.

Verwoerdt, A. (1981). *Clinical Geropsychiatry* (2nd ed.). Baltimore: Williams and Wilkins.

Vickers, R.V. (1976). The therapeutic milieu and the older depressed patient. *Journal of Gerontology,* 31.

Waxman, H.M., Carner, E.A., and Blum, A. (1983). Depressive symptoms and health service utilization among the community elderly. *Journal of the American Geriatrics Society,* 31:417-420.

Zung, W.W.K. and Green, R.C. (1972). Detection of affective disorders in the aged. In C. Eisdorfer and W.E. Fann (eds.) *Psychopharmacology and Aging* (pp. 213-224). New York: Plenum.

Community Care for the Frail Elderly: The Case of Non-Professional Home Care Workers

Eileen Chichin

SUMMARY. With the aging of the population there will be a grow-ing demand for non-professional home care workers to augment family caregivers in the care and support of the frail elderly. Despite the present and future importance of these workers, little is known about their job problems and satisfactions and their relationships with clients and their families. This paper presents an overview of what is known about this vital component of home care and suggests policy and research implications.

INTRODUCTION

Changing demographics and a growing awareness of the need for flexibility in long-term care have begun, albeit slowly, to influence the amount of services delivered to elderly individuals in their homes. Since the 1930s there has been a steady increase in the proportion of older persons within the population. Projections into the next century suggest that, by the year 2020, 25% of the United States population will be over age 65, with the greatest increase being found among those 85 and over. And, by virtue of their greater longevity, women will comprise a significant majority of the aged population.

Although biomedical advances have lengthened life expectancy,

Eileen Chichin is Brookdale Doctoral Fellow, Brookdale Research Institute on Aging, Fordham University, New York, NY 10023.

the later years of life may be accompanied by one or more chronic illnesses. While the majority of older persons are relatively healthy, those considered the "old-old" (over age 85) are likely to suffer from one or more disabling conditions. These include impairments of vision and hearing, cardiovascular disease, diabetes and arthritis. While such conditions may often be controlled to a degree by diet, exercise and/or medication, they tend to limit mobility and independence (Oktay, 1985), conferring varying degrees of frailty on this segment of the population.

Concomitant with the increased number of frail older persons in U.S. society are changes in the size and composition of the family. The family has always functioned as the major social support of the older person, especially in times of illness (Shanas, 1979). In fact, the availability of family as a support system to an increasingly dependent older individual is the key variable in preventing institutionalization (Brody et al., 1978). However, three-generation families residing in the same household have become the exception rather than the rule (although family members continue to maintain an emotional bond described as "intimacy at a distance" [Rosenmayr and Kockeis, 1963]). There has been a trend toward smaller nuclear families, many of which become fragmented as a result of divorce, with the result that single-parent households are commonplace. These changes in the size and structure of the family have limited and will continue to limit its ability to provide informal care to its aged and frail members.

Compounding these problems is the economic plight of many in American society, making the two-income family the rule rather than the exception. Those persons who had previously assumed responsibility for the care of aged family members in the community are no longer available (Treas, 1977), although many women who work outside the home also care for an aged parent (National Center for Health Services Research, 1986).

In addition to demographic influences, a number of policy issues impact upon the care of the frail elderly. Chief among these is the implementation of such cost-containment policies as the Medicare Prospective Payment System. With its emphasis on early discharge, the Prospective Payment system has resulted in large numbers of older persons leaving the hospital "quicker and sicker," placing a heavy burden on the community which is inadequately prepared to carry it.

Another major problem is this country's failure to adopt a coherent national long-term care policy designed to meet the needs of an aged and chronically ill population. The health care industry in the United States has long been "cure-oriented," and, to date, seems unable to assume the "care-oriented" philosophy necessary to deal with the multiple medical, economic and psychosocial problems of the older person. The emphasis on acute high-tech health care is counterproductive in a situation in which supportive services for chronic conditions are the primary need. The greatest proportion of the medical health care dollar buys days and weeks of sophisticated medical machinery in intensive care units in acute care hospitals. Less than 3% of medical expenditures pay for community care with the result that the chronically ill frail elderly living in the community are likely to fall through the cracks of the fragmented and underfunded system of community care.

The majority of older people, Brody (1981) tells us, are not sick and dependent, but rather healthier and more independent than the elderly of the past. They require only the "normal, garden-variety of reciprocal services that family members of all ages need and give each other on a day-to-day basis and at times of emergency or temporary illness." However, the small percentage of elderly having greater degrees of functional and cognitive impairments as a result of chronic illness find it necessary to seek a higher level of aid than the family may be prepared or able to offer. When families are unavailable or overburdened, help must be sought elsewhere. Older people resort to the use of formal assistance when the "level of technical skill or knowledge or the time involvement is beyond the informal support elements" (Cantor, 1979).

The combined effects of demographic influences and inadequate health care policies have encouraged the growth of formal caregiving services to work in concert with informal caregivers. Toward this end, the home care industry has grown by geometric proportions in order to accommodate the needs of an aging and chronically ill population. Despite the importance of the industry and its rapid expansion, relatively little is known about this important component of long-term care. The few studies which have been done focus primarily on utilization patterns, with some attention to client satisfaction (Bass and Rowland, 1983; Branch, Callahan and Jette, 1981; Hughes, 1985; Kleffel and Wilson, 1975; Pastorello, 1982; Remy and Hanson, 1981). Almost nothing is known about home care workers in general, and non-professional home care workers in particular, despite the fact that the latter are the foundation of the home care industry. This paper will overview what is known about this vital component of home care, and suggest policy and research implications.

HOME CARE: THE INDUSTRY

Historically, paid home care has been in existence since the beginning of the twentieth century when its focus was primarily in the areas of maternal and child assistance. Today, however, it tends to serve a predominately elderly clientele. In the United States, it is estimated that there is a ratio of one homemaker-home health aide to every 1000 citizens. In contrast, Sweden, Norway and the Netherlands have a ratio of one home care worker to every 100 citizens (Moore, 1982). The lower U.S. statistic is the result of a lack of access due to limited Medicare/Medicaid coverage, and possibly the low regard with which the non-professional home care worker is held. This is in contrast to some other countries, where home care work is valued as "exemplifying the highest reach of the human spirit" (Fine, 1986).

As it continues to grow, the home care industry in the United States is beset by a variety of problems. On the broadest level, the focus of policy in the field has consistently been on the design and administration of programs (Berger and Anderson, 1984) which, at present, may have proprietary or not-for-profit status, and be free-standing or hospital-based. The industry has inadequate standard-setting and monitoring of home care workers on the state level, and an absence of coherent policy on the federal level (Layzer, 1981, 1-2). Rapid expansion without controls leaves the home care industry ripe for a plethora of problems and abuses — a lesson which should have been learned from the rapid growth of nursing homes and the subsequent scandals that plagued the industry. At present, voluntary accreditation of home care agencies is available through the

National HomeCaring Council, which sets standards for the structure, staffing, service delivery, community relationships and evaluation of agencies (Robinson, 1986). These standards insist, for example, upon 60 hours of basic classroom training for home health aides. While this may be an important first step, it is of minimal value in, for example, New York City, where the greater number of non-professional home care workers are home attendants, not home health aides, or in California, where 80% of home care workers are self-employed and not under the jurisdiction of an agency.

In addition to policy issues, the home care industry has other difficulties. One is the insistence upon viewing the needs of the client residing at home from two perspectives: health-related and social. Although a holistic approach to the care of the elderly suggests that health and social needs are interrelated, there continues to be an insistence upon dichotomizing them into separate functions. This division is further split by the problem of titling. Non-professional home care workers have a variety of titles — homemaker, home health aide, home attendant, chore person, to name a few — a function of multiple funding sources rather than the nature of the tasks performed by the worker. As a result, individuals with differing titles are often performing the same tasks. This creates fragmentation and inefficient service delivery, exemplified, for example, by a Medicare program which funds a home health aide for certain short-term acute care situations, a Medicaid program which may cover a home attendant if the recipient is indigent, and Title XX of the Social Security Act, which provides federal reimbursement for "social services" (Fine, 1986). Usually, the chore person, the homemaker, and the home attendant are employed by a "social" agency, while home health aides work for "health" agencies (Hall, 1983).

WHO IS THE CLIENT?

Persons in need of non-professional home care services have the same needs as other individuals. What differentiates the two groups is that the former are unable to fulfill their needs alone or without the assistance of family, friends, or neighbors. These needs may include help with cleaning, shopping, cooking, or going out of doors. Frailer individuals may be unable to feed, bathe, or toilet themselves. When no informal support system is available, or if the constraints of time, skill, or willingness preclude its ability to do what is needed, older persons or their families must turn to the formal system for assistance.

While the older individual is the identified client, very often the family benefits from the services of the home care worker. Informal caregivers provide the bulk of care to frail elderly (Brody, 1981; Brody et al., 1978; Cantor, 1983; Lindsey and Hughes, 1981; Shanas, 1979; Smyer, 1980), but pay a heavy price in the form of varying degrees of emotional, physical, and financial strain (Cantor, 1983). The respite provided by a home care worker can alleviate these feelings of strain, enabling the family and friends to perform their caregiving tasks for longer periods and with greater ease.

WHO IS THE WORKER?

The only study done to date which focuses on the work situation of the home care worker (Donovan, 1986) suggests that almost half of all home care workers are foreign-born and almost all are female. This latter finding is to be expected, since this work attracts those who are poor and poorly educated, and, as a result, have limited job opportunities. Also, paid caregiving is an outgrowth of the woman's traditional role, the result of sex-role stereotyping which often places women in job roles that are extensions of their personal lives (Pines, Aronson and Kafrey, 1981).

As mentioned earlier, the actual role and definition of home care workers is confusing and ambiguous, with chore workers, home health aides and home attendants having similar tasks listed in their job descriptions. In New York City, home attendants are described as persons who "provide personal care and perform household tasks including shopping, meal preparation, and cleaning" (Caro and Blank, 1985). This generalizing of their duties under the umbrella terms "personal care" and "household tasks" creates difficulties for both the worker and the client. Lack of a clear definition causes role conflict for the worker when clients and staff have differing expectations (Haemmerlie and Montgomery, 1982). The role and duties of home care workers are much less rigidly described than their counterparts in hospitals or nursing homes (Auman and Conry, 1985), with the result that workers are often unsure of their specific job roles.

The non-professional worker in the home is faced with enormous responsibilities. They are often the first to notice changes in the client's condition (Jenkins, 1984), and in emergency situations, are the only persons available to assist clients. They may be forced to resolve problems or deal with situations for which they have been inadequately prepared (Auman and Conry, 1985). Nonetheless, the home care workers' proximity to and intimate contact with their clients often place them in a situation similar to that of aides in nursing home settings who, in addition to providing person care to their clients, may also provide a high level of emotional support (Waxman, Carner and Berkenstock, 1984).

Although comprised of necessary and vital tasks, much of home care work is seen as unpleasant, demanding or menial (Fine, 1986). Maslach (1982) in her work on burnout, suggests that every society has its "dirty" work. While the work itself is of utmost importance, those who do it are held in low esteem. With respect to health care, Fine (1986) believes that such services are similarly divided into the "honorable" and the "dirty." The non-professional worker in the home is usually viewed as performing the latter, despite the fact that her work includes the most intimate level of personal care, and those tasks often perceived by family members to be the most burdensome (Hooyman, Gonyea and Montgomery, 1985).

In addition to the low regard afforded their work, non-professional home care workers have been found to experience a variety of problems in the workplace. In addition to caring for clients who may suffer from a range of physical conditions or functional limitations, they must also deal with different and sometimes difficult personalities. Relationships with families may be positive or negative, and the worker may view the family as boon or bane. While some home care workers may be regarded almost as a member of the family, others feel that clients and their families look upon workers as little more than maids. Workers may, on occasion, be subjected to verbal abuse, especially from clients who are cognitively impaired, or they may be asked to do things that are not part of the job, such as the laundry of adult children. Occasionally workers may experience difficulty responding to requests and complaints from clients or their families, or be unable to initiate their own requests. They may have problems completing assigned tasks because of interpersonal behaviors, and often have a sense that they are performing inadequately (Berger and Anderson, 1984). Preliminary findings of current studies (see, for example, Cantor and Grau, in progress) suggest that some home care workers feel their training is inadequate to prepare them for many of the situations they routinely encounter in the client's home.

While some workers enter the home care field because of their inability to get another job, others view home care as an entry into the health care field. However, opportunities for advancement are minimal or non-existent because of the absence of a career ladder. If one does not possess the resources to leave the home care field and obtain other training, she — or he — finds that once a home care worker, always a home care worker.

In addition to interpersonal problems in the workplace, inadequate supervision and training, and absence of a career ladder, financial remuneration is a major problem for non-professional home care workers. In 1988, for example, in New York City, a home attendant earned $4.15 an hour, with an increase of thirty cents after one year of employment. The laws which cover overtime pay exclude non-professional home care workers, so that a twenty-four hour live-in worker is compensated for only twelve hours of work per day (New York Times, 28 Jan 1988). Although they may wish to, agencies are often unable to provide decent benefits for their workers because of low Medicaid/Medicare reimbursement rates.

Isolation becomes another problem for home care workers, as they have little contact with the employing agency. While some workers actually prefer this level of autonomy, others may feel helpless and alone, and consider themselves a forgotten component of the health care team (Turner, 1983).

While a large number of workers remain in home care for a number of years, high turnover rates are not uncommon. Attrition in the home care field is felt to be the result of low pay and poor benefits (Moore and Layzer, 1983). Those who remain often do so because of their inability to get another job. Nonetheless, many consider their work important, develop emotional ties with their clients

(Kaye, 1986), and believe that their provision of personal care and respite for families is their most important contribution (Burns and Ciaccia, 1985). It is moving to note the testimony of one home care worker on homemaker-home health aide issues before the National Association for Home Care Annual Meeting in October, 1985: "Everything we homemakers, or whatever name you decide to give us, do with our clients, 99 per cent of us do it through love" (Lopez and Ponder, 1986).

HOME CARE:
IMPLICATIONS FOR POLICY AND PRACTICE

There are abundant implications for policy and practice in the field of home care on several levels. In the national arena, there is a need for comprehensive long-term care policies which would incorporate home care for frail elderly into a system of other necessary services. In conjunction with this is the formulation of uniform regulations and procedures to monitor the industry. Concomitantly, research on the national level must address such issues as utilization patterns which, when studied in the past, have tended to use small and/or non-representative samples. Typically utilization is driven by entitlements to various state, federal or local programs. Relatively little is known about variations in access and utilization among different populations as defined by minority/majority membership, urban/rural residence or socio-economic class. Even less is known about the private pay home care market. Data on annual national out-of-pocket expenditures, amount and level of care delivered, worker training and supervision, and agency sponsorship is sorely lacking.

The fact that workers are variously defined and titled on the basis of the multiple funding sources which finance non-professional home care leads to artificial distinctions between "health" and "social care," role confusion among workers and their clients, and inequities in job benefits. Ideally, this horizontal fragmentation would be replaced by a vertical career ladder in which high quality job performance would open doors to additional training and career advancement. Such a national effort would serve to retain the most motivated and skilled workers as well as contribute to the planning and provision of care specifically matched to client need. Additional studies of both workers' and clients' attitudes toward nonprofessional home care are needed to help in the development of appropriate levels of care, training for more advanced positions, and worker selection criteria.

Other issues have to do with the fact that home care is labor intensive human service work. Little is known about the factors which contribute to successful matches between workers and clients in terms of the development of, if not rapport and friendship, at least mutual respect. For example, are clients and workers more satisfied when they share membership in the same or similar ethnic group? Is this less important than say, for example, personality characteristics, or the desire to care for certain types of clients rather than others? This raises questions about how quality of care should be evaluated particularly in cases when clients cannot speak for themselves or are difficult to manage as a result of psychiatric illness or organic brain impairment. On site supervision — both to evaluate care and to support the worker and the client — is seldom an inherent part of the delivery of care. As a result client/worker mediation is generally in response to crisis situations that might have been prevented with earlier intervention.

In conclusion, it must be noted that home care is a women's industry — a predominately female workforce sharing a burden previously borne primarily by women in families and serving a population in which older women comprise a significant majority. It is a classic example of "women's work," and, as such, is undervalued, underpaid, unsung. Thus, while it deserves attention on its own merits, it does so to a greater degree as a women's issue.

REFERENCES

Auman, J. and Conry, R. (1985). An evaluation of the role, theory and practice of the occupation of homemaker. *Home Health Services Quarterly, 5* (3-4), 135-58.

Bass, S.A. and Rowland, R.H. (1983). *Client satisfaction of elderly homemaker services — an evaluation.* Gerontology Program, the College of Public and Community Services, University of Massachusetts, Boston, MA.

Berger, R.M. and Anderson, S. (1984). The in-home worker: serving the frail elderly. *Social Work,* 456-61.

Branch, L.G., Callahan, J.J. and Jette, A.M. (1981). Targetting home care services to vulnerable elderly. Massachusetts Home Care Corporations. *Home Health Care Services Quarterly, 2* (2), 41-57.

Brody, E.M. (1981). 'Women in the middle' and family help to older people. *Gerontologist, 21,* 471-480.

Brody, S.J., Poulshock, S.W. and Masciocchi, C.F. (1978). The family caring unit: a major consideration in the long-term care system. *Gerontologist, 18,* 556-61.

Burns, S. and Ciaccia, W. (1985). Home health aides: the changing role: one agency's experience. *Home Health Care Nurse, 3* (1), 35-37.

Cantor, M. (1979). Neighbors and friends: An overlooked resource in the informal support system. *Research on Aging, 1,* 434-463.

Cantor, M. (1983). Strain among caregivers: a study of experience in the United States. *Gerontologist, 23,* 597-603.

Cantor, M. and Grau, L. (in progress). Stress and strain among home care workers. Funded by United Hospital Fund and Morgan Guaranty. New York: Fordham University.

Caro, F.G. and Blank, A. (1985). *Home Care in New York City.* New York: Community Services Society.

Donovan, R. (1986). *The health and social needs of home care workers: preliminary report.* New York: Hunter College School of Social Work.

Fine, D. (1986). The home as the workplace: prejudice and inequity in home health care. *Caring 5,* (4), 12-19.

Haemmerlie, F.M. and Montgomery, R.L. (1982). Role conflict for aides in a homemaker aide program for frail elderly persons. *Psychological Reports, 51,* 63-69.

Hall, H. D. (1983). The National HomeCaring Council's standards for paraprofessional services: A critical guide. *Pride Institute Journal for Long-Term and Home Health Care, 2* (3), 24-25.

Hooyman, N., Gonyea, J. and Montgomery, R. (1985). The impact of in-home service termination on family caregivers. *Gerontologist, 25*(2), 141-145.

Hughes, S.L. (1985). Apples and oranges? A review of evaluations of community-based long-term care. *Health Services Research, 20*(4), 461-488.

Jenkins, E.H. (1984). Homemakers: The core of home health care. *Geriatric Nursing, 5*(1), 28-30.

Kaye, L. (1986). Worker views of the intensity of affective expression during delivery of home care services for the elderly. *Home Health Services Quarterly, 7*(2), 41-54.

Kleffel, D. and Wilson, E. (1975). *Evaluation Handbook for Home Health Agencies.* Washington, DC: U.S. Government Printing Office.

Layzer, E. (1981). *Individual Providers in Home Health Care.* New York: National HomeCaring Council.

Lindsey, A.M. and Hughes, E.M. (1981). Social supports and alternatives to institutionalization for at-risk elderly. *Journal of the American Geriatrics Society, 29*(7), 308-15.

Lopez, D. and Ponder, C. (1986). The independent provider: testimony before the October 1985 Homemaker-Home Health Aide Hearing. *Caring,* 5(4), 40-41.

Maslach, C. (1982). *Burnout: The Cost of Caring.* Englewood Cliffs, NJ: Prentice Hall.

Moore, F. (1982). Homemaker-home health aide service essential to home care. *Caring,* 12-13.

Moore, F.M. and Layzer, E. (1983). Supporting the homemaker-home health aide as a valuable player on the home health care team. *Pride Institute Journal for Long-Term and Home Health Care,* 2(3), 19-23.

National Center for Health Services Research, quoted in Older Women's League press release, "Family caregivers—a fact sheet" (November 1986).

New York Times (28 Jan 1988). New York's home health care system facing a labor crisis. Sec. B:1.

Oktay, J. (1985). Maintaining independent living for the impaired elderly. *Aging, No. 349,* 14-18.

Pastorello, T. (1982). *Cost-effectiveness analysis of alternative programs in long-term care: substantive and methodological evaluative research within the Loretto Geriatric Center System.* Syracuse, NY: Syracuse University School of Social Work.

Pines, A.M., Aronson, E. and Kafrey, D. (1981). *Burnout: From Tedium to Personal Growth.* New York: The Free Press.

Remy, L.L. and Hanson, S.P. (1981). *Evaluation of the Emergency Family Care Program: San Francisco Home Health Services: Component One: The Basic Evaluation.*

Robinson, N. (1986). Standard-setting and accreditation by the National Home Caring Council. *Caring,* 5(4), 34-39.

Rosenmayr, L. and Kockeis, E. (1963). Propositions for a sociological theory of aging and the family. *International Social Science Journal, XV*(3), 410-426.

Shanas, E. (1979). The family as a social support system in old age. *Gerontologist,* 19(2), 169-174.

Smyer, M. (1980). The differential usage of services by impaired elderly. *Journal of Gerontology, 35,* 249-55.

Treas, J. (1977). Family support systems for the aged: some social and demographic considerations. *Gerontologist, 17,* 486-91.

Turner, P. (1983). Homemaker-home health aides as members of the home health care team. *Pride Institute Journal for Long-term and Home Health Care, 2*(3), 26-7.

Waxman, H.M., Carner, E.A. and Berkenstock, G. (1984). Job turnover and job satisfaction among nursing home aides. *Gerontologist, 24,* 503-509.

Stress and Adaptation Patterns of Older Osteoporotic Women

Karen A. Roberto

SUMMARY. This study explored the ways in which osteoporosis affected the lives of 115 community-dwelling older women. Stress and adjustment patterns were the main variables examined. The women perceived more stress in their lives since being diagnosed with osteoporosis than before the diagnosis. Pain, loss of roles, and other limitations placed on the women due to their condition contributed to their feelings of stress. Both short and long term coping strategies were developed by the women to help them adapt to their illness.

Osteoporosis results from the excessive and prolonged loss of bone mass to the point that microscopic or more obvious fracturing has occurred (Notelovitz & Ware, 1985). Genetic, mechanical, nutritional and hormonal factors appear to be responsible for these fractures (Heaney, 1983). Genetic factors influence fracture risk insofar as large-boned persons are more protected than are small-boned persons. While all individuals lose bone mass as they get older, persons with large amounts of bone mass work from a higher peak mass and by age 70 to 80 still have relatively more bone mass than persons of the same age who started with smaller skeletons (Heaney, 1983). Mechanical loading (i.e., physical exercise, movement, etc.) is responsible for variation in bone mass around the genetically determined level. Increased loadings results in in-

Karen A. Roberto is Coordinator, Gerontology Program, Department of Human Services, University of Northern Colorado, Greeley, CO 80639.

This study was funded by a grant from the AARP Andrus Foundation. This is a revised version of a paper presented at the Fourth National Forum on Research in Aging: Health, Wellness and Independence, Lincoln, NE, September, 1987.

creased bone mass and decreased loadings result in decreased bone mass (Heaney, 1983). In general, physical activity declines with age, even in the most active individuals. Since bone mass is a function of mechanical factors, it follows that bone mass will inexorably decline with age. There is also growing evidence that nutritional, hormonal, and chemical factors, such as calcium, vitamins, estrogen, and alcohol, play important roles in age-related bone mass loss by influencing the rate and level from which age-related loss occurs (Heaney, 1983).

GENDER DIFFERENCES

Older women are particularly susceptible to bone mass loss and far exceed men in the percentage of osteoporotic fractures. A decline of bone mass begins for both men and women in their early 20s with a loss of trabecular bone (the interior meshwork of the bones) from the spine (Notelovitz & Ware, 1985). From the start women lose bone mass more rapidly than men. By the time a woman reaches 80, she will have lost 47% of her trabecular bone while her male counterpart will have lost approximately 14% (Notelovitz & Ware, 1985).

Men and women also experience a slight loss in cortical bone mass until they are around 50 years of age. Cortical bone is the compact layer of bone which forms the outer shell of the bones. However, when women experience menopause they begin losing cortical bone twice as fast as men do. During the first five to six years following menopause their bone mass loss is actually six times as rapid as for men (Notelovitz & Ware, 1985). Following this time, the bone loss slows to a similar rate as seen in men, but, because of the acceleration of loss during the postmenopausal period, a higher proportion of older women develop cortical osteoporosis with advancing age. It has been estimated that 50% of all women will suffer from cortical osteoporosis by the age of 70 and 100% by the age 90 (Nordin, 1983).

Estrogen replacement therapy has been suggested as one means to supplement the post-menopausal woman's diminishing estrogen reserve. Estrogen has been found to prevent cortical bone loss for as long as the woman uses it (Christiansen, Christiansen, McNair, Hagen, Stocklund, & Transbol, 1980; Hutchinson, Polansky, & Feinstein, 1979). However, controversy exists regarding the long-term risks of estrogen therapy. Several studies have demonstrated an increase risk of endometrial cancer among women who have taken estrogen for more than one year (Notelovitz & Ware, 1985; Ryan, 1975). There is also concern that the use of estrogen may increase the risk of breast cancer (Notelovitz & Ware, 1985).

While the loss of estrogen is a natural part of the aging process, some possible causative or contributory influences on the development of osteoporosis have been identified that women can exert more control over. For example, a consistent regime of weight-bearing exercise (e.g., jogging or walking) has been suggested as a retardant of the progression of osteoporosis (Avioli, 1983; Notelovitz & Ware, 1985; Oyster, Morton, & Linnell, 1984). Other preventive measures include meeting the recommended daily allowance (RDA) of calcium and vitamin D, limiting the amount of protein and fat in one's diet, avoiding excessive use of alcohol and caffeine, and abstaining from cigarette smoking (Avioli, 1983; Budoff, 1983; Kamen & Kamen, 1984; Notelovitz & Ware, 1985).

STRESS

Living with a chronic condition, such as osteoporosis, can create unwarranted stress for the older woman. Physical, emotional, or even imagined events may constitute stressors that impact upon the osteoporotic woman's ability to function. Assessment of the amount and type of stress experienced by a chronically ill person is an important step in understanding the disease process. Three stages have been identified to determine the degree of stress an individual may experience: primary appraisal, secondary appraisal, and coping (Holroyd & Lazarus, 1982; Lazarus, 1966; Lazarus & Folkman 1984). Primary appraisal of the event is based upon the person's understanding of him or herself, the event, and prior learning. If the person perceives the stressor as threatening or as having caused pervious harm or loss, then secondary appraisal takes place. Here, the person judges how much control over the situation he or she has. Holroyd and Lazarus (1982) state that this decision is influenced by previous experience in similar situations, generalized beliefs about the self and the environment, and the availability of personal and environmental resources (p. 23). The final stage, coping, can be identified by the actions taken to relieve the stressor. Following this effort, the individual reappraises the original stressor to determine whether it has been diminished or if other additional coping methods are necessary.

Several studies have demonstrated an association between stressful life events and the development of such physical health problems as heart disease and cancer (Holmes & Masuda, 1974; Rahe & Arthur, 1978; Rosenman & Chesney, 1982). According to the life events model, the experience of significant recent life change is considered to cause stress and to require adaptational energy and resources to cope (Holmes & Rahe, 1967). Psychiatric disorders (e.g., anxiety and depression) have also been related to stress. One popular model, the vulnerability hypothesis (Dohrenwend & Dohrenwend, 1981), suggests that chance exposure to stressors triggers illness onset in already vulnerable people. While the source of the vulnerability varies depending upon the disorder being studied, the resources available to the person such as social supports, money, or personal coping skills, are considered mediating factors that determine the impact of the stressor on the person and therefore affect the probability of illness (Rabkin, 1982, p. 567). Hence, both of these models reinforce the importance of appraisal by the individual of the event and the situation surrounding it.

ADAPTATION TO CHRONIC ILLNESS

The growing literature about osteoporosis, and chronic illness in general, pertains mainly to the medical aspects and medical management of the disease. The psychodynamics of chronically ill individuals have not been well described. We do know that chronic illnesses tax the resources of individuals and force them to deal with their life sustaining condition. Thirteen adaptation tasks of chronically ill adults have been identified by Miller (1983): (1) maintaining a sense of normalcy; (2) modifying daily routines and adjusting lifestyle; (3) obtaining knowledge and skill for continuing care; (4) maintaining a positive self concept; (5) adjusting to altered social relationships; (6) grieving over losses concomitant with chronic illness; (7) dealing with role change; (8) handling physical discomfort; (9) complying with prescribed regiment; (10) confronting the inevitability of one's own death; (11) dealing with the social stigma of illness or disability; (12) maintaining a feeling of being in control; and (13) maintaining hope despite an uncertain or downward course of health.

Most of these tasks are relevant to a woman with osteoporosis. For example, osteoporosis is expensive. For an elderly woman already on a limited income, the cost of medical and rehabilitative care can be overwhelming. Another loss associated with osteoporosis is independence. Even in the simplest case, such as a fractured forearm, a woman is limited in performing routine duties. With more severe fractures, dependency on others increases substantially. Osteoporosis can also be very painful, hence the woman must learn to handle the discomfort. In addition, the physical deformities caused in cases of vertebral fractures (i.e., stooped posture, dowager's hump, and protruding abdomen) can greatly affect the woman's self-esteem and confidence.

Strauss and his colleagues (1984) suggest that if health care personnel, service providers, family members and others are going to be effective in aiding chronically ill persons there must be an understanding of the social and psychological problems facing them in their daily lives. They recommend a framework for understanding the daily experiences of chronically ill persons that include identifying the key problems and basic strategies used for dealing with these problems. This information, however, has not been systematically obtained from elderly women with osteoporosis. Therefore, the purpose of this study is to expand our knowledge of living with osteoporosis by focusing on the problems facing women who suffer with this devastating disease. Specifically, this paper explores the ways in which osteoporosis has affected the daily lives of its victims, the stress created by this disease, and how the women have adapted to living with this chronic condition.

METHOD

Sample

A purposive sample of 115 older women, all of whom were diagnosed as osteoporotic by a physician, were interviewed for this study. They ranged in age from 57 to 93 (M = 70.3). The women were living in their own homes, either with their spouse (47.0%), alone (41.7%), or with another family member or friend (11.3%). The women had a mean educational level of 13.6 years and reported their mean income to range between $900 and $999 per month. When asked to rate their overall health at the present time, 10.0% of the women perceived themselves in poor health, 31.0% said they were in fair health, 47.0% felt their health was good, and 12.0% reported being in excellent health. The women reported having an average of 3.14 other illnesses in addition to their osteoporosis. The most common conditions reported were arthritis (71.3%), allergies (43.0%), circulation trouble (32.7%), and digestive difficulties (30.7%).

Procedure

An interview schedule was developed specifically for this study. It consisted of two parts: (1) a written survey which was administered orally to each of the participants; and (2) a tape recorded guided interview. Open-ended as well as forced choice items were used to gather information about the women. Data was obtained on the physical, psychological, and social aspects of living with osteoporosis.

All of the women volunteered to participate in this study. Advertisements, requesting their participation, were placed in the major newspapers serving the Denver-metropolitan area and the front range of Northern Colorado. Notices were also placed in the newsletters of area organizations serving seniors and local churches. Several physicians in the sampling area also distributed written information about the study to their patients who were eligible to participate. If a woman was interested in participating in the study she was instructed to contact the project staff for further information and to schedule an appointment to be interviewed. In most cases, the interview took place in the women's home. The interviews took between two and three hours to complete.

RESULTS

Diagnosis of Osteoporosis

The women had first been diagnosed as having osteoporosis an average of 5.0 years ago, with 42.0% of the respondents being diagnosed within the last year. Reaction to the diagnosis varied. Half of the women (51.0%) said they were not that upset by the diagnosis. They saw it as something they would just have to live with. Another group of women (30.0%) found it very hard to believe and did not really understand what osteoporosis was. The third group of women (19.0%) said they expressed a lot of emotions ranging from sadness to anger to denial.

While osteoporosis is often equated with broken bones, 46.0% of the women in this study had not experienced an overt fracture. For those who had, fractures of the vertebra (48.2%) were the most prevalent. Other types of fractures included wrist (10.3%), leg or ankle (8.6%), and hip (7.0%). Approximately 26.0% of the women reported having multiple types of fractures. Regardless of whether or not a specific fracture had occurred, 86.0% of the women reported suffering with acute or chronic pain which they equated with their osteoporosis.

Several of the women experienced changes in their physical appearance as a result of the osteoporosis. The most frequent changes reported were the loss of height (40.5%), rounding of the shoulders (33.3%), and a protruding stomach (20.7%). Multiple physical changes were not uncommon among the women. When asked if these physical changes created any difficulties for them, 69.0% said "yes." The most common complaints were that their clothes did not fit right; the changes were painful and uncomfortable; and they did not like how they looked.

Stress

The *Perceived Stress Scale* (PSS) (Cohen, Kamarck, & Mermelstein, 1983) was used to examine the amount of stress in the women's lives. This scale was originally designed to measure the degree to which situations in one's life are appraised as stressful (p. 385). It has 14 items. For each item, respondents were asked how often they felt or thought a certain way. Possible responses were (0) never, (1) almost never, (3) sometimes, (4) fairly often, and (5) very often. The items were summed for a total PSS score. The older women were asked to complete the scale in relation to having osteoporosis using three different points in time as reference: before diagnosis, at the time of diagnosis, and at the present time. Using Cronbach's Alpha, reliability scores for the scale were .87 for each of the three times of measurement. The women expressed a significantly greater amount of stress currently (M = 21.07) in their lives than before their diagnoses (M = 18.41), $t(109) = -3.70$, $p <$ .001. The greatest amount of stress was perceived at the time of diagnosis (M = 22.57). No significant relationship was found between how the women reacted to the diagnosis and their perceived level of stress at the time of diagnosis.

Reactions to each of the individual items were compared using paired t-tests (Table 1). The women's responses for eight of the fourteen items, indicated a higher stress level currently than before the diagnosis. Specifically, the women currently perceived themselves as becoming more upset when something unexpected happened; felt more nervous; felt less effective in coping with change; had less confidence about their ability to handle problems; were not as likely to feel things were going their way; were not able to cope with all the things they had to do; felt less on top of things; and felt less in control of the way they spent their time.

Adaptation Patterns

During the guided interview, the women were asked, "When your osteoporosis is really bothering you, what kinds of things do you do that help you *cope* with it." While 19.0% of the women said that they just went on with their day and did not let their osteoporosis bother them, the other women mentioned at least one thing that

Table 1

Mean Perceived Stress Scores Before and After Diagnosis of

Osteoporosis

Stress Item	Before	Currently	t-tests
1. Becomes upset because something happened unexpectedly	1.50	1.70	-2.66**
2. Unable to control important things in your life	1.77	1.85	-.95
3. Feel nervous and "stressed"	1.89	2.09	-2.23**
4. Deal successfully with irritating life hassles	.92	1.08	-1.84
5. Effectively cope with important changes occurring in your life	.70	.91	-2.96**
6. Feel confident about ability to handle personal problems	.56	.95	-5.07***
7. Feel things were going your way	1.00	1.24	-2.70**
8. Could not cope with all the things that you had to do	1.62	1.76	-1.68
9. Able to control irritations in your life	.83	1.11	-3.73***
10. Feel you were on top of things	.85	1.26	-4.89***
11. Angered because things happened outside of your control	1.89	1:92	-0.41
12. Thinking about things that you have to accomplish	2.72	2.67	0.57
13. Able to control the way you spend your time	.62	.50	-2.01*
14. Feel difficulties were piling up so high that you could not overcome them	1.44	1.61	-1.73

n = 114
***p < .011; **p < .01; *p < .05

helped them cope. The most common coping mechanisms used were taking pain relievers (44.9%), lying down and resting (33.6%), and using a heating pad or taking a hot bath (31.8%) (Table 2). As might be expected, women experiencing pain with their osteoporosis used a significantly greater number of coping mechanisms than those who did not report pain, $t(104) = -3.66$, $p < .001$. The total number of coping mechanisms was also positively correlated with the total amount of perceived stress in the women's lives ($r = .17$). Women who perceived their current lives as being more stressful used a greater number of coping mechanisms.

The women were also asked to describe the specific *types of adjustments* they had made in their daily lives because of their osteoporosis. On average, the women had made 1.7 adjustments in their daily routines. The most frequently reported adjustments were giving up housework (35.8%), using a supportive device (32.0%) and limiting social and recreational activities (22.0%) (Table 3). The women who reported experiencing pain with their osteoporosis were significantly more likely to make a greater number of adjustments in their daily lives than those not experiencing pain, $t(107) = -2.97$, $p < .01$. The total number of adjustments was also positively related to the total number of coping mechanisms used. Women who had to make a greater number of adjustments in their

Table 2

Most Common Coping Mechanisms Used by the Women[a]

Take pain relievers	44.9%
Lie down and rest	31.8%
Use heating pad or take a hot bath	31.8%
Exercise	17.9%
Sedentary activities (watch TV; read; etc.)	12.3%
Sit down with pillows	9.4%

[a] multiple response

n = 115

daily routines also used a greater number of coping mechanisms (r = .36).

A discriminant analysis was used to distinguish between women who have had to make adjustments in their daily routines and those who had not. Five variables which were believed to have an influence on adjustment patterns were entered into the equation: age, length of diagnosis (in months), whether or not they experienced any pain (dummy coded), and current stress level. Four variables had sufficient discriminating ability to enter the analysis: age, fracture versus no fracture, pain versus no pain, and current stress level. A significant function was produced, accounting for 20.0% of the variance. The function was weighted primarily by whether or not pain existed (.70) and whether or not a fracture had occurred (.48). The women who had made adjustments in their lives were older, more likely to have experienced a fracture, more likely to be experiencing pain, and perceived a greater amount of stress in their current lives.

Table 3

Types of Adjustments Made by the Women[a]

Giving up housework	35.8%
Using a supportive device (cane, back brace, walker, etc.)	32.0%
Limiting social and recreational activities	22.0%
No lifting	19.3%
Resting more	14.7%
Be careful walking	12.3%
Slowing down pace of life	12.3%
No reaching	6.4%

[a]multiple response

n = 115

DISCUSSION

The results of this study indicated that women with osteoporosis often have to make several changes in their daily lives as a result of their condition. For many women, this was a very stressful experience. The amount and type of stress reported can perhaps best be explained in terms of the specific problems or adjustments osteoporosis brought with it.

Stress may have been brought on by the pain often associated with this disease. Pain can be defined as a complex multidimensional phenomenon which according to Chapman (1977) has four dimensions: sensory, motivational-emotional, conceptual-judgmental, and social-cultural. Using these four dimensions, the relationship between pain and stress in the lives of the older women in this study can be explored. The process begins with the sensory dimension at the point of physical injury or distress. For the osteoporotic woman this would be the pain associated with any fracture or in the case of a collapsing vertebra a mid or lower backache largely due to muscle spasms and ligament strain (Notelovitz & Ware, 1985). The motivational-emotional dimension occurs when the woman feels the pain and becomes aroused and motivated to terminate the sensation. These two dimensions correspond to the primary appraisal phase of stress identification (Holroyd & Lazarus, 1982; Lazarus, 1966). If the pain was minimal or viewed as non-threatening to the older woman, it was likely that she did not attend to it. If, on the other hand, it was perceived as harmful or unbearable she was more likely to deal with it. The methods she chose to relieve the pain involved a conceptual judgement (the third dimension) based upon prior experiences or current expectations of what methods were available to ease the situation. This stage also includes a social-cultural dimension which is contingent upon the course of the woman's social interactions (Ruoff & Berry, 1985) or secondary appraisal of the situation (Holroyd & Lazarus, 1982). If the older woman perceived herself as not being able to control the pain due to the lack of personal or environmental resources she was more likely to view her life as stressful. The women's overall responses on the Perceived Stress Scale lend support to this conceptualization.

The women used medical, physical, and psychological mechanisms to relieve the immediate symptoms of their osteoporosis. Reliance on pain medications was the most common coping strategy used. Other strategies required the women to break away from their normal routine in order to rest or to choose activities that required little or no physical movement. In order to incorporate these mechanisms into their daily lives, the women often had to reorganize their lifestyles, commitments, and activities. For example, participation in prior recreational activities such as skiing, bowling, and dancing were no longer possible for many of the women since being diagnosed with osteoporosis. Even less strenuous activities such as preparing a dinner or playing cards were not feasible due to the pain and discomfort of the disease. While social roles and relationships may be disrupted by these coping mechanisms, there needs to be a concerted effort by the woman, her family and friends, as well as professionals to ensure that these strategies do not create a life of isolation for her.

In addition to temporary coping mechanisms, the majority of the women identified long term adjustments they have had to make in their daily lives as a result of having osteoporosis. While many of these adjustments eased the impact of their disease, they also may have created stress. For example, the restriction of physical movements and the use of supportive devices were adaptations made by several women which can also be seen as stress producing problems. The possibility of injury from falling, lifting, or reaching may restrict the women's mobility. The previously accessible environment may now contain barriers erected by their lessened agility or perceived vulnerability (Lubkin, 1986) which could have led to the feelings expressed on the stress scale of being less in control of their lives. Other changes, such as not being able to do housework and limiting social and recreational activities, also may have created an atmosphere of dependency and isolation and served as a precursor for stress.

The number of specific adjustments made seemed to be related to the state of the disease. That is, women who had an overt fracture and who reported having pain were more likely to have made adjustments in their daily routine. These same women also experienced the greatest level of stress in their lives. This finding, while not surprising, demonstrates the need for greater understanding of the type of changes to expect as the disease progresses. Involvement in peer support groups may be advantageous for these women in order to share and learn from others what to expect from this disease. In fact, when asked if they would like to participate in a support group for women with osteoporosis, 68% of the women in this study said they would be interested. Educational strategies, such as workshops, seminars, and written materials, are also needed to teach the older women and their potential network members (i.e., family members, friends, health care professionals, counselors, etc.) about the changes that frequently occur as a result of having osteoporosis and effective means of coping with them.

REFERENCES

Avioli, L. (1983). The management of the geriatric osteoporotic women. In L. Avioli (Ed.), *The osteoporotic syndrome: Detection, prevention, and treatment*, (pp. 145-153). New York: Grune & Stratton.

Budoff, P. (1983). *No more hot flashes*. New York: Warner Books.

Chapman, C. (1977). Psychological aspects of pain patient treatment. *Archives of Surgery, 12*, 767-772.

Christiansen, C., Christiansen, M., McNair, P., Hagen, C., Stocklund, K., & Transbol, I. (1980). Prevention of early postmenopausal bone loss: Controlled 2-year study in 315 normal females. *European Journal of Clinical Investigation, 10*, 273-279.

Cohen, S., Kamarch, T., & Mermelstein, R. (1983). A global measure of perceived stress. *Journal of Health and Social Behavior, 24*, 385-396.

Dohrenwend, B. S., & Dohrenwend, B. P. (1981). *Stressful life events and their contexts*. New York: Watson.

Heaney, R. (1983). Prevention of age-related osteoporosis in women. In L. Avioli (Ed.), *The osteoporotic syndrome: Detection, prevention, and treatment*, (pp. 123-144). New York: Grune & Stratton.

Holmes, T., & Masuda, M. (1974). Life change and illness susceptibility. In B. S. Dohrenwend and B. P. Dohrenwend (Eds.), *Stressful life events: Their nature and effects*, (pp. 49-72). New York: Wiley.

Holmes, T., & Rahe, R. (1967). The social readjustment rating scale. *Journal of Psychosomatic Research, 11*, 213-218.

Holroyd, K., & Lazarus, R. (1982). Stress, coping, and somatic adaptation. In L.

Goldberger and S. Breznitz (Eds.), *Handbook of stress: Theoretical and clinical aspects*, (pp. 21-35). New York: Free Press.

Hutchinson, T., Polansky, S., & Feinstein, A. (1979). Post-menopausal estrogens protect against fractures of hip and distal radius: A case-control study, *Lancet, 2,* 705-709.

Kamen, B., & Kamen S. (1984). *Osteoporosis: What it is, how to prevent it, how to stop it.* New York: Pinnacle Books.

Lazarus, R. (1966). *Psychological stress and the coping process.* New York: McGraw-Hill.

Lazarus, R., & Folkman, S. (1984). *Stress, appraisal, and coping.* New York: Springer.

Lubkin, I. (1986). *Chronic illness: Impact and interventions.* Boston: Jones and Bartlett Publisher, Inc.

Miller, J. (1983). *Coping with chronic illness: Overcoming powerlessness.* Philadelphia: F.A. Davis Company.

Nordin, B. (1983). Osteoporosis. In V. Wright (Ed.), *Bone and joint disease in the elderly*, (pp. 167-180). New York: Churchill Livingstone.

Notelovitz, M., & Ware, M. (1985). *Stand tall!: Every woman's guide to preventing osteoporosis*, New York: Bantam Books.

Oyster, N., Morton, M., & Linnell, S. (1984). Physical activity and osteoporosis in post-menopausal women. *Medicine and Science in Sports and Exercise, 16,* 44-50.

Rabkin, J. (1982). Stress and psychiatric disorders. In L. Goldberger and S. Breznitz (Eds.), *Handbook of stress: Theoretical and clinical aspects*, (pp. 566-584). New York: The Free Press.

Rahe, R., & Arthur, R. (1978). Life change and illness studies: Past history and future directions. *Journal of Human Stress, 4,* 3-15.

Rosenman, R., & Chesney, M. (1982). Stress, type A behavior, and coronary disease. In L. Goldberger and S. Breznitz (Eds.), *Handbook of stress: Theoretical and clinical aspects*, (pp. 547-565). New York: The Free Press.

Ruoff, C., & Berry, G. (1985). Chronic pain: Characteristics assessment, and treatment plans. *Postgraduate Medicine, 78,* 91-97.

Ryan, K. (1975). Cancer risks and estrogen use in the menopause. *New England Journal of Medicine, 293,* 1200.

Strauss, A., Corbin, J., Fagerhaugh, S., Glaser, B., Mames, D., & Wiener, C. (1984). *Chronic illness and the quality of life (2nd ed.)*, St. Louis, MO: C.V. Mosby Company.

Community Care of Older Women Living Alone

Jay Magaziner
Doris A. Cadigan

SUMMARY. This paper compares the formal and informal care used by women living alone and women living with others using data from a household survey of women over 65. In contrast to those living with others, who use few formal services and receive most of their care from the children they live with, those living alone rely on a diverse group of informal caregivers and formal services, many of which are provided in their homes. Women living alone also report using mechanical devices more often, and are less confident that assistance will be available in the event of illness. Results are discussed from psychological and organizational perspectives.

Over the past decade, the number of persons living alone in the United States has increased in all age and sex groups (Glick, 1979; U.S. Bureau of the Census, 1983). Because women over 65 outlive men over 65 by about 4 years, widowhood leads to a high rate of living alone for elderly women (NCHS, 1985). In fact, demographic projections indicate that within 15 years, women living

Jay Magaziner is affiliated with the Department of Epidemiology and Preventive Medicine, University of Maryland School of Medicine, Baltimore, MD. Doris A. Cadigan is with the National Center for Health Services Research, Rockville, MD.

This research was supported by a grant from the National Institute on Aging (AG04366) to Dr. Magaziner.

The authors would like to thank Renee Sandler for her assistance in preparing the manuscript, and Eleanor Simonsick for her helpful comments on an earlier version of this paper.

An earlier version of this paper was presented at the 39th Annual Scientific Meeting of the Gerontological Society of America, Chicago, IL, November, 1986.

121

alone will constitute the majority of the elderly population in this country (Glick, 1979). Some researchers have suggested that older women who live alone are either particularly vulnerable to health problems, due to the effects of isolation; others suggest that while they are no more frail than other elderly, their disabilities are more problematic since they lack adequate informal support systems (Brody et al., 1978; Bishop, 1986). This paper uses data from the first wave of a three year longitudinal study of community resident older women to examine factors which enable impaired elderly women to continue to live independently in the community.

HEALTH STATUS AND LIVING ARRANGEMENTS

Despite their growing numbers and suspected vulnerability little research has focused on the health consequences of living alone for the community dwelling elderly. Studies of severe pathology indicate that people of all ages who live alone are more likely to be ill (e.g., Sainsbury, 1955; Hare, 1956; Schneidman and Farberow, 1957; Galle et al., 1972). While the few studies of the aged confirm this finding (Gruenberg, 1954; Redick et al., 1973; Magaziner, 1988; Gove and Hughes, 1980; Zubin et al., 1983), such studies may have limited applicability to the community resident aged since they concentrate on severe problems: suicide, alcoholism, mental hospitalization—the very conditions that remove people from the community. In addition, research on the probability of institutionalization suggests that older persons who live alone are at greater risk of entering a nursing home than are elderly people in other living situations (Nielson et al., 1972; Palmore, 1976; Greenberg and Ginn, 1979; Branch and Jette, 1982; Katz et al., 1983). Moreover, studies of community dwelling elderly suggest that those who live alone are not necessarily in the poorest health. In fact, those who live alone report fewer symptoms of mental disorder and exhibit higher morale than their counterparts living with children, but rate more poorly than those living with a spouse (Mindel and Wright, 1982, 1985). Research also indicates that community dwelling elders who live alone see themselves as no less healthy or less able to perform routine activities of daily living (ADL) than those elders in other living arrangements. (Butler and Newacheck, 1981; Lawton et al., 1984; Mindel and Wright, 1985; Magaziner et al., 1986).

In sum, it appears that once age and other demographic factors are accounted for, those living by themselves are no more impaired than their counterparts in other living arrangements. Our own work (Magaziner et al., 1988) indicates that not only are those who live alone no worse off in terms of their physical, mental and functional health than those in other situations, but they may even be healthier. In fact, those who live with people other than a spouse appear most impaired because a substantial portion of such persons choose that arrangement on account of a health problem. It appears that older women choose to live alone or with their spouse until their health fails to the point that living alone becomes untenable, then they either move in with others, or leave the community for a nursing home or similar setting.

While instructive, such research tells us little about the factors that enhance or hinder the ability of older persons to continue independent living. This is a particularly important issue for women because men usually live with a wife until death. Since women typically outlive their husbands, and since current cultural norms support independent living for elderly people, most women will live alone for some portion of their older years.

In addition, we know surprisingly little about whether and how the availability of and use of social and community supports varies by living arrangement. When illness or disability strikes, the availability of such resources, and the individual's ability to mobilize them may make the difference between continued independent living and institutionalization. The ability to mobilize such resources, and the manner in which such resources are utilized, may also vary by living arrangement.

COMMUNITY CARE

About 20% of the community dwelling elderly need long term care, and the absolute number of persons requiring long term care will increase dramatically as we enter the twenty-first century (Kingson et al., 1986). While residence in a nursing home or similar facility is one alternative for long term care, older persons typically prefer living independently in the community (Lopata, 1971; Chevon and Korson, 1975; Soldo and Lauriat, 1976; Schorr, 1980). In fact, living alone can be viewed as a commodity, one that elderly people "purchase" when they have the resources, including the health or available support from others, to do so (Bishop, 1986). The network of such potential community helpers is vast: family, friends, neighbors, religious groups and social clubs, service agencies such as meals on wheels, visiting nurses, and home aides.

In attempting to understand the types of care that enable older persons who live alone to remain in the community longer, we follow the conceptual leads of Cantor and Little (1985) and of Litwak (1965). Cantor and Little define community care as that which enables people to fulfil three needs: socialization, activities of daily living, and personal assistance during times of crisis. They identify two systems of caregiving: the formal and the informal. Furthermore, they suggest that elders choose care sources in a hierarchical manner, first seeking care from the informal system, particularly close relatives, and then turning to the formal system when informal sources cannot or will not meet their needs. The use of one system does not imply not using the other. In fact, Litwak (1965) hypothesizes that the needs of impaired older persons are best met with a combination of formal and informal supports, each doing the tasks to which it is best suited.

Formal system. The formal system consists of community groups, formal organizations and professionals who deliver care to disabled elders. Included in this category are formal programs set up by community and/or religious groups to offer assistance, and programs delivering a specific service such as meals on wheels, or a van service for the handicapped. Also included in the formal support system are nonprofessional helpers such as home aides, housekeepers, and nursing assistants, as well as professional supports such as physicians and visiting nurse services. According to Litwak (1965), the strength of the formal organization lies in its ability to serve large numbers and to do so with a relatively high degree of professional expertise. Formal systems cannot however, deal effectively with nonuniform tasks and unique events. These tasks are better suited to the flexibility of the informal support system.

Informal system. The informal care system consists of family, friends and neighbors. Traditionally, most long term care for the elderly has been provided by families, particularly the wives, daughters, and daughters-in-law of the disabled older person. With the exception of financial matters and decision making, every study on caregiving points to daughters as providers of the preponderance of direct day to day care in the home (Troll, 1977; Brody, 1981; Cantor and Little, 1985). For both social and demographic reasons, such women are increasingly unavailable as caregivers — an increasing portion of women working outside the home and the declining birthrate has reduced the ratio of potential caregivers to the elderly population (Treas, 1977).

The informal care system need not work independently of the formal system, however. The formal system can provide intermittent respite services, or some daytime assistance when family members are working. When total supervision and assistance are unnecessary, formal and informal services permit an older woman to remain in her own home. According to Sussman (1985), the informal system is necessary for the successful use of the formal system, and often acts as a "broker" securing necessary formal services and handling bureaucratic maneuvers.

Community care for those who live alone. Those who live alone differ from people who live with others in that they do not have a "built in" informal support system. Yet many older women with deficiencies in performing activities of daily living manage to continue independent living. As an extension of these observations, the remainder of this paper will explore the type of care older women receive in the community and how this care may vary by living arrangement. In this way, we may be able to identify factors that enable some women to continue independent living, in spite of health problems.

STUDY DESIGN

To identify factors that might allow functionally impaired elderly women to continue independent community living, we compare two groups of functionally impaired older women — one group living alone and one group living with others. Given that many elders living with others may have functional limitations which predispose them to that arrangement, we use a matching design, where the live with others group and the live alone group are matched on functional ability and cognitive impairment.

Study Sample

In the larger study from which this analysis derives, 807 women 65 years or older living in a relatively homogeneous, stable urban community were identified through a random sample of households in a 20 census tract area in Northeast Baltimore. The mean value of owner occupied homes in this area was $38,400 in 1980. Eighty-seven percent of the total population, and 98% of those over 65 were white. An enumeration of 6,540 households yielded 1,200 homes occupied by at least one woman over 65. These women were asked to participate in a three year prospective study consisting of annual in-home interviews and 2 short phone interviews between each home interview. The enumeration effort yielded a response rate of 95%, the community interview, 68%.

Analysis Plan

The current analysis contrasts a group of elderly women who live alone with a group who live with others, where the two groups are matched on ability to perform instrumental activities of daily living. All subjects are unable to perform at least one task independently. In addition, all cases included in this analysis have either no or only mild cognitive impairment.

To "match" the two groups, we first excluded those women who were married, all of whom lived with their husbands. We felt that living with one's husband was not equivalent to living with non-spouse others. Then we selected only those women who had some impairment in instrumental activities of daily living. For each of seven activities individuals received a score of 0 (could do item independently), 1 (needs help), or 2 (is unable to do). The items include using the telephone, going places out of walking distance, going shopping, preparing meals, doing housework, taking one's own medication and handling money.

As a second step, we eliminated those women who had more than mild cognitive impairment. We feel that cognitive impairments would be a nearly insurmountable impediment to independent community living. In fact, none of the women in our baseline sample who lived alone have severe cognitive deficits. We measure cognitive functioning using the Folstein Mini-Mental State Exam (Folstein et al., 1975). The Mini-Mental State Exam is a brief assessment of cognitive functioning that measures orientation, registration, recall, attention, calculation, and language. The test resembles a clinicians assessment, but is designed to be administered by a lay interviewer. The scores on the exam range from 0 to 30, with 23 or less indicating mild impairment and 16 or less indicating severe impairment. The analysis includes only those women who scored better than 23 on the Mini-Mental State Exam.

Using these criteria, we matched 62 women living alone and 54 women living with others. The two groups are also similar in marital status, with never married women accounting for 8% of the live alone group and 7.4% of the live with others group. About 89% of each group is widowed; the remainder are divorced or separated. Those who live with others tend to live with their children; 85% report living with a child or grandchild, 7% live with friends. The remainder live with other relatives, paid helpers, boarders, or in one instance, a parent.

Table 1 presents the results of the match. There are no significant differences between those who live alone and those who live with others, on the matching criteria, other background characteristics, or other health factors.

On the matching criteria, the live alone group and live with others group score similarly on the instrumental ADL scale and the Mini-Mental State Exam. The groups are also similar in age, education, and in the proportion who ever worked.

To ascertain that the groups are similar in health status, we also compared the two groups on several health characteristics. The live alone group reports somewhat more restricted activity days during the last six months (days when one could not do normal activities on account of illness) than those who live with others, but this difference is not statistically significant. The two groups are similar in the number of physician visits and days in the hospital they report over the same six month time period.

Table 1

Comparison of Women
Background Characteristics and Matching
Criteria by Living Arrangement

	Live Alone	Live With Others	P-value
Matching Criteria			
Instrumental ADL	2.77	3.15	.307
Mini-Mental State Exam Score	26.71	26.88	.636
Background Characteristics			
Age	78.03	77.22	.514
Education (highest grade completed)	9.14	8.98	.758
Percent having ever worked	77%	72%	.523
Health Characteristics			
Depression (CESD)	10.40	10.42	.988
Number of physician visits in last six months	2.87	3.22	.563
Restricted activity days in last six months	16.75	12.80	.585
Number of hospital days in last six months	2.52	2.15	.735

We also wanted to be sure that the two groups did not differ in mental health. Depression and dementia are the two most prevalent mental problems for older persons. As mentioned earlier, the matching criteria assured that the two groups did not differ on cognitive status. We also compared the two groups on their level of depressive symptoms, using the Center for Epidemiologic Studies Depression Scale (CESD) (Radloff, 1977). The CESD asks respondents to report the frequency of 20 depressive symptoms over the past seven days on a four point scale. Scores range from 0 to 60, with 16 or more indicating significant symptoms. The two groups did not differ in their level of depressive symptoms.

ANALYSIS OF COMMUNITY SUPPORT SYSTEMS

To describe the community support systems of these two groups of women, we use information from the first home interview of our study. As part of the interview, the women were asked which of a number of community resources they used and the extent of their informal supports. In addition, for each activity of daily living they were unable to do independently, the interviewer asked the women who helped them with that task. The analysis of community supports proceeds in three phases. First, we compare the two groups on use of various sources of formal supports. Second, we compare the two groups on the availability and perception of sources of informal supports. Finally, we examine who actually helps the two groups of women with specific ADL deficits. Because of the exploratory nature of this analysis, we use the criteria of $p < .1$ for statistical significance when discussing results in the text. Exact probability values are reported in the tables.

Use of Formal Supports

We compared those women living alone and those living with others on their use of a number of formal support sources. Table 2 displays the results of this comparison.

In comparison with similarly impaired women who live with others, a larger percent of those who live alone use formal supports. Most notably, those who live alone report using housekeeping services about ten times as often as those who live with others (42% verses 4%). Those who live alone also receive in-home physician visits more often than those who live with others (14% verses 6%). While not statistically significant, we note a trend in which those who live alone use other formal services such as senior/community center programs, social work services, meals-on-wheels, and in-home nursing services more often than those who live with others.

Table 2

Percent of Women in Each Living Arrangement
Using Formal Support Services

	Live Alone	Live With Others	P-value
Proportion Using Senior/ Community Center Programs	25%	17%	.303
Social Work Service	7	6	.827
Meals on Wheels	5	2	.369
In-home nursing Service	3	2	.639
House Keeping Services	42	4	.000
In-home physician visits	14	6	.106

Informal Supports

We compared the two groups both on the size of their potential informal supports, as well as their perception of the availability of those supports to care for them if they need help. Table 3 reports the results of this analysis.

Women who live with others have somewhat more living children than those who live alone (2.41 verses 1.82), reflecting the fact that the women in this group who live alone are more often childless than those who live with others. Both groups report similar numbers of relatives (to whom they feel close) and neighbors (whom they know well enough to have a friendly talk). Those who live alone report more close friends than those who live with others, but this difference is not statistically significant. We note a trend, however, in that those who live alone report more of these informal supports, other than children. Those living with others are more likely to report having a confidant (90% verses 98%), but are less likely to belong to clubs or organizations (37% verses 22%).

The two groups also report different perceptions of the availability of support. Those who live alone are less confident in the availability of others to help them. While 98% of those living with others

Table 3

Comparison of Women on Informal Supports by Living Arrangement

	Live Alone	Live With Others	P-value
Network Size			
Number of living children	1.82	2.41	.100
Number of close relatives	2.65	2.63	.963
Number of close friends	3.06	2.59	.371
Percent having a confidante	90%	98%	.067
Number of organizations and clubs	.37	.22	.083
Perception of Support			
Percent indicating someone to care for them if sick for a short time	91%	98%	.123
Percent indicating someone to care for them if sick for a long time	58	77	.037
Percent indicating there was someone to call in an emergency	94	100	.045

indicate that they believe someone would help them if they were sick for a short period of time, only 90% of those living alone express such a belief. While not statistically significant, this finding is consistent with the rest of our results. Those living alone are significantly less likely to believe that someone would care for them if they were sick for a long time, and are also significantly less likely to indicate that there was someone they could call on in an emergency. In sum, the two groups differ more on their perception of the availability of help than in the more "objective" measures of network size.

Help with ADL Impairments

Finally, we wish to examine whether or not impaired women who live alone receive help in activities of daily living from the same sources as women who live with others. Given the small numbers available for comparison, we could not compare source of help for specific impairments (for example, we could not compare the sources of help the women used for specific ADL tasks, such as meal preparation). Rather, we compare the proportion of women in each living arrangement receiving help from particular sources for *any* ADL impairment. The advantage of this comparison is that it is suitable for the size of our comparison groups. The disadvantage is that it does not consider the frequency or amount of help the women receive from each source. Hence, it is more a comparison of breadth of help sources, rather than quality or quantity. The results of this analysis are displayed in Table 4.

Looking first at sources of formal support, we find that women who live alone are considerably more likely to report receiving help with their ADLs from sources of formal support. Thirty-three percent of those who live alone receive ADL help from a paid worker, in comparison with 6% of those who live with others. Those who live alone are also more likely to receive help from community agencies than those who live with others (17% versus 6%). Both of these differences are statistically significant at p < .05.

Turning to informal support, more than half of the women in both living arrangements report receiving help from their children, and their children's spouses. However, a significantly larger proportion of those women who live with others report receiving help from such relatives (68% versus 52%, p < .000). Those women who live alone are more likely to report receiving ADL help from other relatives — siblings, nieces, nephews, cousins, and other more distant relatives. This difference (35% versus 18%) is statistically significant. The two groups did not differ in reporting help from friends and neighbors.

Finally, we look at the two other indicators of ADL assistance needs and support: unmet need and use of mechanical aids to help with ADLs. Neither group reports much unmet need (12% of those who live alone, 7% of those who live with others) and the difference between the two groups is not significant. The women who

Table 4

**Percent of Those Living Alone and
Living With Others Using Indicated Support
Sources to Help With Specific ADL's**

	Live Alone	Live With Others	P-value
Formal Sources			
Percent reporting help from a paid worker	33%	06%	.000
Percent reporting help from community agencies	17	06	.039
Informal Sources			
Percent reporting help from children and children-in-law	52	68	.064
Percent reporting help from other relatives (siblings, nieces, nephews, cousins)	35	18	.039
Percent reporting help from friends and neighbors	16	11	.434

live alone did report significantly more use of mechanical aids (16% versus 6%).

DISCUSSION

Our analysis compares two groups of older women, with similar needs for assistance with instrumental activities of daily living; one group lives alone, the other lives with others, most often their children. Given that most older persons prefer to continue living independently, the purpose of this analysis was to identify aspects of community care that might enhance the ability of older persons to continue independent living despite a need for assistance.

Despite similarities on demographic and health characteristics, the two groups appear quite different in their use of formal and informal sources of community care. Women who live alone appear less reliant on their children, and also use a wider variety of sources of assistance than those who live with others. Women living with others appear to receive most of their assistance from their children, with whom they often share a home. Importantly, the two groups do not differ significantly in their reports of unmet need for assistance, although more of those who live alone report using mechanical devices, such as walkers, canes, and special eating tools, rather than people to meet their ADL needs.

While the use of formal services is generally quite low in both groups, those who live alone use more of every service, particularly home physician visits, and most notably housekeeping services. Over 40% of the women who live alone use some housekeeping service, and 33% of all the women who live alone report getting help from a paid worker with specific ADL tasks. With the exception of senior/community center programs, no more than 6% of those who live with others report using any single source of formal support, or receiving help with specific ADL tasks from any source of formal supports.

As would be expected from prior work, both groups report substantial help from informal sources of support, particularly children. Those living with others have more living children and are more likely to report having a confidant. Those living alone report more close relatives, friends, and club memberships. While those living with others report getting help with specific ADL tasks mostly from children, the women who live alone report receiving help not only from their children, but also from other relatives, friends and neighbors.

These results suggest that older women who live alone are able to call on, or choose to call on, a more diverse set of persons and organizations to assist them. While our data do not provide information on the quality of the care being given, we can begin to evaluate the impact of these different community care systems from psychological and organizational perspectives.

While currently having no more unmet needs and being no more depressed than women living with others, those who live alone may have more psychological vulnerabilities. The women living alone are less likely to perceive that someone would care for them should they be ill for a long time. This may reflect their absence of "built in" support from persons they live with. Alternatively, those living with others may be overestimating the ability and/or willingness of their kin to care for them in the community.

The community care networks of the two groups can also be evaluated from an organizational perspective. While our data do not permit an evaluation of the quality or actual delivery of care, we can examine the networks' potential stability. The balance theory of coordination (Litwak, 1965) argues that community care is optimized by relying on both formal and informal providers. Using this perspective, one might conclude that those who live alone are advantaged because they rely on a diverse set of resources containing both formal and informal elements. In reality, the situation is much more complex. When care comes from multiple sources, whether formal or informal, someone must be willing to coordinate services. Family members often act as "brokers" between the older person and care providers (Sussman, 1985). Hence, the strength of a care network may depend on the availability of such "brokers."

Those living with others who rely largely on their children may have a "strong" broker, since the child they live with probably fills that role. However, since they rely on fewer informal providers, and virtually no formal ones, the loss of their primary caregiver/ broker may jeopardize the ability of the older person to remain in the community. Demographic realities suggest that a replacement family caregiver (another daughter/in law) may be in short supply. Additionally, the network's ability to procure formal services is untested.

Women living alone may also be vulnerable to the loss of a broker. While they may be able to coordinate care for themselves most of the time, acute illness or increased disability may render this option untenable. In fact, the women in our sample who lived alone did indicate that they were less likely to believe that someone would take care of them in the event of serious illness than the women living with others. While their diverse network may offer potential for substituting one caregiver (or type of caregiver) for another, women who live alone may be vulnerable nevertheless. A substantial portion of women living alone also rely on their children for instrumental aid; hence they are also vulnerable in the event of a loss of these caregivers. For both groups, the direct aid and/or brokerage provided by children may not be replaceable by formal services.

Several caveats are in order. First, the sample from which our comparison cases are selected included only women from a mostly white, homogeneous urban community. The nature and effect of community supports may be very different for men and other ethnic groups. Second, our comparison groups are not severely disabled; all the women are cognitively intact and might best be described as "frail" rather than disabled per se. Finally, the analysis is based on a small number of cases observed at only one point in time. Ideally, one would want to observe these or similar groups over time to answer questions about the stability and effectiveness of community care networks.

While our data have limitations, they do indicate that those living alone differ from those living with others in the nature and use of community care networks. These differences may have important policy implications given secular demographic and social changes. The growing proportion of very old persons in our society, the declining birthrate, and the trend for women to work outside the home portend the increasing unavailability of middle aged women as primary caregivers for older people. Our analysis suggests that formal services such as housekeeping assistance and in-home medical services may help frail people retain independence. Such services may also be helpful to frail persons living with others; it may reduce the often cited potential for "caregiver stress," and hence delay or prevent transfer to institutional care. At the least, this analysis demonstrates the importance of considering both the diversity of community care arrangements for older persons, as well as social and demographic changes when formulating policy for the care of older people.

REFERENCES

Bishop, C.E. (1986). Living arrangement choices of elderly singles: Effects of income and disability. *Health Care Financing Review, 7*, 63-73.

Branch, L., & Jette, A. (1982). A prospective study of long-term care institutionalization among the aged. *American Journal of Public Health, 72*, 1373-1379.

Brody, E.M. (1981). Women in the middle and family help to older people. *The Gerontologist, 18*, 471-480.

Brody, S.J., Poulshock, W., & Masciochhi, C. (1978). The family caring unit: A major consideration in the long-term support system. *The Gerontologist, 18,* 556-561.

Butler, L.H., & Newacheck, P.W. (1981). Health and Social factors relevant to long-term care policy. In J.W. Meltzer, F. Farrow, and H. Richman (Eds.), *Policy Options in Long-Term Care.* Chicago: University of Chicago Press.

Cantor, M., & Little, V. (1985). Aging and social care. In R.H. Binstock and E. Shanas (Eds.), *Handbook of Aging and the Social Sciences.* New York: Van Nostrand Reinhold.

Chevon, A. & Korson, J.H. (1975). Living arrangements of widows in the U.S. and Israel, 1960 and 1961. *Demography, 12,* 505-18.

Folstein, M.F., Folstein, S.E., & McHugh, P.R. (1975). "Mini-Mental State": A practical method for grading the cognitive state of patients for the clinician. *Journal of Psychiatric Research, 12,* 189-198.

Galle, O.R., Gove, W.R. & McPherson, J.M. (1972). Population density and pathology: What are the relations for man? *Science, 176,* 23-30.

Glick, P.C., (1979). The future marital status and living arrangement of the elderly. *The Gerontologist, 19,* 301-309.

Gove, W.R., & Hughes, M. (1980). Reexamining the ecological fallacy: A study in which aggregate data are critical in investigating the pathological effects of living alone. *Social Forces, 58,* 1157-1177.

Greenberg, J., & Ginn, A. (1979). A multivariate analysis of the predictors of long term care placement. *Home Health Care Services Quarterly, 1,* 75-79.

Gruenberg, E.M. (1954). Community conditions and psychosis in the elderly. *American Journal of Psychiatry, 110,* 888-896.

Hare, E.H. (1956). Mental illness and social conditions in Bristol. *Journal of Mental Science, 102,* 349-357.

Katz, S., Branch, L.G., & Branson, M.H. et al. (1983). Active life expectancy. *New England Journal of Medicine, 309,* 1218-1223.

Kingson, E.R., Hirshorn, B.A., & Cornman, J.M. (1986) *Ties that Bind: The Interdependence of Generations.* Washington DC: Seven Locks Press.

Lawton, M.P., Moss, M.,& Kleban, M. (1984). Marital status, living arrangements and the well-being of older people. *Research on Ageing, 4,* 39-51.

Litwak, E. & Meyer, H. (1966). A balance theory of coordination between bureaucratic organizations and primary groups. *Administrative Sciences Quarterly, 11;* 31-58.

Lopata, H. (1971). *Widowhood in an American City.* Cambridge: Schenkman.

Magaziner, J. (1988). Density and Psychopathology: A reexamination of the negative model. *Psychological Medicine, 18,* 419-431.

Magaziner, J., Cadigan, D.A., Hebel, J.R. & Parry, R. (1988). Health and living arrangements among older women: Does living alone increase the risk of illness? *Journal of Gerontology: Medical Sciences, 43,* 127-133.

Magaziner, J., Yuhas, M.K., & Day, N.L. (1986). Health and resources of community resident aged living alone. *Maryland Medical Journal, 35,* 905-909.

Mindel, C.H., & Wright, R. (1982). Differential living arrangements among the elderly and their subjective well-being. *Activities, Adaption and Aging, 6,* 323-345.

National Center for Health Statistics (1985). Advance report, final mortality statistics, 1983. *Monthly Vital Statistics Report,* Public Health Service, Hyattsville, MD, Sept. 26, 1985.

Neilsen, M., Blenkmam, M., & Bloom, M. et al. (1972). Older persons after hospitalization: A controlled study of home aide service. *American Journal of Public Health, 62,* 1094-1101.

Palmore, E. (1976). Total chance of institutionalization among the aged. *The Gerontologist, 16,* 504-507.

Radloff, L. (1977). The CES-D scale: A self-report depression scale for the research in the general population. *Applied Psychological Measurement, 1,* 385-401.

Redick, R.W., Kramer, M., & Taube, C. (1973). Epidemiology of mental illness and utilization of psychiatric facilities among older persons. In E.W. Busse and E. Pfeiffer (Eds.), *Mental Illness in Later Life.* Washington: American Psychiatric Association.

Sainsbury, P. (1955). *Suicide in London: An Ecological Study.* London: Chapman Hall.

Schneidman, E., & Farberow, N. (1957). *Clues to Suicide.* New York: McGraw Hill.

Schorr, A. (1980). *"Thy Father and Thy Mother . . . " a Second Look at Filial Responsibility and Family Policy.* SSA Pub. No. 13-11953. Social Security Administration. Washington, US Government Printing Office.

Soldo, B.J., & Lauriat, P. (1976). Living arrangements among the elderly in the United States: A log-linear approach. *Journal of Comparative Family Studies, 7,* 351-366.

Sussman, M.B. (1985). The family life of old people. *Handbook of Aging and the Social Sciences.* New York: Van Nostrand Reinhold.

Treas, J. (1977). Family support systems for the aged: Some social and demographic considerations. *The Gerontologist, 17,* 486-91.

Troll, L., Miller, S., & Atchley, R. (1977). *Families in Later Life.* Belmont, CA: Wadsworth.

United States Bureau of the Census (1983). Marital status and living arrangements: March, *Current Population Reports,* Series P-20, 380.

Zubin, J., Magaziner, J., & Steinhauer, S. (1983). The metamorphosis of schizophrenia: From chronicity to vulnerability. *Psychological Medicine, 6,* 551-571.

Just Being Friendly Means a Lot—
Women, Friendship, and Aging

Hedva J. Lewittes

SUMMARY. This article examines friendship patterns and interactional skills among older, noninstitutionalized women. It draws on two studies, one quantitative and the second qualitative, of friendship undertaken by the author. Friendship is viewed in relation to age, related socio-environmental transitions and psychological growth in later life including the issues of intimacy, reciprocity and relational identity.

Friendship among older women helps to maintain physical and mental health and contributes to continued psychological growth (Lowenthal and Haven, 1968; Eisenberg, 1979; Lynch, 1977). As women age they are increasingly likely to suffer losses of important relationships and roles. However, their ability to make and maintain friends throughout adulthood aids them in adapting to the transitions of aging (Lowenthal, Thurner and Chiriboga, 1975; Lewittes, 1982; Lenz and Myerhoff, 1985). Friendships are both influenced

Hedva J. Lewittes, Department of Psychology, SUNY Old Westbury, NY 11568.

by the psychological concerns of later life and are a key element in their successful resolution.

This article will examine friendship patterns and the interactional skills of women. Research and theory, based primarily on the experiences of noninstitutionalized women in contemporary U.S. society, will be reviewed. Two research projects conducted by the author will also be discussed. In the first study, to be referred to as the questionnaire study, (Lewittes and Mukherji, 1984), 98 white and 87 black women with an average age of 71, responded to a series of multiple choice questions focusing on intimacy, helping, and shared activity in two of their close friendships. The subjects were neither married nor institutionalized at the time of the study and represented a range of socioeconomic backgrounds. They were recruited from senior centers, church groups, and via community networks from suburban and urban neighborhoods in the Long Island and the greater New York City area.

The second study (Lewittes, 1986), entailed interviews of both members of four friendship pairs. In sessions lasting about one hour, the women gave open ended responses to a series of structured questions about coming to the senior center and making new friends and, in particular, about their relationships with the friend who was being interviewed. At the time of the interview, the friendships were of three to four years duration. The subjects were white, widowed and ranged in age from 65-79. They had worked at clerical and sales jobs and had adequate economic resources. All had children, at least one of whom lived nearby and whom they saw frequently. They were selected by the Center Director who was familiar with their relationships.

TRANSITIONS AND FRIENDSHIP: WIDOWHOOD, RETIREMENT, AND GEOGRAPHIC RELOCATION

While the transitions of earlier adulthood often involve the strain of taking on multiple roles and dealing with the competing demands of family and work, in later adulthood transitions typically involve multiple losses. While change and loss are experienced throughout the life cycle (Levinson, 1978; Allen and Pickett, 1984), with age losses are harder to replace. Widowhood, retirement and geographic relocation are common experiences among older women. Given that the aging process varies enormously from one individual to the next, for many women these losses function as "timing events" in that their occurrence initiates or deepens feelings of getting old (Neugarten, 1982).

Such timing events may be stressful and contribute to physical illness. Nor is it unusual for women to experience two or three major changes within a short period of time. Since female gender identity may be partially defined in relation to others, such events can lead to a loss of a sense of self and depression (Gilligan, 1982; Chodorow, 1978; Scarf, 1980). Friendship can serve as a critical source of help in coming to terms with these changes. As older women may have fewer obligations, more time is available to put into friendship affording the opportunity to develop both themselves and their relationships in new ways.

Widowhood

It is well known that women have a longer life expectancy than men, that the chance of widowhood increases with age and that women are more likely to be widowed than men (Hess, 1985). Children are a vital source of support for widows (Longino and Lipman, 1985). However, widows' need for support may strain their relationships with adult children. Both children and the widow fear and resent the possibility of her increased dependency. These dynamics are most pronounced when the child is a white middle class male (Hiltz, 1978). Thus, friends are an important resource for meeting some of the additional needs of widows and by so doing relieving family tension. Indeed, in one study, contact with neighbors and friends had more impact on widows' positive morale than contact with children (Arling, 1976). In recent years, widow to widow programs have sprung up. Such programs are recognized as effective because understanding and equal give and take among peers may be more possible than with children (Silverman, 1982).

During the early grief work period, widows need to express feelings including sorrow, anger and guilt. Unfortunately, in our society these emotions are often responded to with anxiety and withdrawal. During the process of adjustment to the death of a spouse feelings of vulnerability and the need to reestablish a sense of control are common. Often, quiet companionship and a minimum of interference are desired (Lopata, 1973). Other widows may be best at accepting feelings and in knowing how to help. One widow described her friendship with another: "She's a good listener. There's no advice, but she listens."

In Lopata's important study of urban widows, loneliness was the most frequently mentioned problem. Widows missed talking about daily events and experiences, a companion for activities, and someone who appreciated them as a unique person. Friendship, usually aided by telephone conversations, can mediate loneliness as demonstrated by Lopata's finding that loneliness was more likely among those who lacked widowed friends.

Widowhood involves not only grief work, but resocialization into new roles. Part of this process includes developing and extending one's friendship network. Economically comfortable widows who are healthy enough to be mobile often have numerous friends with whom they attend cultural events, travel, and participate and volunteer in group activities. Many Black women receive both concrete assistance and social support from friends who are members of their church (Ortega, Crutchfield and Rushing, 1983). For some women, being widowed provides the opportunity to develop new personal friendships that augment earlier relationships which were established on the basis of being a couple (Lewittes, 1986).

Age and socio-economic status influence friendship patterns among widows. Younger widows who are still in the labor force are usually more mobile and affluent, assets which assist in maintaining old and establishing new friendships. Women with more education are also more likely to have more friends (Lopata, 1973), possibly because education creates opportunities for socialization and interests which can form the basis for friendships.

Retirement

The study of women and retirement has been hampered by sexist assumptions about women and work. Not only has women's labor force participation been overlooked, but the role of work in women's self concept has been ignored. Recent research suggests that retirement is indeed a significant life event for women (Szinovacz, 1983). While adjustment to retirement can be as difficult for women as it is for men, the psychological concerns and circumstances of retirement are somewhat different. For women, fears before retirement and problems in adapting to it tend to focus on the loss of relationships (Levy, 1980). Decreased social contact may be more problematic for women, not only because they value personal interaction, but also because their work friendships are an integral part of the sense of meaning provided by employment. Additionally, women are more likely than men to face retirement around the same time as widowhood, increasing the importance of work-related friendships. A quote from one of the interview study subjects is illustrative:

> It was the saddest part of my life. Ooh, I can't work? What am I? I worked for 20 years straight through and when my husband passed away I felt like I had somebody to go to. My co-workers were great and just being with them I had someplace to go. And when the doctor said I couldn't work any more, it was like, what do I do now?

Research indicates that women often do not continue their work friendships after retirement (Szinovacz, 1983). In general, prior planning for, and having relationships and activities outside work, improves retirement adjustment. One study suggests that both men and women increase the number of their friendships during the transition to retirement, and that women's friendships during this period were more complex and multidimensional when compared to pre-retirement men and women at earlier phases of adulthood (Weiss and Lowenthal, 1975). However, the impact of women's increasing labor force participation on friendship and retirement remains largely unexplored. Increased economic status as a result of labor force participation may facilitate mobility and access to friends. On the other hand, women who have worked full time throughout adulthood and who have also fulfilled the roles of wife and mother, may differ little from male retirees who lacked the time to develop friendships and interests outside the work and family context.

Geographic Relocation

For older people, the neighborhood or immediate residential environment is often the best source of friendship (Arling, 1976). Among the current cohort of elderly, many older persons have "aged in place." As a result, the neighborhood is likely to contain important long term relationships (Hess, 1985). In addition, those elderly who have lived their adult lives in urban ethnic communities have often socialized with a fairly fixed group of kin and neighbors (Lopata, 1975).

Retirement, physical and economic limitations, as well as inadequate transportation, all increase the dependence of many older people on their immediate residential area. In addition, neighborly relationships are an important source of assistance and security. Neighbors watch out for each other, can help in an emergency, and check on someone who is ill and homebound.

In general, the elderly are less geographically mobile than other age groups (Hess, 1985). However, when they do move their motivations for and patterns of migration are different from those of younger adults (Sullivan and Stevens, 1985). Not infrequently, women relocate from retirement communities to be closer to children as a result of failing health (Lewittes, 1986; Lewittes and Mukherji, 1984). While moving is stressful at any age (Brown and Harris, 1978), it is particularly so for older women because of the importance of neighborhood-based social relations. The following quote illustrates the problem:

> I left all my friends. It was very hard in the beginning. I stayed in the house and got addicted to soap opera. It was getting to the point where I didn't want to go out. . . . Moving to another town, I didn't know anyone here. (Lewittes, 1986)

Although telephone contact enables old friends to remain in touch, making new friends following relocation is necessary in order to maintain desired levels of social interaction and support. Well planned residential housing, senior centers, and religious groups facilitate the older person's integration into the new community and opportunity for friendship (Hochschild, 1982; Myerhoff,

1978; Lewittes, 1986). Indeed, when such programs are available relocation may expand the older person's social horizons.

FRIENDSHIP AND PSYCHOLOGICAL GROWTH IN LATER LIFE: INTIMACY, RECIPROCITY AND THE RELATIONAL IDENTITY

In examining the friendships of older women it is necessary to look both at continuity and change. Older women characterize their friendships in much the same way as younger adult women; intimacy and reciprocity are central to their definition. In addition, throughout the life cycle friendships continue to contribute to the process of the formation of women's relational identity (Gilligan, 1982). However, older women's friendships must also be examined in light of the physical and social changes and the accompanying psychological needs of later life. Thus a model of psychological development that looks both at the unique problems to be solved in later life and at the potential for continued growth is important to an understanding of friendship.

Intimacy

One of the earliest theories about older people's relationships posited that "social disengagement" occurred in tandem with biological decline (Cumming and Henry, 1961). Many theorists, however, do not see disengagement as inevitable (Butler, 1982; Hochschild, 1982). Rather, they argue that withdrawal is a response to restrictive and discriminatory social circumstances and attitudes. Thus, the belief that isolation is "normal" becomes a self-fulfilling prophecy. In contrast to the social disengagement theory, Robert Butler, a leading geriatric psychiatrist, has begun to describe the characteristics of psychological health in later life. Building on Erikson's model of development, he posits that each person must achieve a balance between conflicting forces in order to successfully adapt (Erikson, 1959). Two of the features Butler identifies which are relevant to friendship in later life are intimacy, which grows out of the resolution of the conflict between affiliation and loneliness; and, interpersonal responsiveness, which grows out of the conflict between self-disclosure and reticence. A growing number of studies supports these contentions by indicating that older people maintain a network of friends and that intimacy and the ability for self-disclosure are associated with mental health (Peters and Kaiser, 1985).

In order to understand the impact of intimacy on older people it is necessary to distinguish between the close friend or confidant and the broader network of casual friends, neighbors and acquaintances. It is sometimes assumed that lonely old people simply require social contact rather than friendships that are meaningful. In fact, it is the intimate friend that is particularly important to psychological health, especially during a crises (Lowenthal and Haven, 1968). Research suggests that the majority of older people have a small core of confidants, and that the presence or absence of even one is more critical to morale than the number of persons in the social network (Strain and Chappell, 1982). Confidants may or may not be family members. In the questionnaire study, about one third of the close friends named by both Black and white women were also family members (Lewittes and Mukherji, 1984). In addition, close friends and confidants are also often long term friends (Bell, 1981; Roberto and Scott, 1986). In the questionnaire study, subjects had known their close friends for an average of over 20 years. Other studies have similar findings (Bell, 1981; Peters and Kaiser, 1985; Roberto and Scott, 1986).

Men and women differ in regard to intimate friendships. Older women are more likely than men to have had, maintain and to make close friends (Powers and Bultena, 1976). A man's confidant is most often his wife. This may be due, in part, to the greater likelihood that older men are married. However, married women's intimate friends may include, but usually extend beyond their husbands.

The close friendships of adult women of all ages include self-disclosure, or in popular terminology, the ability to "open up" to one another (Hacker, 1981). Older women are no exception. In the interview study the chemistry between close friends is described as an ease of communication.

I could talk to her for . . . it's funny. She's the one who can make you talk. I don't know what it is. We have long conversations, long. It's funny, it's unusual. She just keeps talking and I keep talking. (Lewittes, 1986)

In the questionnaire study, intimate self-disclosure seemed to be the most important aspect of close friendships. The statement "I share my thoughts and feelings with my friends," and "I tell my friend things I do not tell anyone else," were rated as more important than statements describing concrete help or shared activities. The statement "she listens without judging" was also highly rated (Lewittes and Mukherji, 1984). Typically when women explain the difference between family and friends, the issue of being judged is raised. Relatives, even if they are close, often have expectations of each other and a personal stake in each other's actions and decisions. They may not be able to listen with the same distance and objectivity as friends.

Many older women are deprived of any kind of physical intimacy to the detriment of their physical and mental health. Touching and hugging friends can help to fill this need. One women described her first visit to the senior center and how physical contact played a role in the process of making friends.

She (a staff member) had this group form a circle and she introduced me to all the ladies and they all came over and shook my hand and kissed me on the cheek. She made me feel so good and so at home. (Lewittes, 1986; p. 5)

There is some debate in the literature as to the role intimacy plays in the friendships of older Black women. Some studies find that friendships among Black elderly are less intimate and more loosely defined than among whites (Creecy and Wright, 1979; Sterne, Phillips and Rabushka, 1974). However in the questionnaire Black women rated the statements describing intimate self-disclosure as highly as did white women. Additionally, Black women were more likely than their white counterparts to choose different statements to describe two close friends. Thus, rather than having a looser definition of friendship, they actually make sharper distinctions between friends and the function of friendships (Lewittes and Mukherji,

1984). Several aspects of the questionnaire study distinguish it from other studies and may account at least in part for the different findings. For example, women were questioned about specific close friends, rather than friends in general, and older Black women were studied separately from Black men. Also, study subjects were residentially stable, having lived in their current location for an average of 17 years.

Intimacy is the outcome of an ongoing process. Butler's conceptualization of a dialectic between two poles, while difficult to demonstrate empirically, is useful in describing this process. In order to achieve intimacy, older persons must often overcome or compensate for circumstances that make affiliation difficult. For example loneliness, the polar opposite of affiliation in Butler's model, is often unavoidable as a result of social losses in later life such as widowhood and retirement.

For some elderly, loneliness is not easily remedied. Interpersonal difficulties of earlier adulthood may be exacerbated by the loss and loneliness of later life stymying the development of new relationships. Continued dependency on memories of a deceased spouse can preoccupy one's life. One widow, nine years after her husband's death, centered her thoughts and conversations around him, his virtues and loss. She expressed dissatisfaction about her current life in spite of the fact that she was healthy and economically comfortable. She excused herself from relating to others— "I could have gone to New Year's dinner with my friends, but when I come home, I'm still alone. So what's the use." However, for others, grappling with loneliness eventually pushed them to become socially involved in new ways. Another woman initially responded to her husband's death with withdrawal. Finally, after about two years, she was ready for a change. Although in her late 60s she learned to drive and joined a senior center where she made new friends and talked with them intimately in a way that she had never previously done with nonfamily members. This women exhibited what one researcher labelled "flexibility" and "elasticity" (Peck, 1985). Ultimately, she was able to expand her social sphere in order to adapt to her new needs and situation.

In Butler's model intimate relationships are not fixed phenomena of which there is some standard of normality or health. Rather, individuals strike a balance that suits their personalities, reflects their values and past experiences, and shifts with changing circumstances (Fiske and Weiss, 1977). In order to accomplish Butler's conception of "interpersonal responsiveness," some degree of self-disclosure is necessary. However, older people also have a need for a certain degree of reticence. Indeed, the current cohort of older people highly value independence and privacy. For example, one woman in the interview study, when asked about the contents of her conversations with a close friend replied, "I don't make trouble with talk." Another, who attended group therapy at her senior center, explained her reasons for participating as: "I didn't have problems, I went to listen" (Lewittes, 1986).

Many older persons make a distinction between the role of family and friends vis-à-vis appropriate topics of conversation. While family is a major topic of conversation between friends, the discussion of some highly personal matters is limited to family members (Lewittes 1986). The current cohort of older women reached adulthood well before the emphasis on "openness" and intimacy that characterized the 1970s and early 1980s. Hence the contexts of intimate disclosure may be more constrained than those of younger persons.

It has also been suggested that the experience of past loss and fear of future loss creates an emotional set in which disclosure is associated with risk (Myerhoff, 1978). For example, Myerhoff's documentary movie, *Number Our Days* (Myerhoff and Littman, 1976) presents a striking portrait of a socially engaged, attractive woman who had outlived both her husband and children. She resisted a romantic relationship because of fear of, once again, losing someone she loved.

Finally, there is some indication that the ability to maintain a close confidant decreases with advancing age (Peters and Kaiser, 1985). As the population ages, and those over 75 increase in proportionately larger numbers, frailty becomes an important detriment to the development and maintenance of close friendships. However, formal programs such as senior centers can provide opportunities for social interaction and the development of social relationships to those who were previously homebound and isolated.

Reciprocity

Reciprocity is an important aspect of all adult relationships and particularly of close friendships (Longino and Lipman, 1985). A reciprocal relationship as defined by Weiss and Lowenthal (1975) is one in which "the emphasis is on helping and support." These authors studied friendship at four transitions of adulthood and found that, at all ages, women valued reciprocity more highly than men, moreover, women in the "pre-retirement stage" valued reciprocity more than their younger counterparts.

The questionnaire study suggests some difference between Black and white women in the kinds of things that were exchanged in friendships. While for both groups emotional support was central, for Black women practical help, such as visiting when sick, was also an important aspect of close friendship. Black women's friendships seemed to parallel Black kinship networks which have been found to provide a greater amount of "functional aid" than white families (Mindel, 1983).

The term reciprocity implies that both members give and receive. Relationships can be characterized as involving similarity or complimentarity in regards to what is exchanged. For example, a study of widows in a San Francisco housing project found a pattern of similarity.

> They all wanted more or less the same things and could give more or less the same things . . . When they did exchange services it was usually the same kind of service as they themselves performed. For example, two neighbors might exchange cornbread for jam but they both knew how to make both cornbread and jam. (Hochschild, 1980; p. 367)

Since the majority of women in this community had migrated from the same area in Oklahoma they had similar life experiences, backgrounds and skills. Such homogeneity is not uncommon in the communities of the elderly. Similarities in ethnic membership, social class, and age all contribute to the likelihood of a pattern of reciprocal similarity. Reciprocal relationships can include both similar and complimentary exchanges. For example, in one of the friendships studied, the more talkative member provided information and stimulation while her quieter partner drove her friend to various activities. It may be that complimentarity provides a control on competition and enables each woman to maintain a sense of her own uniqueness.

There is a growing body of literature which uses exchange theory to examine reciprocity in relationships. Relationships are measured in terms of the equity of input and outcome and the gains and losses of each person in the relationship (Longino and Lipman, 1985). Individuals expect to receive what they have given and feel obligated to return what has been given to them. One study tested the assumption of equity exchange theory in the friendships of older people. It found more discomfort in relationships with inequitous exchange than in those with more equal exchanges. However, contrary to prediction, it was the over-benefited (those who received more than they gave), rather than the under-benefited, who expressed discomfort. The people who gave help were not resentful because they understood their friends inability to reciprocate, while those who received were angry because of their dependency (Roberto and Scott, 1986).

Based on the capitalist conception of a profit motive, it is often assumed that people give in order to receive. This is not, however, true among the current cohort of older women who find it more acceptable to give than to receive from friends. In the San Francisco community previously discussed, several widows cared for people older and sicker than themselves. Their only negative feeling was missing the person they helped when he or she died (Hochschild, 1982).

However, inequitous exchange can be a problem in the friendships of older people. Precisely because of this emphasis on helping others, many older people are extremely reluctant to seek help and or to maintain relationships in which they are on the receiving end. Asking for help may be considered to be impolite or to put one in the position of seeking charity or being pitied. The value of independence, and the belief that when one needs help one goes to family, may keep older people from reaching out. One interview subject commented, "I don't believe in taking advantage of friends. I have my son and daughter-in-law to turn to." When questioned further as to whether she would ask for help at the senior center she continued, "I'm quite sure if I had a problem I'd go right to the staff . . . I don't believe in taking advantage of friends." While it is often assumed that asking assistance from service agencies under-mines pride, under certain circumstances sensitive and caring staff are better able than friends or even family to offer help that main-tains dignity and independence (Lebowitz, Fried and Madaris, 1973). Indeed, in the questionnaire study several women named staff members as one of their close friends.

The Relational Identity

In later life a central aspect of affirming one's identity is coming to terms with death (Butler, 1982). According to Butler, the immi-nence of death creates in people as they age a need to remember, review, and re-integrate their past. Returning to his bipolar model, the successful resolution of the conflict between continuity-historic-ity and discontinuity leads to a sense of legacy. The conflicts be-tween life review and denial leads to the autobiographic process. Resolving these conflicts is part of affirming one's identity and can provide new significance and meaning to one's life. Typically, fam-ily is seen as the main source of legacy. Parents, one's spouse, siblings, cousins and children have shared the past; children and grandchildren give connection to the future. However, friends also contribute to an ongoing sense of rootedness and help to maintain a connection to the past and to oneself in previous stages of life. Friends are more likely than adult children to have had the same subjective experience of past events and to share the need for life review. Family members may have a vested interest in denial, or may not want to remember or discuss sensitive issues.

The role of friends in maintaining a sense of continuity may partly account for the importance of long term friends to older peo-ple (Bell, 1981; Roberto and Scott, 1986; Peters and Kaiser, 1985). Long term friendships facilitate continued intimacy and trust and provide a rich context in which current reactions and needs can be understood. The role long term friendships play in providing conti-nuity is aptly described by May Sarton in her book *A House By The*

Sea. The book, written while she was in her 60s, is based on her journal entries while she was living alone in a house in Maine. She writes,

> There is another member of the family who comes here for a day or so every month. Judith Matlack, with whom I shared a house in Cambridge for many years and who is now in a nursing home . . . for 30 years or more she has been the closest thing to family in my life. Without her presence even though her mind is failing, and she has no memory of all our journeys to Europe together and all our summers in Nelson, there would be no Christmas and no Thanksgiving, and I would feel like an orphan. (Sarton, 1981, p. 12.)

Over time close friends can come to be considered as family, further adding to one's sense of connectedness (Rubin, L., 1985).

Unfortunately, the economic and physical circumstances of older people often make the maintenance of old friendships difficult. Both the loss of old friends and being forced to depend on proximate relationships, contributes to a sense of discontinuity. A study of elderly living in single room occupancy (S.R.O.) dwellings demonstrates how new social contacts cannot automatically replace the psychological importance of long-term friendships (Cohen and Rajkowski, 1982). In this study, when elderly S.R.O. residents were asked to name their friends, they chose old friends with whom they were not currently in frequent contact. This was in spite of the fact that the subjects interacted and even received assistance from other S.R.O. residents. Perhaps, for these people living in the degrading and alienating circumstances of an S.R.O., old friends represented a tie to a past and a self which was more positive.

It may be that the need for legacy makes it less likely that new friends will reach the level of closeness of old ones. In addition to the lack of shared past, the contraction of futurity limits the time available to develop new shared experiences. However, with the increase in longevity, it is possible for friends in their 60s to have ten to twenty years of shared experiences. Similarity in life experiences and values between new friends can contribute to a sense of continuity. One of the subjects in the interview study recounted how she and her new friends first became close.

> On the trip to Atlantic City we really got to know each other. We sat together. She talked to me about her daughter and all about Brooklyn and Queens (where they had both lived in earlier years) and anything we talked about we understood. We talked about the depression, the war . . . (Lewittes, 1986, p. 8)

New friends from the same ethnic or religious backgrounds often give each other a sense of connection to their common past. The community so beautifully documented by Barbara Myerhoff was made up of Jewish elderly who did not necessarily know each other when they were younger. Despite this, they shared the Jewish immigrant experience in the early part of the century and retained common values and a way of life. The knowledge that their way of life would die with them, solidified the bonds between them.

Affirming one's identity involves adapting to the present as well as integrating the past. As people age, coming to terms with the present involves dealing with getting older and often with failing health and chronic or increasing disability. For many people, physical problems create psychological barriers which negatively affect social relations. One very frail woman who did attend a senior center explained that "I walk very slowly. No one wants to walk with me, so, I don't have any friends here." Unfortunately, it is not uncommon in senior centers for the relatively healthy to avoid the frail, and for those in poor health to have lower social status (Hochschild, 1980). Since the healthiest and most active are often highly invested in helping others (Ward, 1979), selfishness is most likely not the root of these attitudes. It is more likely that frailty and physical disabilities arouse anxiety and fear because they mirror the future.

Coming to terms with death and illness are crucial to affirming one's identity and free energy for continued personal development. Butler notes:

Much is made of the wish to maintain a sense of identity. Little attention has been paid to the wish to change identity, to pre- serve and exercise the sense of possibility and incompleteness against a sense of closure and completeness. (Butler, 1982; p. 222)

Involvement in relationships and activities at a senior center or program can also facilitate the learning of new skills providing what Butler calls the "renewal function" which results from the dialectic between self-education and obsolescence. One of the subjects in the interview study described the evolution of her participation in the senior center.

Someone asked me to sit at a table; I think it was a crafts sale. "Sit at our table while we have a meeting." So I sat there for a while and I'm thinking, how could they go to a meeting and I can't go? Why don't I go? (I was talking to myself.) Then finally I said next time they have something I'm going to see what it's all about and that's what I did. There was a friendly visiting committee here. I started that and six months later I was asked to be chairperson. This is all new to me but it's not bad because I'm with other people . . . I learned a lot; how to deal with people; how to listen—outgoing. I felt [before] like I'm no good to anyone any more. What do I know? But it's easy. Just being friendly means a lot. Now I feel I'm part of everything. I feel free.

The intertwining of involvement in a group, friendship and a sense of usefulness illustrated in the above quote has been found in other research as well. A study of the meaning of group participa- tion to older people found that contact with friends was the most frequently mentioned benefit, while helping others and benefitting society were also seen as important (Ward, 1979). Among the Black elderly, church based friendships were related to measures of psychological well-being, while nonchurch friendships were not. These church friends were part of a helping network which functioned as a "pseudo extended family" (Ortega, Crutchfield and Rushing, 1983).

In the interview study, the friendship pairs were typically part of a network of friends. Thus when a woman came to the center and made one new friend, she was introduced to a whole group, many of whom became her personal friends as well. These groups would regularly eat lunch together at the center and accompany each other on trips and to other activities. Further, for the women in the interview study, the senior center seemed to provide a critical social context for the formation and maintenance of friendships. One of the major topics of the telephone calls they made to each other at home was what went on at the center. When they got together for a meal it was usually before or after some center event and most of their excursions were organized by the center staff (Lewittes, 1986).

CONCLUSION:
DIRECTIONS FOR FUTURE RESEARCH

Given the aging of the population, there is a need to more fully explore the rich variety of friendships among older women and their impact on psychological and physical health in later life. Further research is needed on the meanings of friendship to individuals, as well as on the social contexts in which relationships are embedded. Despite their apparent importance, few empirical studies have examined the origins, maintenance and functions of long-term friendships. Studies on the impact of cohort membership and ethnic/racial background are also necessary. This is particularly important in view of the increasing number of Hispanic and Asian elderly in the country. Relatively little is known about friendship patterns and their consequences within these groups. Additional investigation is also needed of older women who have not assumed traditional female roles; women who never married, the childless, and those who are homosexual. For many of these women, friendship is a primary source of intimacy and social support. Hopefully, a more comprehensive understanding of friendships will also encourage service agencies to facilitate and support these relationships.

REFERENCES

Arling, G. (1976). The elderly widow and her family, neighbors and friends. *Journal of Marriage and the Family*, 38, 757-868.

Allen, K. R. and Pickett, R. S. (1984). Perceptions of normative versus variant life events: A comparison of the life courses of a selected sample of never-married and never-married elderly women. Paper presented at the Northeast Gerontological Society Conference, Philadelphia, PA.

Bell, R. (1981). *World of Friendship*. Beverly Hills: Sage Publications.

Bensmen, J. and Lillienfeld, R. (1979). Friendship and alienation. *Psychology Today*, 13, 56-66, 114.

Brown, G. W. and Harris, T. (1978). *Social Origins of Depression*. New York: Macmillan.

Butler, R. N. (1982). Toward a psychiatry of the life cycle. In S. Zarit (ed.). *Reading in Aging and Death*. New York: Harper and Row.

Chodorow, N. (1978). *The Reproduction of Mothering*. Berkeley: University of California Press.

Cohen, C. I. and Rajkowski, H. (1982). What's in a friend? Substantive and theoretical issues. *Gerontologist*, 28, 261-266.

Creecy, R. F. and Wright, R. (1979). Morale and informal activity with friends among black and white elderly. *Gerontologist*, 19 (60), 544-547.

Cumming, E. and Henry, W. E. (1961). *Growing Old: The Process of Disengagement*. New York: Basic Books.

Eisenberg, L. A. (1979). A friend not an apple a day will keep the doctor away. *The American Journal of Medicine*, 66, 551-553.

Erikson, E. (1959). Identity and the life-cycle. *Psychological Issues*, 1 (1) New York: International Universities Press.

Fiske, M. and Weiss, L. (1977). Intimacy and crises in adulthood. In N. Schlossberg and A. Entine (eds.), *Counseling Adults*. Monterey, CA: Brooks/Cole.

Gilligan, C. (1982). *In a Different Voice*. Cambridge, MA: Harvard University Press.

Hacker, H. M. (1981). Blabbermouths and clams: Sex differences in self-disclosure. *Psychology of Women Quarterly*, 5 (3), 384-402.

Hess, B. (1985). America's Elderly: A demographic overview. In B. Hess and E. Markson (eds.). *Growing Old in America, 3rd Edition*. New Brunswick, NJ: Transaction Books.

Hess, B. (1979). Sex roles, friendship, and the life course. *Research on Aging*, 1, 494-515.

Hiltz, S. R. (1978). Widowhood: A roleless role. *Marriage & Family Review*, 1 (6), 1-9.

Hochschild, A. R. (1982). Communal life-styles for the old. In B. Hess (ed.), *Growing Old in America, Second Edition*. New Brunswick, NJ: Transaction Books.

Lebowitz, B. D., Fried, J. and Madaris, C. (1973). Sources of assistance in an urban ethnic community. *Human Organization*, 32, 267-271.

Lenz, E. and Myerhoff, B. (1985). *The Feminization of America*. Los Angeles: Jeremy P. Tarcher, Inc.

Levinson, D. (1978). *Seasons of a Man's Life*. New York: Ballantine Books.

Levy, S. M. (1980). The adjustment of the older woman: Effects of chronic ill health and attitudes retirement. *International Journal of Aging and Human Development*, 12, 93-110.

Lewittes, H. (1986). The process of friendship formation between women at a senior center. Paper presented at the National Council on Aging Conference, Washington, DC.

Lewittes, H. and Mukherji, B. R. (1984). The best friends of older black and white women. Paper presented at the Annual Northeast Gerontology Association Conference: Philadelphia, PA.

Longino, C. F. and Lipman, A. (1985). The support systems of women. In W. T. Sauer and R. T. Coward (eds.). *Social Support Networks and the Care of the Elderly*. New York: Springer.

Lopata, H. Z. (1973). *Widowhood in an American City*. Cambridge, MA: Schenkman.

Lowenthal, M. F. and Haven, C. (1968). Interaction and adaptation: Intimacy as a critical variable. *American Sociological Review*, 33 (20), 20-30.

Lowenthal, M. F., Thurner, M. and Oniriboga, D. (1975). *Four Stages of Life*: San Francisco, CA: Jossey-Bass.

Lynch, J. J. (1977). *The Broken Heart: The Medical Consequences of Loneliness*. New York: Basic Books.

Mindel, C. H. (1985). The Elderly in Minority Families. In B. Hess and E. Markson (eds.) *Growing Old in America, 3rd Edition*, New Brunswick, NJ: Transaction Books.

Myerhoff, B. (1979). After 15 years of feminism, where is women's friendship? *Ms*. 13 (12) June, 85-87.

Myerhoff, B. (1978). *Number Our Days*. New York: Simon & Schuster.

Neugarten, B. (1982). Middle age and aging. In B. Hess (ed.). *Growing Old in America: Second Edition*. New Brunswick, NJ: Transaction Books.

Ortega, S. T., Crutchfield, R. D. and Rusing, W. A. (1983). Race differences in elderly personal well-being. *Research on Aging*, 5, 101-118.

Peck, T. (1985). The role of relationships in women's adult development. Paper presented at the Annual Convention of the American Gerontological Association, New Orleans, LA.

Peters, G. R. and Kaiser, M. A. (1985). The role of friends and neighbors in providing support. In W. J. Sauer and R. T. Coward (eds.), *Social Support Networks and the Care of the Elderly*. New York: Springer.

Powers, E. A. and Bultena, G. L. (1976). Sex differences in intimate friendships in old age. *Journal of Marriage and the Family*, 38, 739-746.

Roberto, K. A. and Scott, J. P. (1986). Equity considerations in the friendships of older adults. *Journal of Gerontology*, 41 (2), 241-247.

Rubin, L. B. (1985). *Just Friends*. New York: Harper and Row.

Sarton, M. (1977). *A House by the Sea*. New York: W. W. Norton.

Scarf, M. (1980). *Unfinished Business*. New York: Doubleday.

Silverman, P. (1982). Widowhood and preventive intervention. In S. H. Zarit. *Readings in Aging and Death*. New York: Harper and Row.

Sterne, R., Phillips, J. E. and Rabushka, A. (1974). *The Urban Elderly Poor*. Lexington, MA: D. C. Heath.

Strain, L. A. and Chappell, N. L. (1982). Confidants: Do they make a difference in quality of life? *Research on Aging*, 4, 479-502.

Sullivan, D. A. and Stevens, A. S. (1985). Snowbirds: Seasonal migrants to the sunbelt. In B. Hess, E. Markson (eds.). *Growing Old in America: Third Edition*. New Brunswick, NJ: Transaction Books.

Szinovacz, M. E. (1983). Beyond the hearth: Older women and retirement. In B. Hess and E. Markson (eds.). *Growing Old in America: Third Edition*. New Brunswick, NJ: Transaction Books.

Ward, R. A. (1979). The meaning of voluntary association participation to older people. *Journal of Gerontology*, 34 (3), 438-445.

Weiss, L. and Lowenthal, M. J. (1975). Life course perspectives on friendships. In M. F. Lowenthal, M. Thurnher and D. Chiriboga (eds.). *Four Stages of Life*. San Francisco, CA: Jossey-Bass.

Gender Differences
in the Relationship
of Widowhood
and Psychological Well-Being
Among Low Income Elderly

James E. Lubben

SUMMARY. The present study examined the influence of widowhood on the psychological well-being of low income elderly women and men while controlling for a number of mediating variables. Both widows and widowers were found to have lower psychological well-being than their married counterparts once health and social network differences were controlled. Health status and social networks were the major predictors of psychological well-being. Married women reported many more stress related ailments than any other group. Among women, friends contributed more to psychological well-being than family contact. Among men, family rather than friends were more highly correlated with psychological well-being. Implications for clinical practice and future research are discussed.

James E. Lubben, University of California, School of Social Welfare, Los Angeles, CA 90024.

The data used in this analysis were derived from the California Senior Survey, which was the comparison group for the California Multipurpose Senior Services Project (MSSP), a U.S. Health Care Finance Administration (HCFA 1115) research and demonstration project administered by the Health and Welfare Agency of the State of California (Grant #11-P-07553). The results and views reported are totally the responsibility of the author and do not reflect official policies of the State of California.

The author would like to thank Diane de Anda and Ruth Zambrana for their helpful comments on various drafts of this article. Also acknowledged are Gloria Crane, Nancy Engles and Roberta Parker for their research assistance in the early stages of this article.

It is speculated that women suffer fewer psychological consequences from widowhood than elderly men (Berardo, 1970; Stroebe
& Stroebe, 1983; Brubaker, 1985). One reason suggested from this
difference is that marriage may not provide the same protection for
women that it does for men (Turner, 1983). Nearly a hundred years
ago, Durkheim (1951; 274-275) stated that "women can suffer
more from a marriage if it is unfavourable to her than she can benefit by it if it conforms to her interest. This is because she has less
need of it." Accordingly, a woman probably suffers less when her
husband dies than a man does when his wife dies.

However, Lopata (1987) states that there is a dearth of empirical
evidence regarding purported sex differences in experiencing widowhood. Moreover, widowers, who are much fewer in number than
widows, have tended to quickly remarry and thus be understudied.
Those in better health are most apt to remarry which may account
for the greater incidence of health problems among elderly men
who remain widowed (Lopata, 1984). Such differences in health
status may partially explain why widowers report lower mental
health than married men (Palmore & Luikart, 1972; Larson, 1978;
Markides & Martin, 1979; Palmore, 1981; Baur & Okun, 1983;
Ward et al., 1984; Okun 1987).

Sex differences observed in mortality studies have encouraged
speculation that elderly women suffer fewer psychological consequences than men from widowhood. For example, Helsing and associates (1981) reported that widowers have higher adjusted mortality rates for most causes of death than married men whereas
mortality rates were about the same for widows as for married
women. Likewise, Gore's (1973) study of traumatic deaths observed few differences between elderly widows and married women
although elderly widowers were more likely than married men to
commit suicide and be victims of homicide, fatal motor accidents
and other fatal accidents. Similar data led Berardo (1985) to suggest
that many men succumb to a "broken-heart syndrome" following
their wife's death.

The death of a spouse can fundamentally change an elderly person's social network which in turn can affect psychological well-
being (Stroebe & Stroebe, 1983). Many studies have demonstrated
a link between social networks and mental health (Greenblatt et al.,

1982; Dimond et al., 1987). However, the death of a spouse may affect the social networks of women and men differently.

The death of a husband may actually enhance an elderly woman's ability to socialize because wives are much more likely than husbands to be consumed by demanding conjugal caretaking responsibilities (Fengler & Goodrich, 1979; Depner & Verbrugge, 1980; Abel, 1987). Further, conjugal caretaking is often unable to keep pace with need as couples age creating additional tension (Depner & Ingersoll-Dayton, 1985). The inability to maintain important social relationships may aggravate this stress because of the role social networks play in moderating or buffering the impact of life stressors (Cassel, 1976; Cobb, 1976; Kaplan et al., 1977; Dean & Lin, 1977; LaRocco et al., 1980; Turner, 1983).

Whereas the death of a husband may allow an elderly woman to spend more time with her friends, the death of a wife is likely to deplete an elderly man's social network. Trela and Jackson (1979) observed that men rely more on their spouse as a confidant than women do. Furthermore, wives often assume responsibility for maintaining social contacts for their husbands in old age (Berardo, 1970; Cummings & Lazer, 1981). Accordingly, Turner (1983) stated:

> because women in our society tend to maintain both normative and interactive integration of kinship systems (and perhaps of wider social networks as well) on behalf of men and themselves, the implications of loss of spouse for men tends to be multiplied. Widows lose only their husbands, but widowers also tend to suffer the loss of some portion of their wider support networks. (p. 120)

Another consideration is the type of social contact. Although family contact has been viewed as instrumental to higher morale (Shanas, 1973), most studies have failed to find a positive correlation between frequency of family interaction and psychological well-being (e.g., Larson, 1978; Lee, 1979). Baur and Okun (1983) found that perceived adequacy of contact with friends significantly predicted psychological well-being among elderly persons and Ward and associates (1984) observed that contact with friends was more important than contact with children in terms of morale. Interaction with friends may be more positive than that with family members because selection of friends is discretionary and peer relationships may provide special rewards (Chappell, 1983).

Traditional gender roles may also influence the need for social support after the death of a spouse. For example, Brubaker (1985) suggested that a wife often assumes the role of housekeeper among elderly couples and her death usually forces her husband to take on this role and to learn new tasks. This is important in that the current cohort of elderly men has been characterized as "a generation of husbands heavily dependent upon their spouses for physical, emotional, and other kinds of support" (Berardo, 1985: 41).

Income is another significant factor associated with psychological well-being (Glenn, 1975; Morgan, 1976; Pearlin & Johnson, 1977). Whereas widowers have tended to fare worse than widows in terms of health and the social network consequences of widowhood, the opposite is true for income. Widows endure more financial hardships than widowers because men generally have better pension plans and social security benefits than women (Muller, 1983; Estes et al., 1984). While current estimates of hardship vary, it has been suggested that one-half of all widows live at or below the income adequacy level determined by the Social Security Administration (Balkwell, 1981). Harvey and Bahr (1974) summarize the importance of income to widowhood stating that the:

> negative impact sometimes attributed to widowhood derives not from the widowhood status, but rather from socioeconomic status. The widowed have appeared to have more negative attitudes than the married because they are much poorer than the married. (pp. 104-106)

These studies suggest several research questions which were examined in the present analyses. The central question was whether a relationship between psychological well-being and widowhood exists in a population of low income elderly after controlling for health status and social networks. Secondly, are gender and marital status related to poor health and social networks which tend to also influence psychological well-being among elderly populations?

Thirdly, what types of social networks are most predictive of psychological well-being by gender? Finally, do social networks indirectly influence psychological well-being by acting as a buffer against life stressers?

STUDY METHODS

Design

The present study was a cross-sectional survey of non-institutionalized Medicaid elderly. The association of widowhood with psychological well-being was examined while accounting for differences in gender, health and social networks. Income differences were also controlled in the study design since all respondents were Medi-Cal (California's version of Medicaid) recipients at the time of the survey.

Participants

The data were drawn from the California Senior Survey (CSS), a random sample of elderly Medi-Cal recipients from eight representative communities within California. CSS respondents were randomly selected from California's Central Identification (CID) files which contain names, addresses and other basic demographic data for all Medi-Cal recipients. Only Medi-Cal recipients 65 years or older were sampled. They were interviewed face-to-face in 1982 and paid fifteen dollars for their participation. Comparisons between the CSS sample and statewide data indicated that the CSS respondents were typical of California's Medicaid elderly population. More complete descriptions of the CSS sampling methodology and sample characteristics have already been published (Lubben, 1984; Miller et al., 1985; Clark et al., 1988).

For the present analysis, only those CSS respondents who reported their current marital status as married or widowed were retained. Further, CSS respondents who had been widowed within six months prior to the interview, or married respondents who were not living with their spouse were eliminated from the study. Respondents in the current study ranged in age from 65 to slightly over 100 years. With respect to gender, there were almost two females for every male. Significant gender differences were noted in marital status in that more than 60% of the men were married compared to less than 20% of the women. Reflecting California's ethnically diverse population, approximately 56% of the sample were White, 16% Black, 10% Mexican-American, 9% Chinese-American, and the remaining 9% were from other racial/ethnic groups primarily other Latinos and other Asian-Pacific Islanders.

MEASURES

Psychological Well-Being

Psychological well-being was measured with the Life Satisfaction Index (LSI) developed by Neugarten, Havinghust, and Tobin (1961). Adams (1969) suggested dropping two items from the original LSI and this become common practice (Harris, 1981). The LSI-A used in the present study included eighteen items which displayed a high degree of internal consistency (alpha = .80).

Health Status

Health status was measured in three ways. The first measure was an abbreviated version of Langner's (1962) ailment checklist. Langner suggested that these ailments were indicative of psychological distress. The list included such ailments as frequent headaches, stomach pains, nervousness, and poor appetite. There was a high degree of internal consistency (alpha = .74) among these ten items in the present sample. They were equally weighted and summed to form the abbreviated Langner stress scale. Thus low scores indicated better health. The second health measure was the single item Subjective Self Health Rating (SSHR) which was obtained in response to a question of how do you rate your overall health at the present time: good, fair, or poor?

The final measure of health status was the Instrumental Activities of Daily Living (IADL). Lawton and Brody (1969) developed the IADL to measure an elderly person's capability to perform a number of tasks important to maintaining social connections, such as, telephoning and transportation. Further, the IADL measures an elderly person's capability to do housework, laundry, and prepare meals. Because these latter tasks have tended to be associated with gender roles, it has been suggested that widowers may be more impaired by IADL limitations than women or married men who often have their wives to help out in these areas. Higher scores on the IADL indicate less self-care capacity. The IADL displayed a high level of internal consistency (alpha = .79) among the present sample.

Social Networks

Social networks were measured using a series of questions which had been developed by the State of California Human Population Laboratory for use in their Alameda County Epidemiological Studies (Berkman & Syme, 1979). Three different variables were used: one measured size of an elderly person's active social network, another measured size of their intimate network, and a third dealt with frequency of social interaction. All three types of measures distinguished family from friend networks. For the present analysis, spousal contact was not counted as family contact.

Size of active social networks was determined from a series of questions which asked how many people the respondent "saw or heard from" on a monthly basis. *Size of intimate social networks* was determined by questions that asked how many family members and friends the respondent felt "close to" (people the respondent felt at ease with, could talk to about private matters and could call on for help). *Frequency of social contact* was evaluated in terms of the family member and close friend seen most often. Response options to these questions ranged from daily to once a year or less.

ANALYSIS PLAN

The influence of widowhood on psychological well-being was examined using parallel multiple regression models for women and men. Separate models were constructed because of the high collinearity of gender with widowhood and the disparate sample sizes by gender. Furthermore, separate models for women and men facilitated analysis of sex differences in the relationship of social networks with psychological well-being. New variables were created to test the stress buffering hypothesis. Using the average effects[1] method, one set of interaction variables was created by multiplying the deviations of the Langner stress scale and each social network variable from their respective means.

FINDINGS

Characteristics

Demographic characteristics are reported in Table 1. Both female and male samples were quite elderly. The mean age of women was 78 years whereas the average male was 77 years. Married respondents in both samples were, on the average, 4.8 years younger than their widowed counterparts. No differences were noted in educational level or ethnicity between the widowed and married respondents in either sample.

Health and Widowhood

Although there were no significant differences in IADL between married and unmarried individuals, there were major differences on the other two health measures. Furthermore, the relationship of marital status with the other health status variables tended to be exactly opposite for women as for men. For example, widows were less likely than married women to rate their health as poor whereas widowers were more than twice as likely as married men to rate their health as poor. Differences between married and widowed women on the Langner scale were especially significant (Table 2). Married women averaged many more ailments than widows (3.5 versus 2.3) whereas the average number of ailments for married men was slightly lower than for widowers (1.8 versus 2.2). These data suggest that the married women were more distressed than any other group of elderly respondents. More specifically, married women were twice as likely as widowed women to report "shortness of breath," "exhaustion," "headaches," "stomach pains," "fainting spells or dizziness," "feeling tired even after a night's sleep" and "nervousness."

TABLE 1

MAJOR CHARACTERISTICS BY GENDER AND MARITAL STATUS
(Percentage Distributions)

	MEN			WOMEN		
	Married	Widowers	X^2: Prob.	Married	Widows	X^2: Prob.
All Persons (N)	(99)	(57)		(78)	(393)	
Age						
65-74 years	51.5	35.1		60.3	29.1	
75-84	42.4	35.1	$X^2 = 16.5$	35.9	51.8	$X^2 = 30.9$
85+	6.1	29.8	p<.001	3.9	19.1	p<.001
Ethnicity						
White	51.0	52.6	$X^2 = 0.04$	55.1	57.6	$X^2 = 0.2$
Non-White	49.0	47.4	n.s.	44.9	42.4	n.s.
Education						
Elem. or Less	49.5	59.6		57.7	54.2	
High School	23.2	26.3	$X^2 = 3.7$	29.5	29.5	$X^2 = 0.6$
Beyond H. S.	27.3	14.0	n.s.	12.8	16.3	n.s.

TABLE 1: (continued)

	MEN			WOMEN		
	Married	Widowers	X²; Prob.	Married	Widows	X²; Prob.
All Persons (N)	(99)	(57)		(78)	(393)	
# of Langner Ailments:						
none	30.3	19.3		14.1	23.9	
1	28.3	29.8		14.1	21.9	
2	21.2	19.3		16.7	15.8	
3	7.1	5.3		14.1	13.7	
4	1.0	12.3	X² = 11.0	6.4	9.7	X² = 19.2
5+	12.1	14.8	p<. 10	34.6	19.2	p<.001
IADLs (# dependent)						
none	7.1	16.1		6.4	10.4	
1	15.2	17.9		24.4	32.1	
2	23.2	14.3	X² = 4.5	18.0	14.3	X² = 3.9
3+	54.6	51.8	n.s.	51.3	43.3	n.s.
Self-Rated Health						
Good	47.4	33.3		32.5	39.2	
Fair	42.3	42.1	X² = 6.4	37.7	39.5	X² = 3.2
Poor	10.3	24.6	p< .05	29.9	20.9	n.s.

TABLE 2

LANGNER AILMENT CHECKLIST BY GENDER

	MEN			WOMEN		
	% with Ailment	Odds Ratio[e]	(95% C.I.)	% with Ailment	Odds Ratio[e]	(95% C.I.)
Shortness of breath	32.7	1.65	(.79, 3.45)	31.4	.63[d]	(.37, 1.05)
Pain in heart/chest	22.4	1.54	(.68, 3.49)	28.8	.89	(.52, 1.53)
Often feel worn out	23.7	1.66	(.74, 3.73)	25.9	.46[b]	(.27, .78)
Frequent headaches	16.7	1.47	(.59, 3.67)	21.9	.57[c]	(.33, .99)
Stomach pains	7.0	1.13	(.29, 4.37)	12.7	.37[b]	(.19, .71)
Fainting or dizziness	22.4	1.94	(.86, 4.35)	34.2	.42[a]	(.25, .70)
Nervousness	23.7	2.21[d]	(1.00, 4.91)	38.2	.56[c]	(.33, .92)

TABLE 2: (continued)

| | MEN | | | WOMEN | | |
	% with Ailment	Odds Ratio[e]	(95% C.I.)	% with Ailment	Odds Ratio[e]	(95% C.I.)
Problems with sleep	22.4	.90	(.38, 2.09)	24.6	.67	(.38, 1.18)
Tired even after usual night's sleep	15.4	2.18[d]	(.86, 5.53)	20.8	.47[b]	(.27, .83)
Poor appetite	7.0	.83	(.21, 3.32)	10.2	.55	(.25, 1.20)

NOTES:

a   p <.001
b   p <.01
c   p <.05
d   p <.10
e   Odds ratios are adjusted for age.

172

Social Networks and Widowhood

Married women had significantly more limited friendship networks than widows but there were no differences among the male respondents with regard to friends (Table 3). Almost half of the married women reported not having any close friends which was twice the rate for widows. Accordingly, married women were much less apt than widows to have frequent contact with friends. Gender specific associations with social networks were also noted. Although there were no differences between widows and married women in family contact, married men had larger family networks than did widowers. For example, widowers were twice as likely as married men to report having neither seen nor heard from a family member in the last month.

Psychological Well-Being and Widowhood

The elderly women in the present study reported a median Life Satisfaction Index (Adams' version: LSI-A) score of 24.0 which was slightly lower than the mens' median LSI-A of 24.5. The LSI-A values in both samples approximated the overall median (24.7) reported by Harris (1981) in his national survey of the aged. Moreover, LSI-A scores observed in the present samples were quite comparable to the low income sub-sample of the Harris (1981) survey which reported a median of 24.1. There were no significant differences in LSI-A scores between married women and widows in the present study. However, married men reported significantly higher average LSI-A scores than did widowers. Although there were no differences in LSI-A scores among women, both married and widowed women had significantly lower LSI-A scores than married men. There were no significant differences in LSI-A scores between widowers and either married or widowed women.

Bivariate Correlations with Life Satisfaction

Table 4 reports Pearson correlation coefficients for all variables entered into the multivariate models. Although self-reported health (SSHR) was highly correlated with LSI-A (r = .42), it was not

TABLE 3

SOCIAL NETWORKS BY GENDER AND MARITAL STATUS
(Percentage Distributions)

	MEN			WOMEN		
	Married	Widowers	X^2; Prob.	Married	Widows	X^2; Prob.
All Persons (N)	(99)	(57)		(78)	(393)	
Active Network Size:[a]						
FAMILY:						
none	7.1	17.5		3.9	7.1	
1-2	6.1	17.5		14.3	16.8	
3-4	10.1	21.0	$X^2 = 17.4$ p<.001	14.3	17.6	$X^2 = 2.5$ n.s.
5+	76.8	43.9		67.5	58.5	
FRIENDS:						
none	34.3	33.3		48.7	28.2	
1-2	19.2	24.6		20.5	32.6	
3-4	21.2	15.8	$X^2 = 1.1$ n.s.	14.1	19.1	$X^2 = 13.0$ p<.01
5+	25.2	26.3		16.7	20.1	
Intimate Network Size:[b]						
FAMILY:						
none	15.2	22.8		10.3	17.0	
1-2	30.3	33.3		39.7	34.6	
3-4	24.2	29.8	$X^2 = 5.6$ n.s.	21.8	23.4	$X^2 = 2.7$ n.s.
5+	30.3	14.4		28.2	24.9	

FRIENDS:					$X^2 = 0.5$ n.s.			$X^2 = 13.2$ p< .01
none	31.3	28.1			43.6	24.2		
1-2	16.2	19.3			20.5	28.5		
3-4	22.2	19.3			11.5	20.0		
5+	30.3	33.3			24.4	27.5		

Frequency of Contact:

FAMILY:					$X^2 = 9.8$ p< .05			$X^2 = 4.9$ n.s.
Daily	42.4	40.4			52.6	51.2		
Weekly	37.4	19.3			29.5	26.7		
Monthly	10.1	15.8			14.1	10.4		
Less Often	10.1	24.6			3.9	11.7		

FRIENDS:					$X^2 = 0.6$ n.s.			$X^2 = 12.3$ p< .01
Daily	23.2	26.3			20.5	30.0		
Weekly	29.3	31.6			24.4	31.3		
Monthly	14.1	10.5			7.7	11.2		
Less Often	33.3	31.6			47.4	27.5		

NOTES: a number of family or friends seen or heard from at least once a month
       b number of family or friends feels close to
       n.s. not significant

175

TABLE 4

BIVARIATE CORRELATIONS WITH LSI-A SCORES

	—MEN— Pearson R	—WOMEN— Pearson R
WIDOWED	-.22[b]	.03
AGE	-.04	.03
IADLs	-.36[a]	-.28[a]
LANGNER STRESS SCALE	-.53[a]	-.44[a]
SOCIAL NETWORKS		
Size of Active Network[e]		
Family	.21[b]	.16[a]
Friends	.22[b]	.22[a]

Size of Intimate Network[e]		
Family	.16c	.17a
Friends	.21b	.21a
Frequency of Social Contact		
Family	.17c	.04
Friends	.19c	.15a

NOTES:

a p < .001
b p < .01
c p < .05
d p < .10
e # family or friends seen or heard from at least once a month
f # family or friends respondent feels "close to"

entered into the regression models because the SSHR was also highly correlated with the Langner stress scale (r = .49). In order to avoid problems with multicollinearity, only one of these two health variables was incorporated into the regression models. The Langner checklist was selected because it generally had a much higher correlation with LSI-A scores than SSHR at all stages of analysis. In fact, the Langner checklist demonstrated a higher bivariate correlation with LSI-A scores than any other variable. Functional health, as measured by the IADL, possessed the next strongest relationship with LSI-A scores. Social networks were also highly correlated with LSI-A scores in both samples although some intriguing gender differences were noted. Among elderly women, contact with friends contributed more to LSI-A scores than family contact. However, family contact was more highly correlated with LSI-A scores among elderly men than contact with friends.

Multivariate Correlational Analysis

Table 5 reports standardized regression coefficients along with total R^2 for the different models. It was decided to construct separate regression models for each type of social network variable because of high collinearity among the social network variables. The R^2 values were quite comparable within each sample regardless of the type of social network measure included in the regression models. However, the models were less able to predict LSI-A scores among elderly women than men. Only 27% of the variation in female scores was explained whereas up to 37% of the variation in male LSI-A scores was explained.

The two health variables, the Langner Scale and IADL, accounted for most of the variance in the models. The Langner scale was most predictive of LSI-A scores. Its standardized beta weight was at least double that of any other variable in any of the regression models.

The social network variables were also strong predictors of LSI-A scores. However, a very different pattern of associations between specific social network variables and LSI-A scores emerged for women and men. A woman's contact with friends was more predic-

TABLE 5

MULTIVARIATE CORRELATIONS WITH LSI-A SCORES BY TYPE OF SOCIAL NETWORK AND GENDER

(Separate models were constructed for each type of social network because of collinearity)

	MEN			WOMEN		
	ACTIVE NETWORK model (beta)	INTIMATE NETWORK model (beta)	FREQUENCY OF CONTACT model (beta)	ACTIVE NETWORK model (beta)	INTIMATE NETWORK model (beta)	FREQUENCY OF CONTACT model (beta)
WIDOWED	-.09	-.12[d]	-.14[d]	-.09[c]	-.08[d]	-.10[c]
AGE	-.01	-.03	.00	.08[d]	.08[d]	.08[d]
IADLs	-.19[b]	-.20[b]	-.20[b]	-.16[a]	-.16[a]	-.16[a]
LANGNER STRESS SCALE	-.44[a]	-.47[a]	-.45[a]	-.39[a]	-.40[a]	-.41[a]
SOCIAL NETWORKS						
Size of Active Network[e]						
Family	.19[b]			.12[b]		
Friends	.12[d]			.18[a]		
(Langner) * (Family)	.02			-.02		
(Langner) * (Friends)	-.08			.05		

	MEN			WOMEN		
	ACTIVE NETWORK model (beta)	INTIMATE NETWORK model (beta)	FREQUENCY OF CONTACT model (beta)	ACTIVE NETWORK model (beta)	INTIMATE NETWORK model (beta)	FREQUENCY OF CONTACT model (beta)
Size of Initimate Network[f]						
Family		.14[c]			.15[a]	
Friends		.09			.15[a]	
(Langner)*(Family)		.05			-.02	
(Langner)*(Friends)		-.11[d]			.08[c]	
Frequency of Social Contact						
Family			.13[d]			.06
Friends			.14[c]			.14[a]
(Langner)*(Family)			.04			-.05
(Langner)*(Friends)			-.02			.03
ADJUSTED R^2	.36[a]	.37[a]	.37[a]	.26[a]	.27[a]	.24[a]

NOTES:
a $p < .001$
b $p < .01$
c $p < .05$
d $p < .10$
e number of family or friends seen or heard from at least once a month
f number of family or friends feels close to

180

tive of her LSI-A scores whereas a man's family network was generally more predictive of his LSI-A score.

Furthermore, the interaction of close friends with the Langner scale suggested a significant stress buffering relationship among elderly women. Specifically, more close friends moderated the effect of more stress. Although a modest interaction between close friends and stress was also observed among elderly men, the sign on the coefficient was negative. Accordingly, having more close friends tended to exacerbate an elderly man's stress rather than moderate it. Thus, a stress aggravating relationship was suggested among men rather than a stress buffering relationship as was observed among women.

Additional analyses on the type of active family network and frequency of family contact also revealed that grandchildren were more influential on LSI-A scores than one's own children. For example, the number of one's own children seen or heard from monthly did not predict LSI-A scores for either women or men whereas the number of grandchildren seen or heard from monthly did.

Although age was not significant at the bivariate level of analysis, there was a slight tendency for it to positively impact on LSI-A scores among elderly women. This tendency conflicts with many earlier studies which reported that age was not significantly related to psychological well-being scores when other factors, such as health and socio-economic status, were controlled (Palmore & Kivett, 1977; Mussen et al., 1982; Bauer & Okun, 1983).

The influence of widowhood displayed a similar pattern among both women and men in the multivariate models. Widowhood, which was not close to being a significant factor among women at the bivariate stage of analysis, became negative and statistically significant. This implies that widowhood also has a negative impact on psychological well-being among elderly women once health status and social network differences are controlled. Although the strong association of widowhood with LSI-A scores among the male sample was greatly diminished once health and social network factors were controlled, widowers still tended to have lower LSI-A scores than married men.

DISCUSSION

The health status variables were the strongest predictors of LSI-A scores among both elderly women and men in the present study. These findings are consistent with earlier findings (Edwards & Klemack, 1973; Morgan, 1976; Bauer & Okun, 1983) which have demonstrated that good health is very important to psychological well-being.

A major finding of the study is that the psychological well-being of married women appears to be greatly impaired by the presence of extensive stress. One reason for higher stress scores reported among married women is that many of them may be burdened by caring for a spouse. An elderly wife caring for a severely dependent husband is often the hidden victim of the husband's illness (Zarit et al., 1985). Even if an elderly married woman received assistance with the caretaking functions, the frail health of a spouse can still create family tensions (Kerckhoff, 1966; Brody, 1985).

Support for a hypothesis of conjugal caretaker strain among married elderly women is suggested when one looks at the sex differences in reported stress. The married women had twice as many ailments as the married men. Because women tend to marry men who are older than they are, elderly wives in the sample were probably more likely to be caretakers than husbands and therefore they would probably not encounter the same strains (Fengler & Goodrich, 1979). Unfortunately, there were no data in the present study on health status or age of spouses to directly test a hypothesis that caretaker strain may have been a factor in lowering LSI-A scores among married women.

The higher prevalence of the Langner stress related ailments among the married women may also be related to thwarted attempts at maintaining friendships. Close friends tended to buffer some of the stress the elderly women experienced. However, almost half of the married women reported not having any close friends. Because friends were more powerful predictors of psychological well-being among women than family, this deficiency of friends among the married women assumes extra significance.

The importance of friends to psychological well-being has been shown in other gerontological studies. Indeed, Larson and associates (1986: 117) recently noted that "one of the major puzzles found in the gerontology literature is the apparent superiority of friends over family as sources of psycological well-being." One possible explanation to Larson's puzzle may be that contact with friends brings mutual enjoyment by generally avoiding stressful encounters, whereas contact with relatives may sometimes require unpleasant social obligations.

The present study, however, suggests that the superiority of friends over family may be gender related. Further, the interaction of the Langner stress scale and close friends among elderly men indicated an aggravating rather than buffering relationship. This surprising result may be unique to low income elderly men and not representative of the general elderly population. However, it may also be that men find it more difficult to discuss physical ailments with close friends than women do. Thus, a more open communication between a woman and her close friends may enable a stress buffering role for friends which is not possible for a man.

Further study is needed to answer Larson's puzzle but it is likely that important sex differences will emerge regarding specific roles played by various types of social network structures among different elderly populations. For example, Hess and Waring (1978) suggested that a "special relationship" exists between mothers and offspring partially because women have been socialized to assume nurturant roles and responsibility for kin keeping whereas men are socialized into roles of rivalry and control. Moreover, caretaking of elderly widowed persons is primarily done by daughters (Stone et al., 1987). Thus, a lifetime of interdependency and family intimacy may make it easier for a woman to accept care whereas a man may have difficulty accepting such help because it symbolizes his loss of mastery. This might also explain why the IADL variable contributed more to the R^2 in the male models than in the female models.

Although all regression models in the present analysis were quite significant, they also suggest that many other factors beside those enumerated in the models influence variations in psychological well-being among elderly populations. Possible additional factors that should be examined in future research include health of spouse and quality of social interaction with family and friends.

Another important question requiring further study is why parent-child interaction appears less predictive of psychological well-being than parent-grandchild interaction. Perhaps changing family roles and concomitant stress might explain this finding. In the present study, some family interaction may have involved situations where established parental roles were especially challenged because of the very old age of both samples. Although family contact usually increases to assure necessary support during convalescence, tensions can be created by role changes and power shifts within the family (Croog, 1970; Cohler & Lieberman, 1980; Scharlach, 1987). Conflicts may further result when support is no longer needed by the patient but the person who assumed new roles during the patient's illness does not want to relinquish them. A chronically ill person may particularly experience such difficulties because new family roles are likely to become entrenched when convalescence is extended or when recovery from an illness is incomplete. It is unlikely that grandchild contact would involve as much stress as child contact which sometimes must deal directly with sensitive issues such as control over legal matters and personal care for parents.

IMPLICATIONS

The major focus of the present study was on the relationship of widowhood and psychological well-being among low-income elderly women and men. Although widowers continued to report lower LSI-A scores than married men at all stages of analysis, it is perhaps more important to focus on women where widowhood became a significant and negative factor once health and social network variables were controlled. Accordingly, the present study suggests that the current focus of gerontological research regarding the influence of widowhood on the psychological well-being of elderly persons should be expanded. Rather than primarily concentrating on why widowers may have less psychological well-being than married men, future gerontological research should also try to understand why married women have less psychological well-being than married men. Although the present study suggests that high stress and restricted contact with friends are probable causes, more clarification of why elderly married women report lower psychological well-being than their male counterparts is needed.

The present study also suggests a methodological research agenda. Better instruments are needed to measure social networks among elderly populations. Additional items dealing with the qualitative aspects of an elderly person's social network probably would have increased the R^2 values (Lowenthal & Haven, 1968; Rook, 1980; Ward et al., 1984; Essex & Nam, 1987; Dimond et al., 1987). Furthermore, the IADL in the present study was more capable of predicting male LSI-A scores than female scores. Perhaps refinement of this commonly used functional health measure would improve description of essential differences among elderly women.

The data also bare important practice implications. There appear to be gender differences in social network patterns which influence successful aging. Therefore, clinicians need to be aware of the specific needs of different elderly groups. For example, the focus of support groups must respond to the particular interests and needs of participants which are related to gender and marital status. Furthermore, the data suggest that a married woman's ability to interact with her friends may be severely constrained. Special intervention programs may help. For example, respite programs may make it possible for a married woman, with spousal caretaker responsibilities to spend more time with her friends. Ultimately, she may be better able to cope with the demands of extended spousal care. Programs to foster increased opportunities for contact with friends may be as meaningful as other interventions, given this study's evidence that close friends may be especially good "medicine" for the psychological well-being of elderly women.

Finally, the study warns clinicians working with severely disabled elderly to also be sensitive to the health status and psychological well-being of conjugal caretakers. Elderly who care for a chronically ill spouse are themselves at increased risk of illness and death (Gerber et al., 1975). The extensive list of stress related ailments reported by married women in the present study is probably a warning of their own imminent health crisis.

NOTE

1. Multicollinearity has often complicated testing for multiplicative interaction effects because the interaction variable is generally highly correlated with at least one of the two independent variables used to create the interaction term. This results in very unstable estimates and greatly enlarged standard errors for both main effect and interaction coefficients. One solution to this problem is the average effect method (Finney et al., 1984) which minimizes multicollinearity and stabilizes the estimates of main effects. A major advantage of the average effect method is that the main effect coefficients are almost same in a multiplicative model as they are in an addictive model. Any differences are usually due to rounding. Thus, data normally presented in two separate tables can be summarized in one.

REFERENCES

Abel, E.K. (1987). *Love is not enough*. Washington, DC: American Public Health Association.

Adams, D. (1969). Analysis of a life satisfaction index. *Journal of gerontology*, 24, 470-474.

Balkwell, C. (1981). Transitions to widowhood: a review of the literature. *Family relations*, 30, 117-127.

Baur, P. & Okun, M.A. (1983). Stability of life satisfaction in late life. *Gerontologist*, 23, 261-265.

Berardo, F.M. (1970). Survivorship and social isolation: the case of the aged widower. *Family coordinator*, 19, 11-25.

Berardo, F.M. (1985). Social networks and life preservation. *Death studies*, 9, 37-50.

Berkman, L.F. & Syme, S.L. (1979). Social networks, host resistance, and mortality: a nine year follow-up study of Alameda County residents. *American Journal of Epidemiology*, 109, 186-204.

Brody, E.M. (1985). Parent care as a normative family stress. *Gerontologist*, 25, 19-29.

Brubaker, T.H. (1985). *Later life families*. Beverly Hills, CA: Sage Publications.

Cassel, J. (1976). The contribution of the social environment to host resistance. *American journal of epidemiology*, 104, 107-123.

Chappell, N.L. (1983). Informal support networks among the elderly. *Research on aging*, 5, 77-99.

Clark, W.F., Pelham, A.O., & Clark, M.L. (1988). *Old and poor*. Lexington, MA: Lexington Books.

Cohler, B.J. & Lieberman, M.A. (1980). Social relations and mental health. *Research on aging*, 2, 445-469.

Cobb, S. (1976). Social support as a moderator of life stress. *Psychosomatic medicine*, 38, 300-314.

Croog, S.H. (1970). The family as a source of stress. In Levine, S. & Scotch, N.A. (Eds.) *Social stress*. Chicago: Aldine Publishing.

Cummings, E. & Lazer, C. (1981). Kinship structure and suicide: a theoretical link. *Canadian review of sociology and anthropology*, 18, 271-282.

Dean, A. & Linn, N. (1977). The stress-buffering role of social support. *Journal of nervous and mental disease*, 154, 403-417.

Depner, C.E. & Ingersoll-Dayton, B. (1985). Conjugal social support: patterns in later life. *Journal of gerontology*, 40, 761-766.

Depner, C.E. & Verbrugge, L.M. (1980). Social networks and health behavior. In McGuigan, D.G. (Ed.) *Women's lives: new theory, research and policy*. Ann Arbor: University of Michigan.

Dimond, M., Lund, D.A., & Caserta, M.S. (1987). The role of social support in the first two years of bereavement in an elderly sample. *Gerontologist*, 27, 599-604.

Durkheim, E. (1951). *Suicide*. New York: The Free Press.

Edwards, J.N. & Klemack, D. (1973). Correlates of life satisfaction: a re-examination. *Journal of gerontology*, 28, 497-502.

Essex, M.J. & Nam, S. (1987). Marital status and loneliness among older women: the differential importance of close family and friends. *Journal of marriage and the family*, 49, 93-106.

Estes, C.L., Gerard, L., & Clarke, A. (1984). Women and the economics of aging. *International journal of health services*, 14, 55-67.

Fengler, A. & Goodrich, N. (1979). Wives of elderly disabled men: the hidden patients. *Gerontologist*, 19, 175-184.

Finney, J.W., Mitchell, R.E., Cronkite, R.C., & Moos, R.M. (1984). Methodological issues in estimating main and interactive effects: examples from coping/social support and stress field. *Journal of health and social behavior*, 25, 85-98.

Gerber, I., Rusalem, R., Hannon, M., Battin, D., & Arkin, A. (1975). Anticipatory grief and aged widows and widowers. *Journal of gerontology*, 30, 225-229.

Glenn, N.D. (1975). The contribution of marriage to the psychological well-being of males and females. *Journal of marriage and the family*, 37, 594-601.

Gore, W.R. (1973). Sex, marital status and mortality. *American journal of sociology*, 79, 45-67.

Greenblatt, M., Becerra, R.M., & Serafetinides, E.A. (1982). Social networks and mental health: an overview. *American journal of psychiatry*, 139, 977-984.

Harris, L. and Associates (1981). *Aging in the eighties: America in transition*. Washington DC: National Council on Aging.

Harvey, C.D. & Bahr, H.M. (1974). Widowhood, morale and affiliation. *Journal of marriage and the family*, 36, 97-106.

Helsing, K.J., Szklo, M., & Comstock, G.W. (1981). Factors associated with mortality after widowhood. *American journal of public health*, 71, 802-809.

Hess, B.B. & Waring, J.M. (1979). Parent and child in later life: rethinking the relationship. In Lerner, R.M. & Spanger, G.B. (Eds.) *Child influences on marital and family interaction*. New York: Academic Press.

Kaplan, B.H., Cassel, J.C., & Gore, S. (1977). Social support and health. *Medical care*, 15, 47-58.

Kerckhoff, A.C. (1966). Family patterns and morale in retirement. In Simpson, I.H. & McKinney, J.C. (Eds.) *Social aspects of aging*. Durham, NC: Duke University Press.

Langner, T.S. (1962). A twenty-two item screening score of psychiatric symptoms indicating impairment. *Journal of health and human behavior*, 3, 269-276.

LaRocco, J.M., House, J.S., & French, J.R.P. Jr. (1980). Social support, occupational stress, and health. *Journal of health and social behavior*, 21, 202-218.

Larson, R. (1978). Thirty years of research on subjective well-being of older Americans. *Journal of gerontology*, 33, 109-125.

Larson, R., Mannell, R., & Zuzanek, J. (1986). Daily well-being of older adults with friends and family. *Psychology and aging*, 1, 117-126.

Lawton, M.P. & Brody, E. (1969). Assessment of older people: self maintaining and instrumental activities of daily living. *Gerontologist*, 9, 179-186.

Lee, G.R. (1979). Children and the elderly. *Research on aging*, 1, 335-359.

Lopata, H.Z. (1984). The widowed. In Palmore, G.B. (Ed.) *Handbook on the aged in the United States*. Wesport, CT: Greenwood Press.

Lopata, H.Z. (1987). Widowhood. In Maddox, G.L. (Ed.) *Encyclopedia of Aging*. New York: Springer Publishing Company.

Lowenthal, M.F. & Haven, C. (1968). Interaction and adaptation: intimacy as a critical variable. *American Sociological Review*, 33, 20-30.

Lubben, J.E. (1984). Health and psychological assessment instruments for community based long term care: The California Multipurpose Senior Services Project (MSSP) experience. Doctoral dissertation, University of California, Berkeley.

Markides, K. & Martin, H.W. (1979). A causal model of life satisfaction among the elderly. *Journal of gerontology*, 34, 86-93.

Miller, L.S., Clark, M., & Clark, W. (1985). The comparative evaluation of California's multipurpose senior services project. *Home health care services quarterly*, 6, 49-79.

Morgan, L.A. (1976). A re-examination of widowhood and morale. *Journal of gerontology*, 31, 687-695.

Muller, C. (1983). Income supports of older women. *Social policy*, 14, 23-31.

Mussen, P., Honzck, M.P., & Eichorn, D.H. (1982). Early adult antecedents of life satisfaction at age seventy. *Journal of gerontology*, 37, 316-322.

Neugarten, B.L., Havighurst, R.H., & Tobin, S.S. (1961). The measurement of life satisfaction. *Journal of gerontology*, 16, 134-143.

Okun, M.A. (1987). Life satisfaction. In Maddox, G.L. (Ed.) *Encyclopedia of Aging*. New York: Springer Publishing Company.

Palmore, E. (1981). *Social patterns in normal aging*. Durham, NC: Duke.

Palmore, E. & Kivett, V. (1977). Change in life satisfaction: a longitudinal study of persons aged 46-70. *Journal of gerontology*, 32, 311-316.

Palmore, E. & Liukart, C. (1972). Health and social factors related to life satisfaction. *Journal of health and social behavior*, 13, 68-80.

Pearlin, L.I. & Johnson, J. (1977). Marital status, life-strains and depression. *American sociological review*, 42, 704-715.

Rook, K.S. (1980). Social networks and well-being of elderly widowed women. Unpublished doctoral dissertation, University of California, Los Angeles.

Scharlach, A. (1987). Role strain in mother-daughter relationships in later life. *Gerontologist*, 27, 627-638.

Shanas, E. (1973). Family-kin networks and aging in a cross-cultural perspectives. *Journal of marriage and the family*, 35, 505-511.

Stone, R., Cafferata, G.L., & Sangl, J. (1987). Caregivers of the frail elderly: a national profile. *Gerontologist*, 27, 616-626.

Stroebe, M.S. & Stroebe, W. (1983). Who suffers more? Sex difference in health risks of the widowed. *Psychological bulletin*, 93, 279-301.

Trela, J.E. & Jackson, D.J. (1979). Family life and community participation in old age. *Research on aging*, 1, 233-252.

Turner, R.J. (1983). Direct, indirect, and moderating effects of social support on psychological distress and associated conditions. In Kaplan, H.B. (Ed.) *Psychological stress: trends in theory and research*. Orlando, FL: Academic Press.

Ward, R.A., Sherman, S.R., & LaGory, M. (1984). Subjective network assessments and subjective well-being. *Journal of gerontology*, 39, 93-101.

Zarit, S.H., Orr, N.K., & Zarit, J.M. (1985). *The hidden victims of Alzheimer's disease*. New York: New York University Press.

Kinship versus Friendship: Social Adaptation in Married and Widowed Elderly Women

Joann P. Reinhardt
Celia B. Fisher

SUMMARY. The qualities of daughter versus same-sex friend relationships were described by 151 married and widowed elderly women. The relation of these qualities to life satisfaction was assessed. Relationship qualities predicted life satisfaction in widowed women but not in married women. Significant predictors of life satisfaction for widows included the emotional support of daughters, the instrumental support of friends and friendship strength. In a comparison of the relationship qualities, both married and widowed respondents described daughters as providing more stimulation, ego support and utility than friends. Respondents also reported that relationships with daughters were stronger than those with friends. Married women described relationships with both daughters and friends as more stimulating than widowed women. The value of assessing qualitative indices compared to quantitative indices of later life relationships is discussed.

To be old is to be female. From age seventy-five and above, the elderly population is largely composed of women (Day, 1985). Due to greater longevity, women live to an advanced old age, many of

Celia B. Fisher, Department of Psychology, Fordham University, Bronx, NY, NY 10458.

This paper is based on a dissertation submitted by the first author to Fordham University under the mentorship of the second author. Portions of the paper were presented at the Annual Meeting of the American Psychological Association in Atlanta, GA in August, 1988. Joann P. Reinhardt, Research Associate, The Lighthouse, Department of Research and Evaluation, 111 E. 59th Street, New York, NY 10022.

them without the presence of a spouse. Being married in old age is correlated with higher subjective well-being (Larson, 1978; Lee, 1978). In contrast to their married or never married peers, the millions of widows in our society are more likely to be poverty stricken, psychologically or emotionally troubled or socially isolated (Bankoff, 1983). Thus, as women age, their interpersonal needs evolve and the fulfillment of such needs impacts life satisfaction. The present investigation examined the influence of informal relationships on life satisfaction among married and widowed elderly women.

Women, as expressive family leaders, spend time and energy in maintaining caring relationships. An important aspect of women's relationships is their overall intimacy or bondedness (Candy, Troll & Levy, 1981; Davidson & Packard, 1981). When asked about their closest relationship, elderly husbands usually name a spouse. Wives, on the other hand, are more likely to name adult offspring or female age peers (Hess & Soldo, 1985). The relationship of mothers to their adult daughters is of specific interest as daughters have been reported to show greater affection and concern for parents than sons (Aizenberg & Treas, 1985; Day, 1985; Hoyt & Babchuk, 1983; Stoller & Earl, 1983). Same-sex friendships are also important to women. Both same-sex kin and same-sex friends are more likely to serve as confidants than cross-sex pairs (Hoyt & Babchuk, 1983).

RELATIONSHIP QUALITY AND LIFE SATISFACTION IN ELDERLY WOMEN

Research focusing on social interaction in later life has demonstrated the importance of close interpersonal relationships for a variety of outcomes including life satisfaction (Connor, Powers & Bultena, 1979; Liang, Dvorkin, Kahana & Mazian, 1980), adjustment in old age (Costa, McCrae & Norris, 1981; Lemon, Bengston & Peterson, 1972) and physical and mental health (Thomae, 1980; Turner, 1980). The quality of activity rather than its quantity has been demonstrated to be important (Connor, Powers & Bultena, 1979; Larson, 1978; Liang et al., 1980; Lowenthal & Haven, 1968; Snow & Crapo, 1982) possibly because close relationships provide role support and self affirmation in old age (Longino & Kart, 1982). The present investigation builds on this work by focusing on the relative importance and meaning of informal relationships with kin and friends among widowed and married older women.

First, we will distinguish between social support and social network. By definition, supportive relationships provide increased psychological stability and improved health and morale in times of stressful life changes. Whether a relationship is supportive is measured subjectively. The concept of social network is, on the other hand, quantitative. Measures of social network include identification of network members, size of the network and frequency of interaction. This structural type of measure is not a precise measure of support (House, 1981). The social network concept allows examination of the extent of a person's involvement in a social field. However, not all social ties are supportive and one's phenomenological perception of support is important.

Researchers have stressed the need to examine the subjective meaning and importance of social relationships in old age (Aizenberg & Treas, 1985; Peters & Kaiser, 1985; Snow & Crapo, 1982; Ward, 1985). Specifically, research is needed to address the question of what needs are served by relationships instead of only asking how many persons are in a network and their frequency of interaction (Connor et al., 1979). Relationship quality has been looked at globally (e.g., presence of a confidant). For example, Snow and Crapo (1982) found that the emotional bondedness or overall intimacy that geriatric medical patients experienced with the person they could "most trust and confide in" was a significant predictor of well-being (p. 610). What is yet to be adequately addressed is the relative importance of different types of support on adjustment and well-being in old age (Gottlieb, 1983).

Researchers most often distinguish between instrumental (tangible assistance) and affective aspects of social support (Cantor, 1979; House, 1981; Kahn & Antonucci, 1980; Lopata, 1975). Wright (1969; 1985) has developed a model which identifies the dimensions or qualities of close interpersonal relationships including those that are both affective and instrumental. These dimensions include rewards or values such as stimulation, ego support and utility, the strength of the relationship and the maintenance difficulty of the relationship. Candy-Gibbs (1982; 1983) demonstrated the salience of such dimensions in the close interpersonal relationships of elderly persons. The present investigation tested the relationship qualities assessed with Wright's model for their relation to life satisfaction in married and widowed elderly women.

KIN AND FRIEND RELATIONSHIPS IN ELDERLY WOMEN

The social networks of elderly persons are made up of kin, friends and neighbors (Cantor, 1979; Ward, 1985; Wood & Robertson, 1978). The relative importance of kin and friends in fulfilling different support needs has not been fully explored (Antonucci & Akiyama, 1987). The nature of such relationships is different in that kinship is ascribed to and is likely to be associated with some sense of obligation while friendship is voluntary, maintained by affective bonds (Lee & Ellithorpe, 1982; Litwak & Szelenyi, 1969). Some researchers postulate that kinship and friendship involve separate realms of activity and are thus non-substitutable (e.g., Arling, 1976; Litwak, 1985; Litwak & Szelenyi, 1969; Ward, 1978). Others hold that kin are the preferred choice for all types of support compared to friends and neighbors who are chosen in a compensatory fashion (Cantor, 1979).

Cantor (1979) has proposed a hierarchical-compensatory model which predicts that the type of support group (e.g., kin versus friend) chosen for a particular task depends on the primacy of the relationship. She has described kin as the first choice for all types of support needs followed by significant others, such as friends, who are chosen in a compensatory fashion. Cantor's (1979) model would predict an advantage for kin over friends in both a global measure of emotional bondedness and in distinctive relationship qualities. The model would further assume increased difficulty in maintaining relationships with friends compared to daughters. By contrast, a task-specific model proposed by Litwak and Szelenyi (1969) holds that group structure dictates its function. Such a model would predict variability in kin versus friend relationships qualities. Literature that has highlighted these potential differences is described below.

Elderly persons seek the prevention of social isolation and the existence of meaningful roles and status in the community. The former we may think of as a stimulation function of relationships and the latter as an ego supportive function. According to Wright (1985), stimulation refers to the extent to which the partner's perspectives and favored activities are expanded, while ego support refers to the extent to which a person helps one maintain a worthwhile impression of oneself. Because friends select one another freely, they are usually similar in such characteristics as age, life status, sex and socioeconomic status (Dono, Falbe, Kail, Litwak, Sherman & Siegel, 1979; Jerrome, 1981). Friendships, bound by cohort and affectivity, may be well suited for the sharing of activities and roles. Since kin can be diverse in terms of generation, they are not as effective as friends in tasks requiring matched interests (Litwak & Szelenyi, 1969). Thus a task-specific model would predict that friends would be valued more than kin relations for both stimulation and ego support.

The utility value of a relationship refers to the giving of one's own time and resources to help the partner meet his/her needs or reach various personal goals (Wright, 1985). Cantor (1979) and Litwak and Szelenyi (1969) would make similar predictions about the utility or instrumental value of relationships by giving kin primacy over friends for such tasks. Kin relations are defined by their permanence and are thus suited for tasks requiring long-term commitment such as the provision of help during extended illness. Research has demonstrated that when elderly persons need instrumental assistance, they rely more on family than friends (Cantor, 1979; Cicirelli, 1981; Stoller & Earl, 1983). Moreover, elderly parents and their adult children have similar beliefs about filial responsibilities expected and received (Cicirelli, 1981; Seelbach, 1978).

KIN AND FRIEND RELATIONS
AND LIFE SATISFACTION

Previous investigations have consistently found relationships with friends to be more predictive of life satisfaction in the elderly than relationships with kin (Arling, 1976; Gottlieb, 1983; Larson, 1978; Lee & Ihinger-Tallman, 1980; Pihlblad & Adams, 1972;

Wood & Robertson, 1978). There are several reasons to be cautious about conclusions drawn from these findings. First, when the term "confidant" is used to examine older women's relationships, it is often unclear whether respondents are referring to a relative or friend. Second, before concluding that kin relationships are not important to morale, we should reexamine the way their support has been operationalized (Ward, 1985). More specifically, we need to assess the value of reports which rely on quantitative indices of social support.

Although important in its own right, a quantitative measure such as interaction frequency ensures the visibility, not the quality of a relationship (Aizenberg & Treas, 1985; Thoits, 1982). In fact, Strain and Chappell (1982) have reported that a high degree of confidants among kin, that is, confidants who were spouses or children rather than friends, was related to higher life satisfaction.

RELATIONSHIPS OF MARRIED VERSUS WIDOWED ELDERLY WOMEN

Widowed elderly need social and emotional support (Lopata, 1978). Confidants are needed to make the widowed feel competent and adequate, self-sufficient and integrated into a network. Such confidants can also help the widowed person accomplish grief work by being interested in their feelings. The widow must rebuild a social system that became disorganized upon the death of the spouse. Losing a spouse creates a vacuum in one's social network and filling this void takes time and support from others (Brubaker, 1985).

When one does begin to replace relational needs once provided by the spouse, widowhood can be a stimulus not only to greater social participation (Kohen, 1983; Rosow, 1967) but also to deeper involvement in relationships. For example, elderly widowed are more likely than elderly married to rely on adult children, friends and siblings for stimulation, ego support and utility (Anderson, 1984; Brubaker, 1985; Kohen, 1983). Consequently, the total relationship strength of kin and friend relationships, that is their interdependence and uniqueness (Wright, 1985), may be stronger in widowed than in married elderly women.

METHODOLOGY

There were three goals in the present investigation. The first goal was to examine the influence of kin and friend relationships on the life satisfaction of married and widowed elderly women. The second goal was to compare the degree to which older women's relationships with daughters and friends differed with respect to stimulation, ego support, utility, total relationship strength, maintenance difficulty, and global quality (emotional bondedness). Finally, the third goal was to assess the impact of marital status on elderly women's reports of relationship qualities.

Sample

The married and widowed women interviewed were elderly urban senior center participants aged 62 and over. Women were first addressed in a large group where the purpose of the study was explained and criteria for participation were discussed. Since proximity may determine the effectiveness of daughters and friends in the provision of different types of support (e.g., help with daily tasks), the proximity of daughters and friends was controlled in the present investigation. Both daughters and friends lived within one hour of the respondents. Women who met the criteria of having both a daughter and a same-sex friend they felt close to who lived within one hour, and who volunteered for participation were interviewed privately by the first author. Women were asked to describe both a daughter and a same-sex close friend who "they felt close to, who they could confide in." Responses to three self-report instruments and demographic information were recorded in the structured interview. Scale presentation was counterbalanced across participants.

Measures

The Life Satisfaction Index-A (Neugarten et al., 1961) was used as a measure of global well-being. The revision of this instrument suggested by Adams (1969) was adopted in the present study resulting in the use of 18 of the 20 original items. Possible scores ranged from 0-18. Snow and Crapo's (1982) Emotional Bondedness Scale was used as a global assessment of relationship quality. Possible scores ranged from 12-36. Finally, Wright's (1985) Acquaintance Description Form was used to measure relationship qualities. Responses assessed the extent to which items applied to the relationship under study. Possible scores ranged from 0-30 with the exception of the total relationship strength scale which had scores that ranged from 0-60.

Characteristics of the Sample

Participant demographic information is presented in Table 1. Participants consisted of 151 elderly Caucasian women (seventy-five married and seventy-six widowed) who ranged in age from 62 to 80. Married respondents (two of whom were actually remarried) were married an average of 44 years and widowed respondents were widowed an average of 14 years. Married and widowed respondents were not significantly different in age ($F(1,148) = 2.98$, ns), education ($F(1,148) = 3.10$, ns) or health ($F(1,149) = 1.88$, ns). On a self-reported health scale, with a possible score range of zero to ten, both married and widowed participants had an average score of six. Income was divided into three groups: 8,000 and below, 8,000-20,000 and 20,000 and above (Streib, 1984). A chi square analysis indicated that the married and widowed participants were significantly different in income ($X^2(2) = 20.2$, $p. < 001$). This is consistent with research indicating that elderly married women are better off financially than elderly widows (Day, 1985; Harvey & Bahr, 1974; Lopata, 1973). Approximately 31% of the married group would not disclose their income compared to 9% of the widowed group. Two of the married participants and three of the widowed participants were working part-time.

Demographic data for the daughters of participants is presented in Table 2. The daughters of married and widowed participants were not significantly different in age ($F(1,148) = 1.26$, ns) or in education ($F(1,149) = 2.82$, ns). Daughters of the married sample were reported by their mothers as significantly healthier than the daughters of the widowed sample ($F(1,149) = 4.79$, $p. < 05$). Daughters were grouped as with spouse/without spouse for the chi square analysis on marital status. No significant differences were obtained in the marital status of married versus widowed respon-

Table 1
Demographic Variables for Married and Widowed Elderly Women

			Marital status	
			married	widowed
Demographic variables			(n=75)	(n=76)
Age [a]	M		70.07	71.63
	$\overline{S}$D		5.42	5.64
	$\overline{R}$ange		63–80	62–80
Number of years married or widowed	M		44.36	14.00
	$\overline{S}$D		11.27	10.41
	$\overline{R}$ange		4–62	1–38
Education (total number of years) [b]	M		10.36	9.74
	$\overline{S}$D		2.10	2.26
	$\overline{R}$ange		5–15	5–14
Self-reported health (on a scale of 0–10)	M		6.93	6.45
	$\overline{S}$D		2.26	2.09
	$\overline{R}$ange		1–10	1–10
Income (frequency of responses in each category) [c]	<8,000		13	45
	8–20,000		30	32
	>20,0000		9	2
	missing		23	7 *

a
 Married elderly women: n=74
b
 Widowed elderly women: n=75
c
 Married elderly women: n=52; widowed elderly women: n=69
*p<.05

dents' daughters ($X^2(1) = .01$, ns). Approximately 80% of the daughters in both the married and in the widowed sample were married. Finally, a chi square analysis which was performed to assess differences in the work status of daughters failed to yield significance ($X^2(1) = .06$, ns). Approximately 70% worked either full or part-time in each group.

The demographic information for the friends described by participants is given in Table 3. The friends chosen by married versus widowed women were not significantly different in age ($F(1,149) = 3.45$, ns), education ($F(1,118) = 1.14$, ns) or health ($F(1,149) =$

Table 2
Demographic Variables for the Daughters of Participants by
Marital Status

Demographic variables		married (n=75)	widowed (n=76)
		Marital status	
Age [a]	M	42.07	43.45
	SD	7.37	7.73
	Range	23-58	28-59
Education (total	M	13.31	12.70
number of years)	SD	2.31	2.14
	Range	9-20	8-18
Self-reported health			
(on a scale of 0-10)	M	8.59	7.92*
	SD	1.85	1.88
	Range	2-10	5-10
Marital Status [b]	Married	58	60
(frequency of	Remarried	3	2
responses in	Widowed	3	2
each category)	Separated	4	5
	Divorced	4	4
	Single	3	3
Distance from [c]			
participant (in	M	23.16	23.69
minutes)	SD	19.49	19.18
	Range	5-70	5-60
Work Status			
(frequency of	Yes	52	54
responses in	No	23	22
each category)			

[a]
 married elderly women: n=75
[b]
 Note. Daughters were grouped as with spouse/without spouse for
      chi square analysis.
[c]
 married elderly women: n=68; widowed elderly women: n=65
*p<.05

2.08, ns). Friends were grouped as with spouse/without spouse for the chi square analysis performed on marital status. The marital status of friends differed significantly for married and widowed respondents ($X^2(1)/13.26, p < .001$). For married participants, married friends were chosen 49% of the time and unmarried friends

Table 3
Demographic Variables for the Friends of Participants by
Marital Status

Demographic variables		married (n=75)	widowed (n=76)
		Marital status	
Age	M	68.08	70.59
	$\overline{SD}$	7.83	8.76
	$\overline{Range}$	40-85	36-88
Education (total number of years) [a]	M	10.47	10.05
	$\overline{SD}$	2.25	2.12
	$\overline{Range}$	8-16	6-16
Self-reported health (on a scale on 0-10)	M	6.85	6.34
	$\overline{SD}$	2.20	2.15
	$\overline{Range}$	1-10	1-10
Marital Status [b]	Married	34	15
	Widowed	33	51
	Separated	1	5
	Divorced	2	1
	Remarried	3	1
	Single	2	3*
Distance from participant (in minutes) [c]	M	13.46	11.89
	$\overline{SD}$	13.11	11.14
	$\overline{Range}$	5-60	5-60
Number of years known friend [d]	M	22.16	19.13
	$\overline{SD}$	17.93	13.98
	$\overline{Range}$	2-52	2-60

[a] married elderly women: n=58; widowed elderly women: n=61
[b] Note. Friends were grouped as with spouse/without spouse for chi square analysis.
[c] married elderly women: n=68; widowed elderly women: n=65
[d] married elderly women: n=67; widowed elderly women: n=63
*$p<.001$

were chosen 51% of the time. This is contrasted with widowed participants who for the most part chose unmarried friends (79%). Only 21% chose married friends. An ANOVA performed on the number of years participants have known their friends failed to yield significant results ($F(1,128)=1.15$, ns). Both married and widowed respondents have known their close friends for approximately twenty years. Most participants reported that their friends were not working. Only three of the married participant's friends and two of the widowed participants' friends worked full-time.

To assess the difference in distance lived from participant, a 2 (marital status: married, widowed) × 2 (relationship type: daughter, friend) analysis of variance with repeated measures was performed. Results demonstrated a main effect for relationship type only ($F(1,131) = 27.63, p < .001$). Respondents reported that their friends lived significantly closer to them than daughters.

RESULTS

Life Satisfaction

The mean score on life satisfaction was 13.49 ($SD = 3.43$; range = 4-18) for married women and 11.74 ($SD = 3.86$; range = 3-18) for widowed women. To assess differences in life satisfaction between married and widowed women, a one-way analysis of variance was performed. Life satisfaction was found to be significantly higher in married women than in widowed women ($F(1,149) = 8.71, p < .01$).

Multiple regression analyses were used to examine the contribution of the Acquaintance Description Form (ADF) variables to life satisfaction in married women and in widowed women. The eight ADF variables used as predictors included the stimulation value, ego support value, utility value and total relationship strength of both daughters and friends. The stepwise procedure was used in the multiple regression analyses (Cohen & Cohen, 1975). Results demonstrated that the ADF variables significantly predicted life satisfaction for widowed women ($F(3,72), p < .001$) but not for married women. As can be seen in Table 4, the variable accounting for most of the variance in life satisfaction in widowed women was utility value/friend (12.0%) followed by total relationship strength/friend (7.1%). which had a negative coefficient, and ego support/daughter (5.4%).

Two additional stepwise multiple regression analyses were performed to examine the extent to which the emotional bondedness in

Table 4
Stepwise Multiple Regression of ADF Variables on Life
Satisfaction in Widowed Women

ADF variables	b	Proportion of variance accounted for (sr)
utility value/friend	.240	.120***
total strength/friend	-.125	.071**
ego support/daughter	.195	.054*

*$\underline{p}$<.05, ** $\underline{p}$<.01, ***$\underline{p}$<.001

Note. Cumulative R Square=.211

friend and in kin relationships contributed to the variance in life satisfaction. Results demonstrated that while the emotional bondedness scales failed to predict life satisfaction for married participants, they did predict life satisfaction in widowed women ($F(1,74) =$ 9.69, $p < .01$). The variable that accounted for a significant portion of the variance in life satisfaction was the emotional bondedness of daughters (11.6% of the variance, b = .297), not the emotional bondedness of friends. Thus, the global measure of relationship quality yielded results similar to the ADF variables.

Relationship Qualities

To examine differences in relationship functions, a 2 (marital status: married, widowed) × 2 (relationship type: daughter, friend) analysis of variance with repeated measures was performed separately for each of the five relationship functions (stimulation value, ego support value, utility value, total relationship strength, maintenance difficulty). Descriptive statistics and F ratios for the ADF scales are given in Table 5.

In brief, descriptions of daughters were scored higher on all relationship functions than friends regardless of whether respondents were married or widowed. Marital status affected relationship quality for only one variable. Widowed women reported both daughters and friends as providing more stimulation value than married women.

The ANOVA conducted on stimulation value yielded a main effect for both relationship type and marital status. Daughters were

Table 5
Descriptive Statistics on ADF Variables for Daughters and
Friends in Married and Widowed Women

		Marital status			
		married (n=75)		widowed (n=76)	
ADF variables		daughter	friend	daughter	friend
Stimulation	M	19.40	17.17	16.83	16.25
value	SD	5.59	6.56	6.64	6.82
	Range	8-30	4-29	1-30	0-30

Marital status $F(1,149)=4.20, p<.05$
Relationship type $F(1,149)=5.38, p<.05$
Marital status X relationship type $F(1,149)=1.85, ns$

Ego support	M	26.63	24.56	25.38	24.54
value	SD	3.11	4.08	4.69	4.33
	Range	17-30	14-30	5-30	10-30

Marital status $F(1,149)=1.44, ns$
Relationship type $F(1,149)=12.74, p<.001$
Marital status X relationship type $F(1,149)=2.26, ns$

Utility	M	23.23	19.27	22.63	18.05
value	SD	4.74	6.85	5.04	6.95
	Range	10-30	5-30	5-30	3-30

Marital status $F(1,149)=1.37, ns$
Relationship type $F(1,149)=52.31, p<.001$
Marital status X relationship type $F(1,149)=.27, ns$

Total	M	51.23	46.39	47.76	46.00
relationship	SD	5.42	9.29	7.96	10.15
strength	Range	36-60	17-60	6-60	11-60

Marital status $F(1,149)=3.36, ns$
Relationship type $F(1,149)=14.16, p<.001$
Marital status X relationship type $F(1,149)=3.07, ns$

Maintenance	M	6.15	6.56	6.13	6.07
difficulty	SD	5.15	6.20	5.84	5.84
	Range	0-25	0-27	0-24	0-27

Marital status $F(1,149)=.11, ns$
Relationship type $F(1,149)=.11, ns$
Marital status X relationship type $F(1,149)=.18, ns$

rated higher in stimulation value than friends by both married and widowed participants. The main effect for marital status demonstrated that married women rated both relationship types higher in stimulation than widowed women. The ANOVA on ego support value yielded a significant main effect for relationship type only. Daughters were rated higher in ego support than friends by both married and widowed participants. The results of the ANOVA conducted on utility value demonstrated a main effect for relationship type only. Daughters provided higher utility value than friends for all participants. The ANOVA on total relationship strength yielded a significant main effect only for relationship type. Daughters were reported as being higher in total relationship strength than friends. There were no significant results for the ANOVA on maintenance difficulty.

Global Relationship Quality

Unlike the pattern of results found for the specific relationship functions, when the global measure of emotional bondedness was used, no differences were found for type of relationship (kin/friend) or for marital status. The mean scores on emotional bondedness for married women describing their daughters and friends were 32.00 ($SD = 2.97$; range = 24-35) and 31.19 ($SD = 3.78$; range = 21-36), respectively. The mean scores on emotional bondedness for widowed women describing their daughters and friends were 30.91 ($SD = 4.43$; range = 14-36) and 31.16 ($SD = 3.63$; range = 22-36), respectively. A 2(marital status: married, widowed) × 2(relationship type: daughter, friend) analysis of variance with repeated measures was performed to assess differences in Emotional Bondedness Scale scores. This analysis did not yield significant effects for either variable.

DISCUSSION

As women survive longer into old age, their interpersonal relationships with their connection to life satisfaction evolve. Social support networks typically revolve around other females, specifically, daughters and friends. Our study demonstrated that relationship qualities with daughters and friends predicted life satisfaction only in widowed respondents. For married women, relationship qualities with individuals other than one's spouse did not predict life satisfaction. One possible explanation would be a ceiling effect for married women who were already high in life satisfaction. Further research may identify aspects of relationships that are related to life satisfaction in married women as well. In addition, other outcome measures may be of interest such as differential aspects of life satisfaction rather than one global score as used in the present study.

When qualitative indices are used in the prediction of life satisfaction, aspects of both kin and friend relationships become important. For widows, the ego support of daughters and the utility value of friends predicted life satisfaction. The importance of the ego support of daughters among widows found here is similar to past research which has demonstrated that emotional support between aged parents and their children is of primary importance (Shanas, 1979). In terms of the utility value of widows' friends, the help they provided with everyday tasks may have been based on convenience since friends lived within an average of ten minutes away compared to daughters who lived within an average of twenty minutes away.

A third predictor of life satisfaction in widows was the total relationship strength of friends. One may wonder why the degree of interdependence and uniqueness that defines total relationship strength would have a negative relationship to life satisfaction in widows. Matthews (1983) maintains that viewing friends as relationships, as opposed to particular individuals upon whom one is dependent for friendship, is more adaptive in terms of preparation for the losses of old age. Being able to replace friends who pass away is seen as being more flexible. Another possibility is that having high life satisfaction could be related to a lower need for friendship strength.

Finally, the finding that the global quality (emotional bondedness) of daughter relationships also predicts life satisfaction in widowed elderly women provides more support for the notion that the expressive support of daughters is important to the well-being of widows.

One of the most striking findings of our work is that elderly women consistently reported relationships with daughters to be more fulfilling than those with female friends. A comparison of relationship qualities within daughter and friend relationships demonstrated the salience of kin for all types of support. Both married and widowed respondents described daughters as providing more stimulation, ego support and utility than friends. Respondents also reported having a stronger relationship with daughters than friends. Interestingly, daughter and friend relationships elicited similar levels of maintenance difficulty and global relationship quality (emotional bondedness) in respondents.

Both daughters and friends lived within one hour of respondents. Within that time span, friends lived significantly closer than daughters. Yet daughters provided more of all relationship qualities than friends. These findings are supportive of Cantor's (1979) hierarchical-compensatory model which emphasizes the salience of kin. Dono et al. (1979) have suggested that when elderly persons are frail and poor, they rely on cross-generational helpers (e.g., adult daughters) who have long-term commitments for support in all areas. However, respondents in the present investigation were neither frail nor poor and they still relied on daughters more than friends to provide all types of support.

The finding that married respondents described both daughters and friends as providing more stimulation value than widowed respondents is contrary to previous findings of increased social activity among widows (Kohen, 1983; Petrowsky, 1976; Rosow, 1967). The lower life satisfaction among widowed participants compared to married participants found in our research as well as in previous work, may be related to this lower level of stimulation found in their relationships (Dono et al., 1979; Hess, 1979). Overall, widows and married women did not differ in the quality of their relationships with their daughters and friends. One explanation for this finding lies in the number of years — 14 — respondents were widowed. It is therefore likely they have worked through their grief and adapted to this loss. Also, widowed participants in the present study were significantly more likely to choose a widowed friend than married participants. Having widowed friends may be especially important for socialization in the widow role.

In light of the significance of daughters in the lives of elderly respondents, future research may profit from studying women who do not have a daughter or who have a daughter who is not physically or emotionally close. Not all elderly women have a close relationship with both an adult daughter and a friend who live nearby. Sons or daughters-in-law as well as siblings could take the place of a daughter or perhaps friends would substitute. Reciprocity is also an important issue concerning the relationships of older adults. Research may benefit by looking at relationships as reciprocal as opposed to unilateral entities. Finally, developmental investigations of kin and friend relationships are needed. Elderly have been found to describe their friends in a more globally favorable way than middle-age adults and as providing less stimulation than the friends of young adults (Reinhardt, 1985). The elderly have a past history of interaction with their children and with longtime friends. Understanding this past history may facilitate the study of interpersonal relationships in old age.

REFERENCES

Adams, D.L. (1969). Analysis of a life satisfaction index. *Journal of Gerontology, 24*, 470-474.

Aizenberg, R. & Treas, J. (1985). The family in late life: Psychosocial and demographic consideration. In J.E. Birren & K.W. Schaie (Eds.). *Handbook of the psychology of aging* (2nd ed). (pp. 169-183). New York: Van Nostrand Reinhold.

Anderson, T.B. (1984). Widowhood as a life transition: Its impact on kinship ties. *Journal of Marriage and the Family, 36*, 105-114.

Antonucci, T.C. & Akiyama, H. (1987). Social networks in adult life and a preliminary examination of the convoy model. *Journal of Gerontology, 42*, 519-527.

Arling, G. (1976). The elderly widow and her family, neighbors and friends. *Journal of Marriage and the Family, 38*, 757-768.

Bankoff, E.A. (1983). Social support and adaptation to widowhood. *Journal of Marriage and the Family, 45*, 827-839.

Bock, E.W. & Webber, I.L. (1972). Suicide among the elderly: Insulating widowhood and mitigating alternatives. *Journal of Marriage and the Family, 34*, 24-31.

Brubaker, T.H. (1985). *Later life families*. Beverly Hills: Sage Publications.

Candy, S.E., Troll, L.E., & Levy, S.G. (1981). A developmental exploration of friendship in women. *Psychology of Women Quarterly, 5*, 456-472.

Candy-Gibbs, S.E. (1982). The alleged inferiority of men's close interpersonal relationships: An examination of sex differences in elderly widowed. Annual Convention Gerontological Society of America, Boston, MA.

Candy-Gibbs, S.E. (1983). The widowed elderly's interpersonal relations: Assessment of intensity and rewards as predictors of sociability and satisfaction with others. Annual Convention Gerontological Society of America, San Francisco, CA.

Cantor, M.H. (1979). Neighbors and friends: An overlooked resource in the informal support system. *Research on Aging, 1,* 434-463.

Cicirelli, V.G. (1981). *Helping elderly parents: The role of adult children.* Boston, MA: Auburn House.

Cohen, C. & Cohen, P. (1975). *Applied Multiple Regression/Correlational Analyses for the Behavioral Sciences.* Hillsdale, NJ: Lawrence Erlbaum Associates.

Connor, K.A., Powers, E.A., & Bultena, G.L. (1979). Social interaction and life satisfaction: An empirical assessment of late-life patterns. *Journal of Gerontology, 34,* 116-121.

Costa, P.T., McCrae, R.R., & Norris, A.H. (1981). Personal adjustment to aging: Longitudinal prediction from neuroticism and extraversion. *Journal of Gerontology, 36,* 78-85.

Davidson, S. & Packard, T. (1981). The therapeutic value of friendship between women. *Psychology of Women Quarterly, 5,* 495-510.

Day, A.T. (1985). Who cares? Demographic trends challenge family care for the elderly. *Population Trends and Public Policy, 9,* 1-15.

Dono, J., Falbe, C., Kail, B., Litwak, E., & Sherman, R. (1979). Primary groups in old age: Structure and function. *Research on Aging, 1,* 403-433.

Glenn, N. & McLanahan, S. (1981). The effects of offspring on the psychological well-being of older adults. *Journal of Marriage and the Family, 43,* 409-421.

Gottlieb, B.H. (1983). *Social support strategies: Guidelines for mental health practice.* Beverly Hills: Sage Pub.

Harvey, C.D. & Bahr, H.M. (1974). Widowhood, morale and affiliation. *Journal of Marriage and Family, 36,* 97-106.

Hess, B.B. (1979). Sex roles, friendship and the life course. *Research on Aging, 1,* 494-515.

Hess, B.B. & Soldo, B.J. (1985). Husband and wife networks. In W.J. Sauer & R.T. Coward (Eds.), *Social support networks and the care of the elderly* (pp. 67-92). New York: Springer.

House, J.S. (1981). *Work stress and social support.* Reading, MA: Addison-Wesley.

Hoyt, D.R. & Babchuk, N. (1983). Adult kinship networks: The selective formation of intimate ties with kin. *Social Forces, 62,* 84-101.

Jerrome, D. (1981). The significance of friendship for women in late life. *Ageing and Society, 1,* 175-197.

Kahn, R.L. & Antonucci, T.C. (1980). Convoys over the life course: Attachment, roles and social support. In P.B. Baltes & O.G. Brim (Eds.), *Life-span development and behavior* (pp. 253-286). New York: Academic Press.

Kohen, J.A. (1983). Old but not alone: Informal social supports among the elderly by marital status and sex. *The Gerontologist, 23,* 57-63.

Larson, R. (1978). Thirty years of research on the subjective well-being of older Americans. *Journal of Gerontology, 33,* 109-125.

Lee, G.R. (1978). Marriage and morale in later life. *Journal of Marriage and the Family, 40,* 131-139.

Lee, G.R. & Ellithorpe, D. (1982). Intergenerational exchange and the subjective well-being among the elderly. *Journal of Marriage and the Family, 44,* 217-224.

Lee, G.R. & Ihinger-Tallman, M. (1980). Sibling interaction and morale: The effects of family relations on older people. *Research on Aging, 2,* 367-391.

Lemon, B.W., Bengston, V.L., & Peterson, J.A. (1972). An exploration of the activity theory of aging: Activity types and life satisfactions among in-movers to a retirement community. *Journal of Gerontology, 27,* 511-523.

Liang, J., Dvorkin, L., Kahana, E., & Mazian, F. (1980). Social interaction and morale: An examination. *Journal of Gerontology, 35,* 745-757.

Litwak, W. (1985). *Helping the elderly.* New York: The Guilford Press.

Litwak, E. & Szelenyi, S. (1969). Primary group structures and their functions: Kin, neighbors and friends. *American Sociological Review, 34,* 465-481.

Longino, C.F. & Kart, C.S. (1982). Explicating activity theory: Formal replication. *Journal of Gerontology, 37,* 713-722.

Lopata, H.Z. (1973). *Widowhood in an American city.* Cambridge, MA: Schenkman.

Lopata, H.Z. (1978). Contributions of extended families to the support systems of metropolitan area widows: Limitations of the modified kin network. *Journal of Marriage and the Family, 40,* 355-366.

Lopata, H.Z. (1979). *Women as widows.* New York: Elseier.

Lowenthal, M.F. & Haven, C. (1968). Interaction and adaptation: Intimacy as a critical variable. *American Sociological Review, 33,* 20-30.

Matthews, S. (1983). Definitions of friendship and their consequences in old age. *Ageing and Society, 3,* 141-155.

Neugarten, B.L., Havighurst, R.J., & Tobin, S.S. (1961). The measurement of life satisfaction. *Journal of Gerontology, 16,* 134-143.

Peters, G.R. & Kaiser, M.A. (1985). The role of friends and neighbors in providing social support. In W.J. Sauer and R.T. Coward (Eds.), *Social support networks and the care of the elderly* (pp. 123-157). New York: Springer.

Petrowsky, M. (1976). Marital status, sex and the social networks of the elderly. *Journal of Marriage and the Family, 31,* 749-756.

Pihlblad, C.T. & Adams, D.L. (1972). Widowhood, social participation and life satisfaction. *Aging and Human Development, 2,* 367-391.

Reinhardt, J. (1985). The strength and rewardingness of friendship in adulthood. Paper presented at the 95th Annual Convention of the American Psychological Association, New York, New York.

Rosow, I. (1967). *Social integration of the aged.* New York: Free Press.

Seelbach, W.C. (1978). Correlates of aged parents' filial responsibility expectations and realizations. *The Family Coordinator, 27,* 341-350.

Shanas, E. (1979). The family as a social support system in old age. *The Gerontologist, 19,* 169-174.

Snow, R. & Crapo, L. (1982). Emotional bondedness, subjective well-being, and health in elderly medical patients. *Journal of Gerontology, 37,* 609-615.

Stoller, E.P. & Earl, L.L. (1983). Help with activities of everyday life: Sources of support for the noninstitutionalized elderly. *The Gerontologist, 23,* 64-70.

Strain, L.A. & Chappell, N.L. (1982). Confidants: Do they make a difference in the quality of life? *Research on Aging, 4,* 479-502.

Streib, G.F. (1984). Socioeconomic strata. In E.B. Palmore (Ed.), *Handbook on the aged in the United States* (pp. 77-92). Westport, CN: Greenwood Press.

Thoits, P. (1982). Conceptual, methodological and theoretical problems in studying social support as a buffer against life stress. *Journal of Health and Social Behavior, 23,* 145-159.

Thomae, H. (1980). Personality and adjustment to aging. In J.E. Birrin & R.B. Sloane (Eds.), *Handbook of mental health and aging* (pp. 285-309). Englewood Cliffs, NJ: Prentice Hall.

Turner, R.J. (1983). Direct, indirect and moderating effects of social support on psychological distress and associated conditions. In H.B. Kaplan (Ed.), *Psychosocial stress: Trends in theory and research.* New York: Academic.

Ward, R.A. (1978). Limitations of the family as a supportive institution in the lives of the aged. *Family Coordinator, 27,* 365-373.

Ward, R.A. (1985). Informal networks and well-being in later life: A research agenda. *The Gerontologist, 25,* 55-61.

Wood, V. & Robertson, J.F. (1978). Friendship and kinship interaction: Differential effects on the morale of the elderly. *Journal of Marriage and the Family, 40,* 367-375.

Wright, P.H. (1969). A model and a technique for studies of friendship. *Journal of Experimental Social Psychology, 5,* 295-309.

Wright, P.H. (1985). The acquaintance description form. In S. Duck & D. Perlman (Eds.). *Sage series in personal relationships* (Vol. 1) (pp. 1-33).

Aging Minority Women:
Issues in Research and Health Policy

Deborah Padgett

SUMMARY. This paper presents an overview of current knowledge about the economic, psychosocial and cultural dimensions of the aging process among minority women in the U.S. Attention is directed to the shorter life span of minority women and its implication for understanding aging, the reality of the "quadruple jeopardy" hypothesis, and the adaptative advantages minority women may have in dealing with growing older. The need to consider cohort effects and ethnic diversity in future research on minority women is stressed.

Clinicians, researchers, and policymakers know so little about the lives of aging black, Hispanic, and native American women that they are often left with little more than stereotypical pictures. While the literatures on aging, on women, and on minorities is abundant, the spotlight rarely falls on this seemingly invisible group.

Deborah Padgett is Assistant Professor, School of Social Work, New York University, New York, NY 10003.

This paper will attempt to synthesize what is known about the economic, psychosocial and cultural dimensions of the aging process among minority women in the United States. Due to the scarcity of empirical research, it will focus on broad thematic areas, highlighting important issues and suggesting topics for future policy-relevant research.

Three perspectives are presented, the first emphasizing the hardships shared by aging minority women ("quadruple jeopardy"), the second focusing on the adaptive psychosocial and cultural strengths which appear to characterize the surviving "old-old," and the third arguing for recognition of heterogeneity within groups and through successive cohorts. While discussion of these perspectives allows comparisons between aging minority women and their middle-class white counterparts, it also provides suggestions for future research and policy initiatives.

DEFINING TERMS:
WHAT IS MEANT BY "MINORITY" AND "AGING"?

While no one will dispute the definition of "female," there is a need to discuss other terms used in this paper. The term "aging," which is usually defined as over 65 years of age, must here take into account the fact that members of minority groups have shorter life spans, may be functionally old well before age 65, and even consider themselves "old" at age 55 (Bengtson et al. 1977). Thus, the term aging rather than "old" or "elderly" is generally preferable when referring to this group. Furthermore, it is useful to distinguish two groups of minority women over age 55: (1) the "younger-aging" who constitute the majority, and (2) the "old-old," a much smaller group of survivors who live beyond age 75.

The term "minority" is used to identify members of ethnic and racial groups who share in common a relative lack of power and suffer the effects of discrimination based upon real or perceived racial or cultural differences (Wagley and Harris 1958). In the main, it refers to blacks, Hispanics, and native Americans, though Pacific Islanders and some Asian ethnic groups may be included in Federal government designations.

The fact that members of some white ethnic groups may also

suffer from discrimination or that some Hispanic and Asian groups appear to be exempt from minority status, makes the concept difficult to operationalize. Nevertheless, it is a useful if less-than-perfect device for analysis. Whenever possible, the discussion will identify specific groups, e.g., blacks or Hispanics.

THE QUADRUPLE JEOPARDY PERSPECTIVE ON AGING MINORITY WOMEN

One of the most salient descriptions of being an aging minority female in our society is embodied in the words "quadruple jeopardy," that is, to be old, poor, female, and of minority status. Jacqueline Jackson coined the term in 1971 specifically to refer to the experience of black women, its origins linked to the earlier use of "double jeopardy" to draw attention to the plight of the black aged in America (Talley and Kaplan 1956). However, Jackson's own critique of the concept leaves little doubt that it is problematic (1985).

Empirical tests of the double jeopardy and quadruple jeopardy hypotheses are hampered by a lack of relevant data on age, income, education, health and psychological well-being. Census data, for example, are considered suspect due to under-counting and inaccuracy in retrieving information from members of minority groups (Bengtson 1979). However, we do know that the burden of poverty is greater for aging minority women. Eighty per cent of black women (Women's Equity Action League 1985) and fifty per cent of Hispanic women (Berger 1983) live in poverty, compared with twenty per cent of all aged women.

It is difficult to assess the relative effects of poverty and racial or ethnic status on the lives of aging minority women. Well-known comparisons of gender and race differences in mortality rates, for example, are not controlled by socioeconomic status. At first glance, these comparisons provide support for the concept of quadruple jeopardy, with black women having an average life expectancy of 73.6 years compared with 78.9 years for white women (National Center for Health Statistics, August 24, 1987). However, the fact that shorter life expectancies for black women are reversed by a "crossover" in mortality rates after age 85 weakens the notion of quadruple jeopardy as a correlate of life expectancy.

Jackson's inspection of suicide rates as crude indicators of life satisfaction also tends to undermine the quadruple jeopardy hypothesis. Age-adjusted suicide rates over age 65 broken down by age and sex reveal that black women consistently have the lowest rates for all age categories. In 1979, for example, black women over age 65 had an age-adjusted suicide rate (per 100,000) of 2.5, compared with 7.5 for white women, 12.8 for black men, and 37.7 for white men (Jackson 1985).

Most primary research on double jeopardy has been cross-sectional rather than longitudinal, as exemplified by a survey conducted in southern California by Dowd and Bengtson in 1978. Their test of double jeopardy involved comparing black, Mexican-American, and white elderly on four dimensions: income, health, social interaction, and life satisfaction. Evidence of double jeopardy was found in income and self-rated health, with minority respondents suffering greater relative declines than their white counterparts.

On the other hand, levels of social interaction and of life satisfaction were similar among all three groups, implying that aging does not necessarily entail greater losses in quality of life for minority group members (Dowd and Bengtson 1978). Farakhan et al. (1984) also found relatively high levels of life satisfaction among retired black elderly in Kansas City. Similar results came from another large-scale multiethnic survey of the elderly in New York City, where Cantor and associates (1985) found higher levels of family assistance and family solidarity differentiated Hispanics from blacks and whites. Only in their tendency to give more financial assistance to children were blacks and Hispanics distinct from their white counterparts.

In summary, the evidence from survey research and available national statistics offers mixed messages of support for the quadruple jeopardy perspective. Relative deprivation in income and self-reported health status is not necessarily linked with lower levels of social support, family interaction, self-reported life satisfaction, or higher mortality rates after age 85.

However, marked disparities in income have clear implications for the health and mental health status of aging minority women which deserve further discussion. Objective measures of health status reveal higher morbidity rates for specific conditions associated with lower income status such as diabetes, hypertension, and kidney disease which take their toll in increased disability and overall reductions in life expectancy.

There are no known studies comparing rates of mental disorders between aging minority and white women, but research in related areas suggests a higher degree of risk for those at lower income levels regardless of racial or ethnic status. The federally sponsored Epidemiological Catchment Area (ECA) studies conducted in three sites found that differences between blacks and whites in lifetime prevalence rates of psychiatric disorders were generally modest and rarely statistically significant (Robins et al. 1984). Indeed, Kessler and Neighbors argue that most racial and ethnic differences disappear when socioeconomic status is controlled (1983). The ECA findings of higher rates of mental disorders in inner-city areas as compared with suburbs and small town/rural areas (Robins et al. 1984) also support this emerging picture of income rather than race-related risk factors.

At the same time, the ECA studies yielded rates of mental disorders which declined with age, dropping sharply after age 45. Contrary to popular impression, the evidence is growing that prevalence of all psychiatric disorders except organic brain syndromes actually decreases with age (Myers et al. 1984).

Whether these lower rates of psychopathology apply to aging minority women remains an unanswered question, but a few words of caution are in order before any extrapolations are made. First, most epidemiological studies measure psychiatric disorders which meet strict DSM-III (Diagnostic and Statistical Manual of Mental Disorders, Third Edition) criteria. Dysphoric symptoms associated with medical problems and transient demoralized states which fall short of syndromes are not usually measured or reported. Second, the instruments or scales used in these population surveys have not been validated for use in different minority groups and are thus subject to inaccuracy due to cultural bias. Finally, the tendency of the aged and members of some ethnic groups to somatize symptoms of distress (attributing problems to physical rather than mental origins) may reduce estimates of prevalence based solely upon the disclosure of psychiatric symptoms (Katon et al. 1984). If we cannot state with certainty that the prevalence of mental disorders is greater for aging minority women, it does seem safe to say that the risks are higher for this group due to income-related factors.

The dilemma presented by juxtaposing low income and poor health with relatively high scores on social interaction and quality of life measures raises interesting questions for future research on quadruple jeopardy. More in-depth studies are needed which help us to understand how some minority women adopt psychosocial coping strategies which enhance their ability to age successfully despite the odds against them.

It appears that the premature mortality rates that adversely affect this group produce a select group of survivors who are, in all likelihood, more hardy than their white age counterparts. For these "hardy" older women the day to day problems of poverty and discrimination do not necessarily recede, but they do apparently become less threatening, thus explaining higher life satisfaction and lower rates of suicide.

Surveys of aging minority women which recognize an age stratum distinction between young-old and old-old offer possible tests of the hypothesis that some aspects of quadruple jeopardy lose salience in the latter group. Of course, longitudinal research is needed to fully study the complex process of survivorship. In the meantime, descriptive studies provide clues to the strengths possessed by these older women which enable them to adapt successfully.

STRENGTHS FOR SURVIVAL: AN ADAPTIVE PERSPECTIVE ON AGING MINORITY WOMEN

Statistics documenting the disparities in income and health status experienced by aging minority women obscure a more complex picture of survival and even successful aging for a select few. While the struggles and hardships do not let up, it appears that many aging minority women are able to draw on strengths — psychological, social, and cultural — which ease the transition to old age. They have spent their lives as strategists, marshalling scarce resources to cope with everyday demands and these coping strategies "pay off" later on in self-reliance.

Of course, those who died prematurely in their 50s and 60s faced the same pressures, and it remains unclear which set of biogenetic and socio-environmental factors shortened their lives. We can, however, learn a great deal by applying an adaptive perspective to those who did survive to identify factors which may enhance survival.

Support for an adaptive perspective on successful aging among minority women comes from a variety of sources, including the survey research mentioned earlier. Cantor et al. (1975), for example, suggest that sharing of limited economic and social resources by Hispanic and black elderly is a positive adaptation to the pressures of poverty. More contextual evidence comes from ethnographic accounts of the lives of older black and minority women provided by cultural anthropologists (Stack, 1974; Aschenbrenner, 1975; Clark and Mendelson, 1969). These studies emphasize strengths arising from family and social networks and shared ethnic identity.

In general, older minority women play integral roles in their family networks as "kintenders," providing instrumental and expressive support to their adult children and grandchildren. Stack (1974) notes that poor black households are largely organized around women, with intergenerational ties maintained continuously over time. Family and household boundaries are flexible to meet shifting economic demands, but a core of female relatives retains domestic authority with older women at the center.

This theme of matrifocality is less applicable to Hispanics and native Americans where males are more directly involved in family and household affairs. Nevertheless, women in these groups enjoy greater prestige and domestic authority as they grow older (Cueller 1978). Providing and receiving social support in kin networks are important survival strategies for these women.

Ethnicity can be another important resource in successful aging. Cuellar's description of older Mexican-Americans in East Los Angeles (1978) illustrates how traditional cultural values reduce feelings of alienation in an Anglo-dominated society. Likewise, Cota-Robles Newton (1980) writes of the Hispanic values of "personalismo" and "dignidad" which characterize positive interaction between young and old and reinforce group identity.

How do minority women compare with their older white counterparts in adaptive strategies for aging? Earlier research in social gerontology, largely confined to the white middle-class, emphasized disengagement and images of decline and loss; but the more recent research cited earlier has challenged this negative picture with findings of extensive social interaction by white and nonwhite respondents alike (Cantor 1985; Dowd and Bengtson 1978). What *does* appear to distinguish the minority aged are higher familial contacts. While whites have more interaction with friends and neighbors, Dowd and Bengtson (1978) found familial contacts to be highest among Mexican-Americans, followed by blacks. In contrast, social interaction patterns of white elderly included both family and non-kin relationships.

Theories of adaptive aging based upon presumed higher overall levels of social interaction and social support among minorities have little support from empirical research. However, their immersion in kin networks and reliance on ethnic identity point to features which may coalesce to form adaptive strategies which are distinct from those of older whites. From an adaptive perspective, this reliance on kinship and ethnicity is not a static carry-over of traditional ways, but is a dynamic response to a changing, often threatening environment.

Understanding the role of lifelong experiences and adaptive (or maladaptive) responses is critical. For minority women, just being alive and surviving to old age testifies to earlier successes in coping with deprivation and hardship. Older white women have not generally had to meet the same challenges; the need to develop strategies for survival has been far less over the course of a lifetime and tends to be greatest at retirement age when abrupt losses in income occur. However, the adaptive strategies of those who have endured lives of poverty and deprivation are likely to be similar to those of minority women.

Differences between minority and white women are more aptly described as occurring along a continuum rather than as discrete. What appears most important for understanding survival are the challenges posed by the surrounding environment and the strengths possessed by individuals—economic, social, and cultural—which enable them to adapt and survive to old age. While useful in some respects, minority-white comparisons entail the risk of obscuring important variation within these broadly-defined groups. Recognizing differences within as well as between groups and subgroups of aging women allows a more complete—and more complex—picture to emerge.

HETEROGENEITY AND COHORT PERSPECTIVES ON AGING: THE MISSING LINKS IN RESEARCH ON MINORITY WOMEN

The key concepts embodied in these perspectives are diversity and change. Both constitute "missing links" in research due to an almost total reliance upon cross-sectional approaches which treat aging populations as homogeneous entities.

Aging women are in fact a highly diverse group, distinguished by inter- and intra-ethnic differences as well as by age stratum differences between the younger aging and the old-old. Black Americans, for example, may be native-born or come from West Indian, Jamaican, or Bahamian backgrounds. Hispanic groups include Mexican, Puerto Rican and Cuban Americans and many others from a variety of Central and South American countries. White ethnic groups may be Polish, Italian, Greek, or Hungarian, to name only a few.

The experiences of older women in America can also be usefully examined from a cohort perspective. As described by Riley (1985), this perspective takes into account changing social and historial circumstances which characterize the unique developmental experiences of each age cohort. Thus, just as modal patterns of aging differ cross-culturally, so do they differ in successive generations (Ryder 1964).

Aging minority women born in this country share certain experiences in common with their white native-born counterparts—two World Wars, the Great Depression—which have influenced them in unique ways. Both cohort groups also matured at a time when sex roles were sharply differentiated and women's work devalued.

Minority women are distinct, though, in having experienced the profound effects of inequality and racial/ethnic discrimination. The castelike stratification system described so eloquently by Myrdal (1956) lasted well into the 1960s and undoubtedly affected their life chances. The fact that so many older minority women have limited education and hold low-status service jobs attests to the effects of lifelong inequality. Indeed, their tendency to play family-tending roles as they age may be in part attributable to their exclusion from white society as both women and as minorities. Although those born abroad could not have experienced the full range of social and historical conditions of this native-born cohort of minority women, they have had to make similar adjustments to inequality further complicated by barriers of language and culture.

A number of changes have transformed American society in recent decades which are likely to affect future cohorts of aging minority women. These include increased equality for women and higher levels of labor force participation across all occupational strata. Whether these advances have "trickled down" to improve the lot of minority women is open to question, particularly since the acceleration of the feminization of poverty beginning in the early 1980s. The hazards of quadruple jeopardy are not likely to disappear overnight.

However, it is likely that future cohorts of minority women will be more educated and hold higher status jobs outside of the home. The overall emancipation of women and changing societal attitudes toward sex roles may well lead to increased mobility and reductions in the number of older women willing to occupy exclusively familial roles. Finally, future cohorts of minority women will almost certainly contain fewer foreign-born, opening the possibility of increased acculturation and more inter-ethnic interaction.

All of this is, of course, speculation. Only longitudinal research can provide answers to questions of how future generations of minority women will make the transition to old age. In the meantime, the cohort perspective offers useful lessons for challenging the fallacious view of aging as a static, universal process.

DISCUSSION: IMPLICATIONS FOR FUTURE
POLICY-RELEVANT RESEARCH

The foregoing discussion of differing perspectives on aging minority women offers a basis for critical analyses of research findings, highlighting gaps in our knowledge and understanding which need to be filled. We know that further documentation of the effects of quadruple jeopardy is needed to highlight relative deprivation in income and in physical and mental health. At the same time, an adaptive perspective is useful because it goes beyond viewing older minority women solely as victims by focusing on the diverse and creative strategies they employ to adapt to changing circumstances. Ultimately, long-term cohort studies incorporating both quantitative data and more qualitative contextual analyses are needed.

Future research will be considerably improved by including recognition of heterogeneity in aging across and within ethnic groups. Such recognition gives further credence to the growing notion that aging is highly variable with few biological imperatives.

Rowe and Kahn (1987) criticize an emphasis on "normal" aging, arguing that most assumed losses in physical and mental health are not intrinsic to the aging process but are instead reversible by use of appropriate interventions. Even more beneficial are programs designed for prevention of these losses before they can occur.

The vast array of social programs and health services for the elderly in this country operate with limited budgets and a lack of coordination which makes preventive efforts difficult to introduce. In addition, social policy has tended to emphasize a curative rather than preventive approach, treating the problems of the elderly as the inevitable consequences of "normal" aging.

Critics often argue that the bulk of gerontological research and policy has focused too narrowly on the needs and concerns of white, educated middle-class Americans. However, policymakers, practitioners, and advocates for the elderly are gradually becoming aware of the need for services and programs which are culturally sensitive and flexible enough to meet the needs of diverse ethnic groups.

While attention to cultural differences is important, this paper has argued that the primary needs of aging minority women are for more economic support and expanded health services — earlier rather than later in life. We cannot assume that programs targeted for individuals over age 65 will benefit these women; assistance is needed at an earlier age. Nor can we assume that high levels of social support and family interaction are substitutes for these basic services. The risks of poor mental and physical health associated with lower income tend to outweigh other factors which enhance survival for the few.

At the same time, there is much to be learned by studying how the older survivors utilize social, cultural, and psychological strengths to adapt to, and overcome, adversity. Social policy that is based upon a firm foundation of empirical research on their needs *and* strengths will produce more viable and humane programs.

REFERENCES

Aschenbrenner, J. (1975). *Lifelines: black families in Chicago*. Prospect Heights: Waveland Press.

Bengtson, V.L. (1979). Ethnicity and aging: Problems and issues in current social science inquiry. In *Ethnicity and Aging: Theory, Research and Policy*. D.E. Gelfand and A.J. Kutzik (Eds.) New York: Springer, 9-31.

Bengtson, V.L., Dowd, J.J., Smith, D.H. and Inkeles, A. (1977). Modernization, modernity, and perceptions of aging: A cross-cultural study. *Journal of Gerontology*, 30; 688-695.

Berger, P. (1983). The economic well-being of elderly Hispanics. *Journal of Minority Aging*, 8; 36-46.

Cantor, M.H. (1985). The informal support system of New York's inner city elderly: Is ethnicity a factor? In *Ethnicity and Aging: Theory, Research and Policy*. D.E. Gelfand and A.J. Kutzik (Eds.) New York: Springer, 153-174.

Cantor, M.H., Rosenthal, K. and Wilker, L. (1975). Social and family relationships of black aged women in New York City. Paper presented at the 28th annual meeting of the Gerontological Society, Louisville, Kentucky.

Cota-Robles Newton, F. (1980). Issues in research and service delivery among Mexican-American elderly: A concise statement with recommendations. *The Gerontologist*, 20; 208-212.

Clark, M. and Mendelson, M. (1969). The Mexican-American aged in San Francisco: A case description. *The Gerontologist*, 9, 90-95.

Cuellar, J. (1978). El Senior Citizens' Club: The elderly Mexican-Americans in the voluntary association. In *Life's Career: Aging*. B.G. Myerhoff and A. Simic (Eds.) Beverly Hills: Sage, 207-230.

Dowd, J.J. and Bengtson, V.L. (1978). Aging in minority populations: An examination of the double jeopardy hypothesis. *Journal of Gerontology*, 33, 427-436.

Farakhan, A., Lubin, B. and O'Connor, W.A. (1984). Life satisfaction and depression among retired black persons. *Psychological Reports*, 55, 452-454.

Grau, L. (1987). Illness-engendered poverty among the elderly. *Women and Health*, 12, 103-118.

Jackson, J.J. (1985). Poverty and minority status. In *The Physical and Mental Health of Aged Women*. M. Haug, A.B. Ford, M. Sheafor (Eds.) New York: Springer, 166-182.

Katon, W., Ries, R.K. and Kleinman, A. (1984). The prevalence of somatization in primary care. *Comprehensive Psychiatry*, 25, 208-214.

Kessler, R. and Neighbors, H.W. (1983). Special Issues Related to Racial and Ethnic Minorities in the United States. Position Paper submitted to the National Institute of Mental Health, Institute for Social Research, University of Michigan.

Myers, J.K., Weissman, M.M., Tischler, G.L., Holzer, C.E., Leas, P.J., Orvaschel, H., Anthony, J.C., Boyd, J.H., Burke, J.D., Kramer, M., and Stoltzman, R. (1984). Six month prevalence of psychiatric disorders in three communities. *Archives of General Psychiatry*, 41, 969-970.

Myrdal, G. (1956). *An American Dilemma*. Boston: Beacon Press.

National Center for Health Statistics: Annual Summary of Births, Marriages, Divorces and Deaths, U.S. 1986. Monthly Vital Statistics Reports. Vol. 35, No. 13, DHHS Pub. No. (PHS) 87-1100. Public Health Service, Government Printing Office, August 24, 1987.

Riley, M.W. (1985). The changing older woman: A cohort perspective. In *The Physical and Mental Health of Aged Women*. M. Haug, A.B. Ford, M. Sheafor (eds.) New York: Springer, 3-15.

Robins, L., Helzer, J.E., Weissman, M.M., Orvaschel, H., Greenberg, E., Burke, J.D., and Regier, D.A. (1984). Lifetime prevalence of specific psychiatric disorders in three sites. *Archives of General Psychiatry*, 41, 949-958.

Rowe, J.W. and Kahn, R.L. (1987). Human Aging: Usual and successful. *Science*, 237, 143-149.

Ryder, N.B. (1964). Notes on the concept of a population. *American Journal of Sociology*, 69, 447-463.

Stack, C.B. (1974). Sex roles and survival strategies in an urban black community. In *Woman, Culture, and Society*. M.Z. Rosaldo and L. Lamphere (Eds.) Stanford: Stanford University Press, 113-128.

Talley, T. and Kaplan, J. (1956). The Negro Aged. Newsletter, Gerontological Society, 3.

Wagley, C. and Harris, M. (1958). *Minorities in the New World*. New York: Columbia University Press.

Women's Equity Action League (WEAL). (1985). Facts on Social Security. Washington, D.C.: WEAL.

Older Women in Nonindustrial Cultures: Consequences of Power and Privilege

Nancy Foner

SUMMARY. In old age, women in many non-Western cultures gain influence, prestige, and freedom. Tensions, however, often develop with disadvantaged younger women who are subject to old women's authority and resent the privileges of their elders. After outlining the benefits of aging for women in nonindustrial cultures, this article examines the particular relations between old and young women that are subject to strain. It is argued that older women have a strong interest in maintaining young women's subordinate position. In a concluding section, the question of how social change affects the position of old women is considered.

For healthy and active older women in many non-Western cultures, the later years are a time when they come into their own. Old age offers them the chance to achieve greater freedom, influence, and prestige within and beyond the family group. In fact, one writer even speaks of mid and late life "women's liberation" in societies around the world (Gutmann 1977:309).

To grasp the importance and implications of these status changes it is necessary to analyze the specific advantages women accumulate as they age in other societies. But this is only a first step. Older women cannot be viewed on their own. They must be seen in relation to younger women. While women's opportunities often expand with age, young women are, for the moment, left behind. They are frequently bound by cumbersome restrictions and at the mercy of old women's, as well as men's, demands and wishes. Where serious imbalances of privilege, power, and opportunities for autonomy

Nancy Foner, Department of Anthropology, State University of New York, Purchase, NY 10577.

exist between successful older women and subordinate young women, tensions and resentments are likely to arise. Moreover, the fact is that men are not the only ones to gain by young women's subordination. Old women in many societies, too, have a strong interest in keeping young women in their place. The bulk of this paper explores these points, drawing on anthropological studies of individual societies at one moment in time—what anthropologists call the ethnographic present. The concluding section takes up the issue of change, including the possibility that old women will lose ground if social changes improve the position of young women.[1]

THE REWARDS OF AGING

Aging automatically brings some rewards to women in many cultures and gives them the edge in competing for others. This does not mean that all older women are equally successful. Luck, skill, and personality, to name just three factors, can affect their achievements. But as long as older women are healthy and able, they can aspire to and obtain numerous benefits.[2]

Perhaps the most important benefit of aging to women in nonindustrial cultures is their increased "people power" in the domestic group. As a woman ages, so do her children—who marry and, in turn, have their own children. By the time a woman reaches old age, she usually has many juniors under her wing. Older women supervise the work of younger women in the household, including daughters, daughters-in-law, granddaughters, and perhaps also junior wives. They may control who eats what and when, and play a key role in marriage and initiation arrangements for junior women (Brown 1985). For their part, younger women of the household relieve mothers and mothers-in-law of more burdensome tasks, and owe the older women respect and obedience.

Many anthropological reports on patrilocal societies, where women join husbands at marriage, show women only fully coming into their own when they have adult sons to provide a support group and younger women to do their bidding. For example, while young married women in the Gusii tribe of Kenya were beholden at every turn to the judgment and authority of seniors, female elders were dominant figures in their homesteads — confident, assertive, and outspoken (LeVine 1978).

Although widowhood may bring an uncomfortable dependence on others, in some societies widows, too, have considerable domestic authority. In traditional Chinese society, an old widow who was the most senior family member alive might assume control of the family estate, exercising "supreme authority over adults" and enjoying "the fruits of domestic power" (Freedman 1966:66-67). Among the Dukawa of northern Nigeria, healthy old widows who returned to their fathers' homes were outspoken and consulted in major decisions in the compound (Salamone 1980).

Older women's power and authority may also extend beyond the domestic sphere. Typically old women wield informal political influence, but sometimes they fill formal leadership roles in the community, ranging from queen mothers to supervisors of initiation ceremonies for young girls. With their work burdens eased by young women, older women have more time and energy for community affairs. They often gain informal political clout in the community because they can exert influence over husbands, sons, or brothers. And their release from restrictions applying to menstruation or childbearing allows for a fuller participation in public life. Women in many African societies are cautious and quiet in public when they are in their twenties. By the time they reach their fifties, they are confident and assertive, drinking beer with men and speaking their minds at community gatherings.

Another reason why older women in many societies sometime achieve respected positions outside the household (particularly in the ritual sphere) is that aging enables them to accumulate important technical and ritual knowledge. In general, old women in preliterate societies are repositories of wisdom and experience — valued for their expertise in such matters as pregnancy, birth complications, and delivery. In a number of societies, they serve as midwives and as ritual specialists who cure illnesses or direct important ceremonies.

Sometimes, aging gives women greater opportunity to control material resources. Elderly widows in some places control much of the family patrimony in their lifetimes. In some societies, aging enables women to accumulate movable property.

Quite apart from their ritual and secular powers, their wisdom, and their property, age and seniority, in themselves, frequently command deference from the young. An old widowed woman among the Tallensi of West Africa who lived with her son had, as senior woman of the house, an esteemed place. In Fortes's words, she was "the central pillar of his domestic establishment." Her rooms were larger than those of the other women and in the position of honor, and valued ancestor medicine shrines were stored there (1949:58-59).

STRAINS WITH YOUNGER WOMEN

While older women are accumulating powers and privileges, young women have to wait their turn. As a rule, young women are expected to defer to and obey their elders — and they frequently do. They may also be bound to older women by ties of loyalty, identification, and, sometimes, affection. Some even accept their disadvantaged position as right and proper. But — and this is a crucial but — young women often resent the privileges of their elders and the restraints under which they, themselves, labor. Young women may not voice their frustrations openly, but tensions may lie beneath the surface.

The most often reported, and probably the most serious, strains between dominant older women and the young are those between mothers-in-law and daughters-in-law who live together in patrilocal extended families — a common arrangement in other cultures. Although tensions may be severest when the daughter-in-law is a new bride, often strains continue beyond this time, well into the mother-in-law's old age.

The daughter-in-law who moves into the household of her husband's family represents a threat from below. If she is slated to take over as mistress of the household when her mother-in-law dies or steps down, she may be impatiently biding her time. Other daughters-in-law represent a different kind of challenge. The way to autonomy and control for them is to persuade their husbands to set up their own households. The mother-in-law, however, is trying to keep her household together — and her sons with her — and she resents any real or imagined attempts by her daughter-in-law to tear it apart.

Young women often have good reason to want to leave. They are supposed to help their mother-in-law and accede to her demands, but the older woman's domination can be quite repressive, especially when there are severe limitations on the daughter-in-law's autonomy. In many societies, the mother-in-law not only inducts the daughter-in-law into the woman's life of the household but supervises her work in the home and fields. An old Pondo man in South Africa called his son's wife "the bell" because "now my wife just sits still and calls when she wants anything, just like a white lady ringing the bell" (Monica Wilson, quoted in Mair 1971:133). In rural Taiwan in the 1950s, a young daughter-in-law was "the family drudge." Working under the close scrutiny of her mother-in-law, she had to respond to the family's needs and cater to the idiosyncracies of all family members. She was expected to be submissive, showing respect and submitting to the will and whims of her mother-in-law (Gallin 1986:36-37).

An older woman's harsh domination may be a kind of revenge for her own days as a helpless daughter-in-law. Finally, she has an adult person to do her bidding, and she may relish her new power. The older woman is also competing with her daughter-in-law for her son's allegiance and affection, and she may fear that her daughter-in-law is trying to lure the young man away. Margery Wolf (1972) describes how a rural Taiwanese mother-in-law carefully nurtured the tie to her son and was intent on keeping it strong. It was her son (or sons) she could count on in times of crises and for protection and care in her declining years. The entry of the daughter-in-law put the relationship with her son in jeopardy, and her jealousy often led her to abuse her authority. She might criticize, scold, or sometimes even beat the younger woman. A vicious circle was set up: "The more resentful and jealous the mother-in-law, the more she tyrannizes her son's wife; the more she is victimized, the harder the girl works to pry her husband out of his natal family, an effort that only serves to intensify the older woman's fears and to escalate the conflict" (Arthur Wolf 1968: 869).

An example from an urbanized village in metropolitan New Delhi also shows a daughter-in-law's unhappy lot. While a daughter-in-law did the heaviest duties in the house — cooking meals and washing clothes and utensils — the mother-in-law controlled the purse strings. A daughter-in-law had to ask for money for even routine purchases. An old woman expected her daughter-in-law to serve her. Young women often complained that they were made to massage their mother-in-law's legs for hours at night until they dozed off from exhaustion, at which point the old woman demanded that the massaging continue (Vatuk 1975).

While we read much about imperious mothers-in-law and downtrodden daughters-in-law in non-Western cultures, material on relations between other old and young women is sparse. There are a few hints that relations between grown daughters and older mothers are uneasy in certain circumstances. Tensions are apt to develop when an adult daughter lives with her mother and is subject to the older woman's constant directions and orders — and when a woman's domestic authority only waxes as her mother's authority wanes. In Burmese villages, for example, when adult daughters lived with mothers, their subordination and desire for autonomy led to tensions (Spiro 1977:116).

In societies where men have more than one wife at a time, relations between an older woman and her young co-wife (or co-wives) can be strained. The two frequently compete for their husband's affection as well as his attention and largesse to their children, and jealousies arise if one is more successful in such matters as bearing many children. When a senior wife has no official authority over junior wives, her attempts to dominate create difficulties.[3]

Strains are also bound to arise between older and young women outside the domestic group but, unfortunately, ethnographic material on this topic is sorely lacking. An intriguing subject that calls for investigation is the tensions that develop in situations where older women exercise considerable authority over young women in the community, including cases where elderly women are awesome figures at rituals, even, on occasion, administering, supervising, or initiating painful procedures that are inflicted on young women.

OLDER WOMEN'S DOMINANCE
AND YOUNG WOMEN'S SUBORDINATION

Privileged older women, it is clear, stand much to gain by keeping young women in their place. Their power and prestige depend in good part on young women's subordination. It is not just that older women in many societies expect young women to show them the proper respect or that they have the authority to issue orders to young women in the household and, at times, in the community. The ability to call on the labor and support of young women (as well as children and frequently young adult men) gives older women increased leisure and is one reason they can participate more fully in the public sphere.

While we are used to thinking about men — old and young alike — keeping young women down, other women are rarely portrayed as dominant oppressors. Yet old women often have a vested interest, perhaps as strong as men's, in perpetuating a system that victimizes young women.

Old women may, in fact, sometimes try to preserve customs that contribute to young women's unfavorable position. Older women are often the ones to administer and uphold feminine modesty standards applying to young women, even on occasion against the wishes of male family members and in opposition to government policy. The case of old Arab Muslim women in Sudanese peasant villages is particularly dramatic. These old women were respected by their sons and had considerable authority over their daughters-in-law. At this stage in life, they approached full membership in their husband's and son's patrilineage and had a keen interest in its welfare and continuity. It was these powerful old women who were the strongest advocates of the excruciating and dangerous — and, it should be noted, outlawed — custom of genital mutilation, performed on young girls and on mothers after the birth of each child to ensure the moral character of women and the honor of the patrilineage (Hayes 1975).

This analysis of hierarchical relations among old and young women also has implications for understanding inequalities between men and women in nonindustrial cultures. For age inequalities among women can operate to maintain and strengthen gender inequalities. Older women are sometimes active agents in upholding or reinforcing social practices that help to keep young women inferior — not only in relation to older women but in relation to men. Among the Black Carib villagers of coastal Belize, for example, older women were "avid exponents and enforcers" of restrictive rules pertaining to childbearing and sexuality that young women had to observe (Kerns 1985). Age inequalities, moreover, may prevent women from uniting to further their interests as women or from even becoming aware that they have common interests as women. Far from inevitably joining together, old and young women often have widely divergent interests and are sometimes divided by deep strains and cleavages.

OLDER WOMEN AND CHANGE

To complete the picture of privileged and dominant older women in non-Western societies, we should consider that two types of changes can affect their position — sometimes for the worse.

One is the broad social changes commonly associated with the term "modernization." According to many modernization theorists, the patterns described in this essay will soon be a thing of the past. Older women's influence and prestige will invariably deteriorate as their societies become more economically developed and increasingly integrated into the "modern" world. Difficult as it is to foretell the future, these dire predictions must be challenged. The erosion of the powers and privileges of older women is only one possible outcome.[4]

In many nonindustrial societies, needless to say, older women will lose — and actually already have lost — considerable powers in the wake of contact with the industrial world. Indeed, increased freedom for young women often undercuts older women's advantaged position. New or expanded wage-earning opportunities for young women, for example, often reduce older women's authority. The young women gain economic resources of their own and have less time to work under older women's supervision. And changes that give young women greater freedom to choose their spouses weaken older women's control over marriage arrangements.

But all is not downhill for older women, and their powers will not necessarily wither away with modernization and economic development. There is no better proof than the very fact that most ethnographic reports describing older women's privileged status draw on data collected in societies that have already experienced extensive contact with Western industrial powers — some based on research done as recently as the late 1970s and early 1980s (see, e.g., essays in Brown and Kerns 1985). In the years ahead, older women in many societies will doubtless be successful in holding onto, perhaps sometimes even increasing, their rewards and prerogatives.

Cultural traditions often die hard, and age norms are no exception. The idea that special statuses belong to older women, and that only postmenopausal women should be freed from certain restrictions, is strongly rooted in some places. Older women may actively work to maintain these restrictions. New cultural movements may arise that give old women an esteemed role as ritual experts (e.g., Amoss 1981). Moreover, economic and family arrangements are likely to ensure that older women retain dominant domestic roles in many societies. Older women's domestic authority may be especially strong in periods when outside economic possibilities for young women are limited and in places where adult men of the family are away from home for long stretches working for wages.

The other kind of change affecting older women — the aging process itself — is a problem everywhere. With advancing years, women may become seriously disabled in body or in mind. Those who become frail and ill tend to lose their standing, their influence, and their independence. They generally retreat to the sidelines and take part less and less in everyday affairs. While frail old women are often cared for lovingly until the end — and women are more likely than men to receive such care because they often have stronger ties of affection to children and grandchildren and can perform useful childrearing and light domestic duties even when fragile — there are cases where they are abused, neglected, or even abandoned (see Foner 1984 on the frail aged).

For healthy and active older women in many cultures, however, the later years are the best part of life, and they may even pretend to be old before their time. Young women, meanwhile, must wait, suffering the consequences of their second-class status and looking forward to the time when they can attain the privileges, powers, and freedom of old age.[5]

NOTES

1. For a fuller discussion of the consequences of age inequality among women in nonindustrial societies see Foner (1984).

2. In addition to (Foner 1984), see the essays in Brown and Kerns (1985) on the positive changes older women experience in nonindustrial societies.

3. There are, of course, many cases where an older woman and her younger co-wife get along. Bonds of cooperation often draw them together. Many times, they lighten each others' workload, and the older woman assists her younger co-wife before, during, and after childbirth. The fact that co-wives usually have their own separate huts and domestic equipment also mitigates problems between them.

4. See Foner (1984) for a detailed critique of the modernization model and aging as well as an analysis of the impact of social change on old people in nonindustrial societies.

5. Of course, there is the possibility that these subordinate young women will end up disappointed if, as they age, social changes occur that seriously cut into old women's powers.

REFERENCES

Amoss, P. 1981. Coast Salish Elders, In P. Amoss and S. Harrell, eds. *Other Ways of Growing Old*. Stanford: Stanford University Press.

Brown, J. K. 1985. Introduction, In J. K. Brown and V. Kerns, eds. *In Her Prime*. South Hadley, Mass.: Bergin and Garvey.

Brown, J. K. and V. Kerns, eds. 1985. *In Her Prime*. South Hadley, Mass.: Bergin and Garvey.

Foner, 1984. *Ages in Conflict: A Cross-Cultural Perspective on Inequality Between Old and Young*. New York: Columbia University Press.

Fortes, M. 1949. *The Web of Kinship Among the Tallensi*. London: Oxford University Press.

Freedman, M. 1966. *Chinese Lineage and Society: Fukien and Kwangtung*. London: Athlone Press.

Gallin, R. S. 1986. Mothers-in-Law and Daughters-in-Law: Intergenerational Relations within the Chinese Family in Taiwan. *Journal of Cross-Cultural Gerontology* 1, 31-50.

Gutman, D. 1977. The Cross-Cultural Perspective: Notes Toward a Comparative

Psychology of Aging. In J. Birren and K. W. Schaie, eds. *Handbook of the Psychology of Aging*. New York: Van Nostrand Reinhold.

Hayes, R. 1975. Female Genital Mutilation, Fertility Control, Women's Roles, and the Patrilineage in Modern Sudan: A Functional Analysis. *American Ethnologist* 2, 617-33.

Kerns, V. 1985. Sexuality and Social Control among the Garifuna (Belize). In J. K. Brown and V. Kerns, eds. *In Her Prime*. South Hadley, Mass.: Bergin and Garvey.

LeVine, S., in collaboration with R. A. LeVine. 1978. *Mothers and Wives: Gusii Women of East Africa*. Chicago: University of Chicago Press.

Mair, L. 1971. *Marriage*. Harmondsworth: Penguin.

Salamone, F. 1980. Levirate, Widows, and Types of Marriage Among the Dukawa of Northern Nigeria. Paper presented to the American Anthropological Association, Washington, D.C., December.

Spiro, M. (1977). *Kinship and marriage in Burma*. Berkeley: University of California Press.

Vatuk, S. 1975. The Aging Woman in India: Self-Perceptions and Changing Roles. In A. de Souza, ed. *Women in Contemporary India*. Delhi: Manohar.

Wolf, A. 1968. Adopt a Daughter-in-Law, Marry a Sister: A Chinese Solution to the Problem of the Incest Taboo. *American Anthropologist* 70: 864-874.

Wolf, M. 1972. *Women and the Family in Rural Taiwan*. Stanford: Stanford University Press.

Puerto Rican Elderly Women:
The Cultural Dimension
of Social Support Networks

Melba Sánchez-Ayéndez

SUMMARY. This ethnographic study of elderly Puerto Rican women living in Boston explored the influence of cultural meanings on patterns of social interaction and support. Women's roles and social relations were found to reflect the importance of motherhood and domestic responsibilities. With aging, women expect and value respect from their children and younger persons and regard this as even more important than affection. These cultural factors affect friendship selection, family interdependence and exchanges as well as relations with the formal health care system.

Studies on the support systems of elderly adults have seldom studied the cultural dimension of the networks of support. More needs to be known about the meaning that social relationships have for the aged as well as the ways in which cultural meanings influence patterns of interaction. Social networks and the supportive relations that ensue from them have a sociocultural dimension that embodies a system of shared meanings. These meanings affect social interaction and the expectations people have of their relationships with others (McDowell, 1981; Jacobson, 1987; Wentowski, 1981).

The purpose of this paper is to contribute more data on the cultural context of support systems, specifically, ethnicity as a variable that influences the process of aging among minority groups in the United States. It will focus on a group of low-income elderly Puerto Rican women living in an ethnic enclave, some of their value orientations, and how the latter influence patterns of daily activity and

Melba Sánchez-Ayéndez, Department of Social Sciences, Graduate School of Public Health, University of Puerto Rico Medical Sciences Campus.

the relationships within supportive networks.[1] Family interdependence and the double standard of conduct for men and women are the principal values upon which the discussion of the dynamics involved in the relations of support will center.

METHODS AND DEMOGRAPHIC CHARACTERISTICS OF THE SAMPLE

A nineteen month ethnographic study of 16 Puerto Rican women 60 years of age and over and living in a low-income ethnic enclave in the city of Boston was conducted.[1] In-depth formal and informal interviews as well as participant observation were the principal methods used for gathering the data. A qualitative descriptive approach was used in the analysis.

The women lived in government subsidized housing. Only one of the subjects lived in the house of one of her children. Their ages ranged from 60 to 84. The median age was 72. Half of the respondents were widows and 31 percent were living with their husbands. Fifty six percent of the respondents had been in the United States for more than twenty years. Half of the women were over 50 years of age when they came to settle in the United States. More than half of the sample (51%) left their homeland to follow their children.

Networks of Support

Children, husbands, friends and neighbors provide a reliable source of support during everyday life and crises. The transactional content of the support given to old adults is mostly instrumental and emotional. As instrumental support, the networks provide the elderly with transportation and escort to places, information, translation of documents written in English, reading and writing of letters in Spanish (for those who are illiterate) and health assistance. Very few of the older women receive financial help from family and friends except during emergencies. Emotional support involves frequent visits and/or telephone calls from kin and friends, as well as, having someone with whom to share problems.

The elderly women also provide instrumental and emotional support to those in their family networks. Baby-sitting, cooking, giving advice or listening to others are among the supportive tasks most frequently performed for adult children and grandchildren.

Escort and company are part of the reciprocity patterns of exchange among friends. Good relations with neighbors are deemed important since neighbors are viewed as useful during emergencies and unexpected events. Neighbors, unlike kin and friends, are not an essential component of the emotional support system. They might become friends but not necessarily. While supportive relations with friends involve the provision of both instrumental and emotional support, those with neighbors are limited to instrumental assistance.

The family, and particularly adult children, plays the main supportive role in the lives of the women who were interviewed. This represents a continuity of the traditional Island pattern. Despite rapid social change during the past thirty years, the family continues to play a central and essential role in the support and governance of its members among Puerto Ricans on the Island and the mainland (Buitrago, 1973; Cantor, 1979; Carrasquillo, 1982; Cruz-López and Pearson, 1985; Rogler, 1978; Safa, 1974; Sánchez-Ayéndez, 1984).

Cultural Values

The elderly Puerto Rican women who participated in the study believe in a double standard of behavior for men and women, as well as in the predominance of male authority and greater female emotional strength. Women are conceptualized as patient and, to a large degree, as forbearing in their relations with men, particularly male family members. Although men are perceived as authority figures, nevertheless, the women also conceive them as emotionally weaker. The term *como niños* (like boys) is often used in relation to men. Men are recognized as not having as much emotional endurance as women.

FEMALE ROLES

A woman's central role is motherhood. The concept of motherhood is interpreted by the respondents as based upon the female biological capacity of childbearing and the notion of *marianismo*.

Marianismo stems from the Catholic tradition and uses as a role model the virgin Mary. Within this framework, motherhood is the woman's main role despite other roles as wife, sibling or laborer. It is through motherhood that a woman realizes herself and derives her biggest satisfactions in life. All of the respondents who are mothers expressed satisfaction or dissatisfaction with their life accomplishments in terms of their offspring.

A woman's reproductive role is perceived as enabling her to be more committed to and to have better understanding of her children than the father. For example:

It is easier for a man to leave his children and form a new home with another woman, or not to be as forgiving of children as a mother is. They (men) will never know what it is like to carry a child inside, feel it growing, and bring that child into the world. This is why a mother is always willing to forgive and make sacrifices; that creature is a part of you. It nourished from you and came from within you. But it is not so with men. To them, a child is a being they receive once it is born. The attachment can never be the same.

The attitude upheld by the Puerto Rican women of childrearing as their main responsibility in life ensues from this conceptualization of the mother-child bond. For them, raising children means more than looking after the needs of offspring. It involves being able to offer them every possible opportunity for a better life, whether during childhood or adulthood. This is to be accomplished even at the costs of personal sacrifices, including self-denial.

Despite the fact that 69 percent of the respondents had worked outside the home at sometime during their early adulthood, and that many of the younger women in their families have joined the wage labor force, the elderly women perceive the house as the center around which the female world revolves. The house is considered the woman's domain. Decisions regarding household maintenance are generally made by women; men seldom intervene. On the occasions when adult children provide financial assistance, the mother is generally the direct recipient of the money. She then gives it to her husband or decides what to do with it. This pattern is related to the notion of household governance and maintenance as a female responsibility and to the conceptualization of men as breadwinners.

A man's main responsibility to the family is of an economic nature. Although fathers are expected to be affectionate to their young children, child care is not perceived as a man's responsibility. The ideal of maleness among Puerto Ricans is interlinked to the concept of *machismo*. *Machismo* refers to a man's need to prove his virility by the conquest of women, a belief in a stronger sexual drive for males, dominance over women, and a belligerent attitude when confronted by male peers. However, maleness involves more than sexual assertiveness and dominance over women. It also alludes to a man's ability to be a good provider, a protector of the family — particularly of children and women — and, to a large degree, able to control his emotions and be self-sufficient.

RESPETO

Similar to other Hispanic groups, Puerto Ricans view *respeto (respect) as the basis for all proper relationships.* According to Lauria (1964) *respeto* implies "generalized deference in all social interactions." It also involves a variety of deferential acts or rituals that are relevant to specific types of social relations.

Respect has two connotations for the women in this study. One is related to age hierarchy. As women grow older they demand respect from their age cohorts and, in particular, from younger generations. Respect is related to increased status as one ages. Therefore, women also expect deference from other adults by virtue of their status as elders. Interlinked with this connotation is the second dimension of respect. This involves the recognition of the elderly person, and of all human beings, as individuals, of a person's inherent value as a singular human being (*dignidad* or dignity). As such, the respondents demand respect from peers as well as those of higher social status.

Respeto is an essential component of parent-child relationships. One of the necessary qualities of a good offspring, according to the informants, is to be *respetuosos* (respectful). Some of the women believe that it is more important that a child be respectful than affectionate to his/her parents. The ideal is that offspring be both affectionate and respectful. Offspring and other adults, as well as young children and adolescents, are not expected to talk back to or shout back at the elderly. This is considered a serious sign of disrespect (*falta de respeto*). Other deferential acts involve asking and listening to the advice elderly individuals offer, and standing up to greet or say farewell to an older person.

Older Puerto Ricans prefer the use of the terms *doña* (for women) and *don* (for men) before their first name, or *señora* and *senor* before their surname, as titles of respect. *Don* and *doña* have a connotation of familiarity, while *señor* and *señora* are formal. The use of the pronoun *usted* (instead of the informal *tú*, both meaning "you" in the singular form) is expected to accompany these deference terms. Strangers and younger generations, with the exception of those in the immediate kinship group, are expected to use these forms when addressing older persons.

Most of the women who participated in the study feel that today *respeto* does not convey the same deferential meaning or have the same intensity as when they were growing up. Some stress that not all younger people use the deferential terms. This lack of formality in the treatment of an older person is seen as disrespectful. They also state that at times, when visiting social and health services agencies, younger people do not offer their seats to them as a sign of deference for their status as elders. Other examples of disrespect cited by the respondents include older family members being yelled at by younger members, and young people making fun of elderly persons on the street.

However, despite changes occurring in Puerto Rican families and communities, ritualized acts of deference are still bestowed upon Puerto Rican older adults. The patterns are more prevalent within the family and friendship networks. Respect is contingent upon the status of the elders as old adults and parents, and not on their functions and power in familial and community structures.

The Cultural Context of the Informal Support Networks

The difference in the cultural conceptualization of men and women affects patterns of interaction of elderly Puerto Ricans, as well as the dynamics involved in their supportive networks and their expectations for family assistance. The daily activities of Puerto

Rican older women center around the family and the household. Among married couples, it is the woman who is in charge of domestic tasks such as cooking, cleaning the house, and doing the laundry, as well as of taking care of grandchildren and the maintenance of family relations. When telephones are present in the household, older women tend to keep in touch with those in their networks through telephone conversations. When women leave the home it is usually to go shopping for groceries, to attend religious services, or to keep doctor or other appointments. They are frequently accompanied by husbands.

Elderly men, although they do stay in the house for long periods of the day, venture out into the community more often than women. They are usually in charge of going to the bank or the post office. Likewise, as part of their almost daily walks, they stop at *bodegas*[2] to buy staples and to purchase newspapers from Puerto Rico.

The difference in patterns of daily activities between men and women is influenced by factors such as health and marital status. For example, in cases when the wife is ill, the husband participates in household chores. In addition, when women live alone their living arrangement necessitates that they venture into the community more often than married women. Adult children perform certain tasks for their widowed mothers and escort them to places. At other times, elderly women accompany each other to medical appointments, the bank and religious services.

SELECTION OF FRIENDS

Cultural definitions of the roles of men and women influence the selection of friends. Friendship is determined along sex lines. Very few elderly women have friends of the opposite sex. Women tend to be careful about men. Mistrust about males is based upon the notion of *machismo*. Since men are conceived as having stronger sexual desires, the possibility of advances from elderly males—whether physical or verbal—to prove virility is a prevalent attitude among elderly women. Therefore, relationships with male members outside the immediate familial group are usually kept at a formal level. None of the respondents named a man as a friend. Many even emphasized the word amiga (female friend) instead of amigo (male friend). One stated:

I've never had an amigo. Men cannot be trusted too much. They might misunderstand your motives and some even try to make a pass at you.

FAMILY INTERDEPENDENCE

Cultural definitions of male and female roles affect the types of exchanges that occur within family networks and interrelate with the value of family interdependence. The Puerto Rican family is characterized by strong norms of reciprocity that emphasize interdependence among the various family members, especially those in the immediate kinship group. Interdependence within the Puerto Rican symbolic framework:

> . . . fits an orientation to life that stresses that the individual is not capable of doing everything and doing it well. Therefore, he should rely on others for assistance. (Bastida, 1979: 70-71)

Within this framework, individualism and self-reliance assume a different meaning from that which prevails in the dominant culture of the United States.

Family interdependence is a value which the Puerto Rican elderly women who participated in the study strongly adhered. They still expect to be taken care of in old age by their adult children. The notion of filial duty ensues from the value orientation of interdependence. Supportive behavior from children is addressed from the perspective of expected reciprocity in exchange for the functions parents performed for children during their upbringing. All the respondents stressed that "good" offspring ought to help their aged parents according to available resources. Seventy one percent of the older women with children said they first turn to their offspring when confronted by a problem of any kind.

Interdependence for this group of Puerto Rican elderly women also means helping their children and grandchildren. Many times they provide assistance, even if not explicitly requested. Being able to perform supportive tasks for their children's families is a source of emotional satisfaction. Within the interdependence framework, assistance is viewed from the context of the maternal role and parental obligations.

Family interdependence is not, however, based upon total equality of exchange. What is of utmost importance to the older women is that the children visit or call frequently, and not that they help all the time. More emphasis is placed on emotional support from offspring than other forms of assistance. This is why frequent interaction with children, whether in the form of visits or telephone calls, is highly valued, more by elderly women than men. The elderly female parent tends to complain more than the male when adult children do not visit or call frequently.

SEX ROLES AND SUPPORT

The difference in the conceptualization of male and female roles also affects the dynamics and types of exchanges which occur within the family network, both in terms of what support is given and received. In relation to support received from offspring, Puerto Rican older women perceive their daughters, because they are women, as being more understanding and better able to comprehend their problems than sons. Daughters are also considered more reliable. Sons are not expected to help as much as daughters or in the same way. Complaints are more bitter when a daughter, rather than a son, does not fulfill expected duties of assistance.

> Men are different, they do not feel as we feel. But she is a woman, she should know better.

In the same vein, daughters are expected to visit and/or call more frequently than sons. As women, they are linked to the domestic domain and held responsible for the care of family members and the maintenance of family relations.

Two-thirds of the respondents who have sons and daughters stated that they confide their problems more often to their daughters, as well as offer advice to daughters on matters related to marriage and children. This does not mean that they do not discuss personal matters with sons or give them advice, but however, the approach is different. For example, in terms of advice given to adult children by the elderly women:

> I never ask my son openly what is wrong with him. I go carefully. I do not want him to think that I believe he cannot solve his problems; he is a man and you know how they are. Yet, as a mother I worry. It is my duty to listen and offer him advice. With my daughter it is different; I can be more direct. She doesn't have to prove to me that she is self-sufficient.
>
> Of course I give advice to my sons! When they have had problems with their wives, their children, even among themselves, I listen to them, and tell them what I think. But with my daughter I am more open. You see, if I ask one of my sons what is wrong and he doesn't want to tell me, I don't insist too much. I'll ask later, maybe in a different way; and they will tell me sooner or later. With my daughter, if she doesn't want to tell me, I'll insist. She knows I am her mother and a woman like her and that I can understand.

Likewise, 57 percent of those respondents who turn to their children when faced with a problem, turn first to a daughter. Female offspring are perceived as more patient and, being women like their mothers, better able to understand.

Motherhood is perceived as the link that creates a spiritual bond among women. Once a daughter becomes a mother, a stronger tie with her own mother is expected. The basis for this tie is the suffering experienced at the moment of childbirth and the hardships involved in childrearing, since childrearing is considered the main responsibility of women. Fatherhood does not create a similar link among men.

Relations between elderly Puerto Rican men and their offspring are somewhat different from those of women. Fathers tend to keep their problems to themselves, particularly financial and emotional ones. This is related to the notion that men are financially responsible for the family and more self-sufficient than women. As a result, many times older women serve as go-betweens and/or mediators communicating a father's personal problems to adult children.

Many elderly fathers play the role of "protector" by escorting their daughters or granddaughters to different places. Relations with sons are more formal and exhibit less overtly affectionate behavior than those with daughters. Fathers are also more distant and careful than mothers in their approach to male adult children. When a son has a problem, the father will not probe if information is not offered willingly. Sons, as men, are perceived as able to take care of their problems. Mothers tend to be more inquisitive than fathers. However, advice to sons is given by both parents although not as frequently as to daughters. Daughters are perceived by fathers as in need of more protection and support than sons. Mothers, on the other hand, perceive sons and daughters as in equal need of support but recognize daughters' vulnerability to sexual harassment and conjugal problems as a result of their status as women.

Although most adult children are sources of assistance during the illness of an elderly parent, it is generally daughters who are expected to provide the majority of help and assistance. Quite often, daughters take sick parents into their homes or stay overnight at the parents' home in order to provide care. Although sons are part of the supportive network that provide health assistance, their role is limited. Sons and daughters share responsibility for things such as taking aged parents to the hospital or to a doctor's office, buying medicines and contributing money if needed. However, daughters more often than sons check on parents, provide personal care, and perform household chores during times of illness.

The Cultural Context of the Formal Networks of Support

The women who participated in this study utilized formal health and social services when needed. As a result they did not rely solely on families and friends for assistance. Yet, ethnicity influences the selection and use of formal systems of support. For example, there is a preference for Hispanic service providers. This preference is based on commonality of language and cultural rules that underlie social relations such as *respeto* and *personalismo*.

The formal support agency personnel most likely to be turned to are caseworkers. The latter provide information on available social and health services, serve as translators and escort programs, as well as make appointments at agencies and hospitals for the elderly. The caseworkers of all respondents were Hispanic, principally Puerto Rican. Most resided in the same neighborhood or surrounding area in which informants lived. A majority have known most of the subjects or their families for a number of years.

PERSONALISMO

When caseworkers visit the homes of the elderly they are always offered something to eat or drink. For the respondents, this was a way of reciprocating for the services provided and the sensitivity with which assistance was offered. Furthermore, it imbued the relationship with personalismo, the preference of dealing with others in terms of a network of personal relations. The caseworker becomes not only someone who provides services, but one with whom the elderly person is acquainted and comfortable.

Six of the 16 respondents expressed a dislike for their caseworker based on what they perceived as lack of *personalismo* in the relations. They complained that caseworkers were overly formal in the way they interacted with them. For example:

> I have invited her (caseworker) many times to come to this house for coffee or something else to drink. She has been working in this community for five months and not once has she come and accepted my invitation. . . Maybe she thinks she is too good for us.
>
> I liked my other caseworker much more. She would come by to visit, chat or eat something. She never turned down my invitations for a cup of coffee or a bite to eat. This one (new caseworker) is good at her work, but she is so formal! She has been here for almost a year and has never accepted my invitation for a cup of coffee or a good dish of rice and beans.[3]

What the respondents complained about was not that caseworkers were inefficient or rude, but that they refused to see them as "something more than cases." This resulted from the violation of the notion of *personalismo*. The desire to establish closer relationships with others is manifested through offers of hospitality. This is conveyed to strangers by invitations for coffee, lunch or dinner in one's home. A continuous refusal to accept such an invitation is interpreted as a rejection of hospitality and the individual's desire to develop a more personal relationship. In the case of service providers, this can result in elders turning to them only for instrumental assistance.

THE CULTURAL VALUE OF RESPECT

Respeto is also an important element in the service provider-elderly relationship. Basic courtesy forms are expected from service providers and utmost importance is attached to the use of the pronoun *usted*. Twelve of the 16 women stated that many times they are addressed by the pronoun *tú* instead of *usted*, and by their first names without adding the title of *doña*. They interpret this as a sign of disrespect, one that creates distance between them and their service providers. Expressions such as the following were typical:

> She is efficient but I don't feel comfortable with her . . . One of the things I dislike about her is that she calls me by my first name and *tú*. I don't like that. She is young enough to be my daughter and owes me the respect that my age requires.

CONCLUSIONS

Cultural rules underlie the exchanges that occur within a support system (McDowell, 1981). The type of support given or received, the way in which it is offered, the persons involved, and occasions in which it is provided need to be understood within the context of the meaning of interpersonal relationships. Attention to the cultural context in which supportive behavior occurs expands our understanding of social support and of the reasons why support networks are kept or altered (Horowitz, 1985; Jacobson, 1987; Wentowski, 1981). The way a group's cultural tradition defines and interprets relationships is a factor that influences how elderly adults use their networks in order to secure needed support in old age.

NOTES

1. The research was supported by the Danforth Foundation; Sigma Xi, The Scientific Research Society; and the Delta Kappa Gamma Society International. It covered the period ranging from October 1981 to July 1983.
2. Grocery stores, generally owned by Hispanics, where native foods can be bought. They also serve as gathering places and information centers.
3. Typical every-day Puerto Rican dish.

REFERENCES

Bastida, Elena. (1979). Family Integration and Adjustment to Aging Among Hispanic American Elderly. Ph.D. dissertation, University of Kansas.
Buitrago, Carlos. (1973). *An Ethnographic Study of a Peasant Community in Puerto Rico*. Tucson, Arizona: University of Arizona Press.
Cantor, Marjorie H. (1979). The informal support system of New York's inner city elderly: Is ethnicity a factor? In D. L. Gelfand and A. J. Kutzik (eds.) *Ethnicity and Aging*. New York: Springer.
Carrasquillo, Héctor A. (1982). Perceived Reciprocity and Self-Esteem among Elderly Antillean Hispanics and their Familial Informal Networks. Ph.D. dissertation, Syracuse University.
Cruz-López, Miguel and Pearson, R. E. (1985). The support needs and resources of Puerto Rican elders. *The Gerontologist*, 25: 483-487.
Horowitz, Amy. (1985). Sons and daughters as caregivers to older parents: Differences in role performance and consequences. *The Gerontologist*, 25: 612-623.
Jacobson, David. (1987). The cultural context of social support and support networks. *Medical Anthropological Quarterly*, 1: 42-67.
Lauria, A. (1964). Respeto, relajo and interpersonal relations in Puerto Rico. *Anthropological Quarterly*, 37: 53-67.
McDowell, Nancy. (1981). It's not who you are but how you give what counts: The role of exchange in Melanesian society. *American Ethnologist*, 7: 58-70.
Rogler, Lloyd. (1978). Help patterns, the family and mental health: Puerto Ricans in the United States. *International Migration Review*, 12: 248-259.
Saffa, Helen I. (1974). *The Urban Poor of Puerto Rico: A Study in Development and Inequality*. New York: Holt, Rinehart and Winston.
Sánchez-Ayéndez, Melba. (1984). Puerto Rican Elderly Women: Adjustment to Age in an Ethnic Minority Group in the United States. Ph.D. dissertation, University of Massachusetts in Amherst.
Wentowski, Gloria J. (1981). Reciprocity and the coping strategies of older people: Cultural dimensions of network building. *The Gerontologist*, 21: 600-609.

Older Women
in Developing Countries

Marsel A. Heisel

SUMMARY. Women's issues are markedly underrepresented in international policy and research discussions. This paper addresses these deficits by delineating the particular conditions of aging women in developing countries. While these women experience many of the age-related problems as their counterparts in developed countries, cultural and economic influences place them at a greater disadvantage.

The phenomenal rise in the number of old and very old women in developing countries, a growth about four times larger than in developed areas of the world, brings about particular issues related to women, aging, health care, and socio-economic development. An overwhelming majority of older women in developing countries are illiterate, poor, socially dependent, and lack personal resources to cope with changing social conditions. Where the old have traditionally been cared for by the extended family, some of the consequences of development, such as migration of children or labor force participation and emancipation of younger women, have created additional problems for older women. While many third world governments have voiced concern in international forums either about the status of women or about aging in general, little, if any, attention has been paid to the plight of older women. This paper is an attempt to examine the combined effects of being old, being a woman, and living in a rapidly changing society. It provides an overview of the social and personal situation of older women in

Marsel A. Heisel, School of Social Work, Rutgers University, Newark, NJ 07102.

developing countries and explores some of the critical issues facing not only older women, but also their families and governments.

The issues surrounding aging and development are obviously very complex, and conditions for the aged, or for older women, are far from being similar in all developing regions or countries. Nevertheless, the focus of this paper will remain predominantly global, looking at general trends in changing population and family structures and the implications of such change for older women. It should be stressed, however, that the problems of older women need to be dealt with within the context of the larger population and with deliberate understanding and empathy, not only for the older women, but also for younger women who are struggling to improve their status in a male dominated society.

AGING AND SOCIOECONOMIC DEVELOPMENT

Until recently, the aging of populations has been perceived as an issue of immediate concern primarily for developed countries, where the overall decrease in fertility rates has led to a substantial rise in the proportion of elderly in their populations. In developing countries, where high fertility and relatively low mortality prevail, the proportion of older persons in the population remains low while their numbers increase substantially. International research and policy discussions on aging have tended to focus on the proportion rather than the numbers of older persons in a population, thus encouraging the view that aging is not an issue of concern for developing nations. Therefore, in the last twenty years or so, while research, policies and services to benefit the elderly have proliferated in more developed regions of the world (such as Europe, North America, Australia and Japan), the issue of aging in less developed regions (such as Africa, Latin America, the Middle East and much of Asia and the Pacific) has remained virtually unrecognized. This lack of concern is well reflected in the minimal attention given the topic in gerontology literature, including international books on aging (e.g., Palmore, 1980; Thomae & Maddox, 1982; Nusberg, 1984).

The World Assembly on Aging, convened in 1982, was the first international forum indicating concern with the question of aging in developing countries (United Nations, 1982). However, the issue of older women, who constitute the majority of the aged and most of whom are physically and economically dependent widows, was left out of almost all reports submitted to the Assembly by governments (Heisel, 1985). The Vienna International Plan of Action on Aging refers to older women almost as an afterthought — only one sentence embedded within one of its 62 recommendations (United Nations, 1983, p. 38, Recommendation 27). A similar neglect is also evident in the Report of the International Conference on Population, 1984 (United Nations, 1984, p. 32, Recommendation 58). Even more surprising is the minimal attention given to older women in developing regions during the United Nations Decade for Women and at the World Conference convened at the end of the decade in Nairobi. The official report of the conference contains only one paragraph on "elderly women," reiterating the International Plan of Action on Aging adopted by the World Assembly on Aging. It does, however, recommend that research should be directed to "the process of premature aging due to a lifetime of stress, excessive work-load, malnutrition and repeated pregnancies" (United Nations, 1985, p. 68 para. 286), a condition which well describes middle-aged and older women in the developing world.

Developing countries, by definition, are poor and the elderly suffer from the consequences of poverty together with the rest of the population. Sometimes they suffer even more because of their age. For example, mortality among the elderly rises sharply during a famine period and remains for a while above previous levels after the famine is over (Siegel & Hoover, 1984). In addition, however, in many parts of the world, old women have suffered throughout their lives from poor health care, malnutrition, and low social status because they were born female. Where resources are scarce, families seem to give priority to the health, education and nutrition of boys and men and neglect females. Consequently, women in developing areas have greater needs for medical, social and economic assistance in old age. Moreover, adapting to social change can be difficult for older women whose lives have been confined to biological and domestic roles and who have had little contact with the outside world.

In developing countries, it has been almost universally assumed that the family will take care of its aging members. There is ample documentation, however, that this assumption is no longer correct.

Most governments of developing nations are cognizant of the fact that families are at times unable to cope with the fundamental needs of their aging members and assert that government must assume some responsibility for the care of the elderly (Heisel, 1985). Nevertheless, there is also the fear that government assistance to the elderly will lead to erosion of traditional family values, and consequently to neglect of the aged and/or to a financial burden beyond the national capacity. An extreme example of this can be seen in Malaysia where, according to a national statement delivered to the World Assembly on Aging of 1982, the government ceased building welfare institutions for the elderly in order to discourage the erosion of traditional family values (Heisel, 1985, p. 58).

With the increase in life expectancy, there are more elderly who need personal care and protection. To a great extent, this is provided by families, not only in traditional societies but also in developed areas, including the United States (Shanas, 1978: Brody, 1985). However, in developing countries the demand for extended care of old and frail parents is coming at a time when women are just beginning to improve their social status and to make entry into the labor force. The question is not whether the care of the aged is the responsibility of the family or of the state, but rather, how the state can assist the family in providing support for the elderly without damaging the small advances in status younger women are beginning to achieve.

DEMOGRAPHIC OVERVIEW

According to United Nations projections based on 1984 assessments (United Nations, 1986a and 1987), by the year 2020 the number of persons aged 60 and over in the world will surpass one billion, comprising 12.9 percent of the total population. Between 1980 and the year 2000, the number of persons in this age group will increase by 228 million. Most of this growth will take place in the developing world in the regions of East and South Asia, Africa and Latin America.

Currently, there is an almost equal number of elderly persons living in the developed and developing regions of the world, but there is a vast difference in their proportions relative to their larger populations. The proportion of those aged 60 years and over is 6.6 percent in less developed regions as opposed to 15.8 percent in more developed countries. This disparity is expected to continue well into the next century. However, nations with very low and constant proportions of elderly persons may, at the same time, be experiencing considerable growth in the absolute numbers of older persons in the population. While the combination of high fertility and reduced infant mortality keeps the proportion of old people low, advances in general health conditions allows more persons to live into old age, resulting in progressively larger cohorts of the elderly.

Developing countries can anticipate a substantial increment in the absolute number of older men and women by the end of this century, and still higher increases after that. Between 1980 and the year 2000, the more developed regions will add 61 million persons aged 60 and over to their populations, while the less developed regions will add 166 million persons in this age category. This increment will be of the order of 73 and 329 million respectively between the years 2000 and 2020, over four times higher for developing regions when compared with developed areas (see Table 1 & Figure 1).

The projected numbers of persons aged 80 and over, who are more likely to be frail and require special assistance, are particularly significant for health and family policy issues. Between 1980 and 2020, the number of octogenarians will double in the more developed regions, rising in absolute numbers from 22 to 46 million persons. However, during this same period, in the less developed regions this number will grow by a factor of five, from 12 million to 64 million persons. Thus, by the turn of this century, the majority of very old persons will be living in developing countries and most of them will be women (see Table 2 and Figure 2).

Today, there are roughly equal numbers of males and females in the world, but the sex ratio differs considerably between developed and developing regions and between younger and older segments of society. In general, women survive longer and hence, at higher ages, outnumber men. This gender imbalance is much smaller in developing areas of the world, because the relative life expectancy of women in these regions is still significantly lower than in more developed areas.

TABLE 1

SIZE OF POPULATION AGED 60 AND OVER BY SEX
FOR THE WORLD AND REGIONS, 1960-2020
(In thousands, medium variant)

	1 9 6 0		1 9 8 0		2 0 0 0		2 0 2 0	
	Males	Females	Males	Females	Males	Females	Males	Females
Developed regions...	49032	69527	68172	105152	98092	136470	134266	173909
Developing regions...	59797	66135	98737	109145	178371	195759	333637	369787
WORLD......	108829	135662	166909	214297	276463	332229	467903	543696

Source: Global Estimates and Projections of Population by Sex and Age.
The 1984 Assessment. United Nations Publication, 1987.

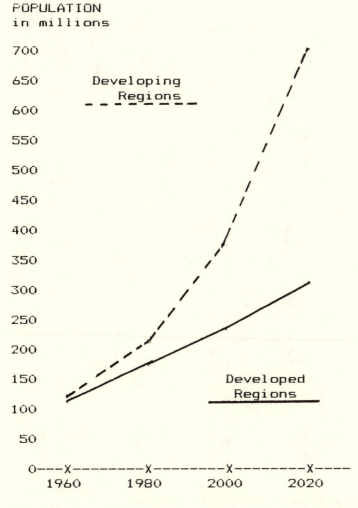

Figure 1. Growth of population aged 60
and over, 1960–2020, in major regions
of the world. United Nations estimates.

TABLE 2

SIZE OF POPULATION AGED 80 AND OVER BY SEX
FOR THE WORLD AND REGIONS, 1960-2020
(In thousands, medium variant)

	1 9 6 0		1 9 8 0		2 0 0 0		2 0 2 0	
	Males	Females	Males	Females	Males	Females	Males	Females
Developed regions....	4285	7448	7067	15757	9597	21739	15599	30908
Developing regions...,	2847	3880	5239	7538	12615	17987	26493	38176
WORLD......	7132	11328	12306	23295	22212	39726	42092	69084

Source: Global Estimates and Projections of Population by Sex and Age. The 1984 Assessment. United Nations Publication, 1987.

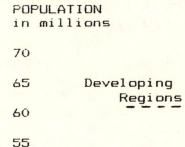

POPULATION
in millions

Figure 2. Growth of population aged 80
and over, 1960-2020, in major regions
of the world. United Nations estimates.

LIFE EXPECTANCY OF WOMEN
IN DEVELOPING COUNTRIES

The average length of life is usually greater for females than for males. Globally, United Nations estimates of life expectancy at birth for 1985-1990, using medium variant, are 59.7 years for males and 62.6 years for females. In more developed regions, this estimate is 70.4 years for males and 77.7 years for females, an advantage of 7.3 years for women. In less developed regions, the corresponding numbers are 57.9 years for males and 60.3 years for females, a sex difference of only 2.4 years (United Nations, 1986a).

Life expectancy, and its interaction with gender, is dramatically different within the developing world. In Latin America life expectancy at birth for 1985-1990 is estimated to be 63.2 years for males and 68.2 years for females, while in Africa this figure is 49.8 years for men and 52.9 years for women. In Asia, the numbers are 60.3 for males and 62 for females. Estimated life expectancy in India is about equal for males and females (respectively 57.8 and 57.9) and in Bangladesh it is 50.1 for men and one year shorter, 49.1, for women (United Nations, 1986a).

Life expectancies at advanced ages are more similar in developed and developing countries, particularly for men. As shown in Table 3, for 1975-1980 life expectancy for men at age 60 was 16.5 years in more developed regions (MDR) and 14.2 in less developed regions (LDR), a difference of 2.3 years. For women aged 60, life expectancy was 19.7 years in MDR, but 4.1 years less, 15.6 years, in LDR. Generally women live longer, and at the age of 60, in MDR, life expectancy of women is 3.2 years higher than men. This advantage drops to 1.4 years in LDR, creating a gap of 4.1 years in the life expectancies of older women in developed and developing regions. These data raise the question as to whether women in developing regions are living to their potential within prevailing conditions.

In a discussion of sex differentials and mortality, Ware (1981) suggests that the process of development includes three stages of mortality: first, higher female mortality at all ages, followed by higher female mortality in childhood and during the reproductive years, and finally lower female mortality at all ages. She points out

TABLE 3

ESTIMATED LIFE EXPECTATION AT AGE 60,
1975 TO 1980, FOR WORLD AND REGIONS

	Males	Females
Developed Regions......	16.5	19.7
Developing Regions.....	14.2	15.6
WORLD.................	14.4	16.0

Source: Siegel & Hoover, International Trends
and Perspectives: Aging. U.S. Bureau
of the Census Publication, 1984

that data from developed countries show the great advantage in life expectancy of females at every age, suggesting that "in societies where males and females receive similar treatment, females live much longer than males" (Ware, 1981, p. 40).

In spite of this biological advantage, in 1985 the overall sex ratio of developing regions was estimated to be 103.7 men per 100 women. Several countries in South Asia, namely Pakistan, India, Nepal, Iraq, show an excess of female mortality (Siegel & Hoover, 1984). It is likely that this is explained by the lower status of females which results in their receiving less medical attention and less food. As older women, they become especially vulnerable as widows, a condition which will be dealt with subsequently.

HEALTH AND DISABILITIES

A review of World Health Organization activities related to the elderly, summarizing reports from 1958 to 1982, concludes that health needs and health service utilization of older people in developed countries is higher than other age groups, and that older women have higher morbidity than men of the same age (Skeet,

1983). As sociomedical surveys indicate, older persons make more visits to physicians than younger persons, have longer episodes of illness, and have higher admission rates to general hospitals and longer hospital stays (Siegel & Hoover, 1982). Among persons aged 60 and older, women have more symptoms than men and there is an increase in prevalence of symptoms with age. Women, more often than men, report tiredness or feelings of faintness, aching or pain in the joints, back troubles, and nervous tension or nervousness. They are also generally less satisfied with life, report more difficulty in coping with activities of daily living, and are more lonely than men (Heikkinen et al., 1983). These results are based primarily on data from more developed regions.

Although there is relatively little empirical information available about the health status of the elderly, and in particular about older women in developing countries, it is clear that illness depends to some extent on the level of development in the countries in which older persons live. Infectious diseases predominate in developing countries, and chronic conditions, such as heart disease and diabetes, in developed areas. However, even in developing countries, there has been a trend away from communicable diseases, accompanied by an increase in chronic conditions that reduce functional ability and require continuous treatment. Recent research by the World Health Organization on aging in four countries in the Western Pacific (Andrews et al., 1986) provides the only comprehensive study to date of the health status of the elderly in developing regions. Hence, it will be discussed in some detail.

Surveys on the health and socioeconomic aspects of aging were carried out in Fiji, Malaysia, the Philippines, and the Republic of Korea. In each country, a sample of 800 persons aged 60 and over, which was reasonably representative of the major subgroups in the population, was studied. Data were collected from the elderly respondents through personal interviews in their own homes using a standardized questionnaire, as well as from informants who lived with the respondent when possible. Proxies or informants were used when direct communication was impossible due to factors such as illness, disability, or loss of cognitive functioning. The questionnaire included items on demography, economic resources, physical and mental health, activities of daily living, interaction with family and friends, and housing.

In all four countries, and in both rural and urban areas, men were more likely to be married than women and women were more likely to be widowed than men. In Fiji, 18 percent of men and 50 percent of women were widowed. These statistics were similar in Malaysia where 11 percent of men and 56 percent of women were widowed. Widowhood, as would be expected, increased with age.

A number of approaches were used to evaluate the health status of respondents including self-assessment of overall health, information on accidents, injuries, and chronic illness, ability to perform the activities of daily living, prevalence of symptoms and health problems, and use of formal health care services. Mental health was assessed through a simple measure of cognitive functioning and a few items relating to symptoms.

Overall, at least half of the study population reported that they felt quite healthy. Observed sex differences in self-assessed health were not consistent throughout the countries. More women than men described themselves as healthy in Fiji (64% women, compared to 53% men). In the Republic of Korea this difference was in the opposite direction, with 45 percent of women and 54 percent of men describing themselves as healthy.

Satisfaction with health did not necessarily correspond with the prevalence of health problems. Of the four national groups, Filipinos reported the highest levels of satisfaction with their health status as well as the highest prevalence of health problems; two thirds of the elderly surveyed reported that they had chronic health problems that impinged on their daily activities. The most common conditions reported were hypertension, pulmonary tuberculosis, peptic ulcers, heart disease, asthma, and abdominal pains.

Responses to questions on specific symptoms revealed a high level of disability, particularly visual and dental problems, which increased with age but showed no particular variance with sex. On the other hand, the ability to cope with activities of daily living (ADL) was consistently high, and most respondents were able to carry out without help all of ten tasks. Manton, Myers and Andrews (1987) subsequently analyzed the ADL data using GOM analysis, a multivariate procedure that made it possible to identify both distinct morbidity patterns and the subgroups that manifest these patterns. One of the groups identified was a predominantly female (95%) group, very old (53% aged 75-84 and 12% over 85), not married, living with children, and having the least education. Physically they were relatively healthy but they had mobility and instrumental ADL (IADL) problems. IADL problems are related to the capacity to live independently in the community, and involve such activities as travelling beyond walking distance, shopping, preparing meals, and handling one's own money. Manton et al. interpreted these symptoms as indicators of significant cognitive impairment, which, in developed countries, would be likely to lead to institutionalization. In developing countries, the combination of traditional values, extended families and greater informal care resources, and the low availability of nursing home facilities kept these women at home. However, in some countries, such as in the Republic of Korea, it appears that disabled elderly men are retained by the family, while elderly widows are likely to be institutionalized (Manton et al., 1987, p. 127). In the developing world, as in developed countries, men are more likely than women to have living spouses to whom they can turn for care and assistance.

One of the main factors affecting health of the aged in developing countries is undernutrition. Megama (1982) reports evidence from Sri Lanka, where the elderly poor are most affected by food shortages during crisis periods. During the famine of 1976, 20% of the increased deaths were among infants while 45% were among those aged 65 and over (p. 242). The situation is particularly bad for older women and widows, Ware (1981), in discussing food intake data from surveys conducted in Bangladesh, reports that older men consume almost as much protein as younger men of working age, but older women receive much less, especially if they are widowed (p. 46). She also notes that Bangladesh is among the few countries where females beyond age 50 experience higher mortality than males and attributes this to the fate of widows without sons to support them (p. 51).

Data on disabilities offer another source of information on health status and functional ability. The proportion of disabled persons among the population aged 65 and over in less developed regions is estimated to far exceed 50 percent (Siegel & Hoover, 1984, p. 28). A report by the United Nations Statistics Office (United Nations, 1986b) provides more specific data drawing on available statistics on disabled persons collected in at least 6 different censuses and surveys in Egypt, Iraq, Jordan, Lebanon, and the Syrian Arab Republic between 1947 and 1981. The term "disability" was used as a general term, covering impairments, disability and handicaps. The study analyzed differences in age distributions of disabled persons by sex.

Among the major findings of interest are statistics on visual impairments, the prevalence of which is highest among the elderly, particularly women. However, from 1960 on, the proportion of blindness among those 70 and over appears to have declined appreciably. This is attributed primarily to reduction in incidence of communicable diseases such as trachoma in the last 25 years, and to increased access to preventive and medical care. Despite this decline in prevalence, the larger numbers of elderly in the population has led to greater absolute numbers of older persons with visual impairment. Within the aged population women are more likely to be blind than men of the same or similar age. For example, of the total reported blind population in the Syrian Arab Republic, 22 percent of women aged 70 or older were blind as compared to 16 percent of men.

The prevalence of mental impairment in developing countries is difficult to estimate, as few epidemiological surveys have been conducted. The U.N. report on statistics of disabled persons (United Nations, 1986b) found higher rates of mental impairment among men than among women, but cautions that this may be the result of underenumeration of females. Mental impairment, particularly mental retardation, is detected at school, usually beyond the age of 10, and few girls go to school. Moreover, the report was based on data from Arab countries, and the Arab culture does not approve of discussing problems of women in public, particularly problems of girls who must appear marriageable. There appears to be no data to support the popular belief that most mental and emotional problems of the aged are the result of development or of "westernization." The compendium of World Health Organization Reports on the health of the elderly concludes that "There is no consistent evidence to support the view that traditional societies have a significantly smaller share of psychosocial disorders in old age than industrialized societies" (Skeet, 1983, p. 58).

Because women live longer than men, and because older women suffer from more chronic illnesses than men of the same age, their demands on health and social services will be greater than those of men. But developing countries are poor, and, according to the World Bank, public and private spending on health in these countries is only 5 percent of that expended in the developed countries. The average per capita health expenditure for 1981-82 was $9 for low-income countries, $31 for middle-income countries, and $670 for industrialized countries (World Bank, 1987). Direct private payments by individuals account for about half of health care expenditures in developing countries, as opposed to about one quarter in developed countries. In developing countries, most older persons are too poor to afford even meager health care, and women are more economically disadvantaged than men. In many developing countries women still cannot own property and since few, if any, have worked in wage-earning jobs, they have little or no economic resources such as social security or pension. Older widows with no children are particularly disadvantaged.

FAMILY SUPPORT AND WIDOWS

In developing countries, the family is the most important source of support both for health care and for economic and social well-being of the aged. However, as reports submitted to the World Assembly on Aging indicate, economic and social changes, particularly migration, have produced a decline in the traditional system of assigning responsibility in the family and in its capacity to cope with some of the fundamental needs of its aging members. There are many old persons without means of support and without near kin who are available or willing to look after them (Heisel, 1987a, p. 568). The greatest proportion of elderly persons without support are older widows, and the family situation of older women in developing areas needs to be discussed within the context of widowhood.

In most developing countries, the proportion of married older females is much lower than in developed regions. Cross national comparisons of data show very large proportions of widowed females, often exceeding two thirds of women aged 60 and over, as compared to very low proportions of widowed males (Heisel, 1985). For example, the WHO study in the Western Pacific reports that in Malaysia, among those aged 60 and over, 11 percent of the men and 56 percent of the women were widowed. Moreover, when compared with a similar WHO study in 11 European countries, the Western Pacific region had much higher rates of widowhood among older women (Andrews et al., 1986). Noting statistics on widowhood for Egypt, India, Indonesia, Jordan, and Syria, Palmore finds that "being an old woman usually means being a widow" (Palmore, 1987, p. 96). However, rarely is this phenomenon mentioned in relevant official government documents (Heisel, 1985).

The large numbers of widowed older women in less developed regions is not so much due to differential mortality between the sexes as it is to the fact that women marry very young and to older men. Widowed women past their childbearing age have almost no chance of remarriage, while widowed men of any age soon marry women significantly younger than themselves. Older men are much more likely to receive social and personal support in traditional families because of their high status as males, economic independence and likelihood of being married and having a spouse to provide needed care. Older women fall short of men on all of these counts and their situation, inside or outside of the family, is more likely to decline with the frailties brought about by old age.

In developing societies, the primary, and often only, source of support for a widow is her children, mostly her sons. But there are substantial numbers of old widows in developing countries who do not have sons, or any children, who will assist them in their old age. Hugo (1985) reports that in parts of Africa (such as in Gabon, Cameroon, Zaire, Central African Republic, Sudan) there are regions where 20 to 50 percent of women aged 50 and older have never borne children. The incidence of childlessness among Indonesian women, primarily due to sterility, exceeds 15 percent. The problem of loneliness of single women, well documented in developed countries, is scarcely ever mentioned with reference to Less Developed Regions. Yet Hugo's work in West Java showed that older widows and never married women who lived on their own had to rely on the charity of the community to survive, and their poverty, deprivation and loneliness was one of the most significant problems of these rural communities (Hugo, 1985, p. 14).

Even for those older women who are the recipients of traditional filial care and respect, the inevitable, and often desirable, social changes create discrepancies in what generations expect from each other. There is barely any research on interrelationships of generations in Less Developed Regions, a subject that deserves much more attention. In countries where social and economic development has been in progress for many years, such as in Turkey, one of the major positive consequences has been an increase in the status of women. As younger women become more educated, join the labor force, and become more equal to men, they also achieve more companionship and equal status in their marital relations. Yet research suggests that where such conditions are beginning to take place, elderly widows are becoming increasingly worried that they will not be cared for by their sons (Heisel, 1987b). It would appear that such intergenerational conflict needs to be resolved by involving older women in the process of development and social change, so that they are able to understand and foster, rather than hinder, the struggle of younger women for social equality.

As the number of very old women in developing countries increases, so will problems related to maintaining at home those who require constant care and attention. To preserve any momentum achieved towards labor force participation and equal status for women, governments and communities will have to assume some of the responsibility in providing such care.

NOTES

1. Throughout this article developing/less developed and developed/more developed are used interchangeably when referring to countries or regions.
2. Throughout this article an aged population is operationally defined as that category of persons 60 years of age or older. This conforms to the definition adopted by the World Assembly on Aging at Vienna and is different from the commonly used limit in the U.S. of age 65. It is, however, the preferred limit of governments of developing nations.

REFERENCES

Andrews, G. R., Esterman, A. J., Braunack-Maye, A. J., & Rungie, C. M. (1986). *AGING IN THE WESTERN PACIFIC*. Manila: W.H.O. Regional Office for the Western Pacific.

Brody, E. M. (1985). Parent cared as a normative family stress. *THE GERONTOLOGIST*, 25:19-29.

Heikkinen, E., Waters, W. E., & Brzezinski, Z. J. (1983). *THE ELDERLY IN ELEVEN COUNTRIES*. Copenhagen: W.H.O. Regional Office for Europe.

Heisel, M. A. (1985). Aging in the context of population policies in developing countries. *POPULATION BULLETIN OF THE UNITED NATIONS*, 17:49-63. United Nations Publication, Sales No. E.84.XIII.13.

Heisel, M. A. (1987a). Population policies and aging in developing countries. In G. L. Maddox & E. W. Busse (Eds.). *AGING; THE UNIVERSAL HUMAN EXPERIENCE*. New York: Springer Publishing Company.

Heisel, M. A. (1987b). Women and widows in Turkey: Support systems. In H. Z. Lopata (Ed.). *WIDOWS: THE MIDDLE EAST, ASIA AND THE PACIFIC*. Durham, Duke University Press.

Hugo, G. (1985). Population ageing: Some demographic issues in developing countries (1985). Background paper prepared for the International Congress of Gerontology, New York, July 12-17.

Megama, S. A. (1982). Aging in developing countries. *WORLD HEALTH STATISTICS QUARTERLY*, 35:239-246.

Manton, K. G., Myers, G. C., & Andrews, G. R. (1987). Morbidity and disability patterns in four developing nations: Their implications for social and economic integration of the elderly. *JOURNAL OF CROSS-CULTURAL GERONTOLOGY*, 2:115-131.

Nusberg, C. (1984). *INNOVATIVE AGING PROGRAMS ABROAD*. Westport, CT: The Greenwood Press.

Palmore, E. (ed.) (1980). *INTERNATIONAL HANDBOOK ON AGING*. Westport, CT: The Greenwood Press.

Palmore, E. (1987). Cross cultural perspectives on widowhood. *JOURNAL OF CROSS-CULTURAL GERONTOLOGY*, 2:93-107.

Shanas, E. et al. (1968). *OLD PEOPLE IN THREE INDUSTRIAL SOCIETIES*. New York: Atherton Press.

Siegel, J. S., & Hoover, S. L. (1982). Demographic aspects of the health of the elderly to the year 2000 and beyond. *WORLD HEALTH STATISTICS QUARTERLY*, 35:133-203.

Siegel, J. S., & Hoover, S. L. (1984). *INTERNATIONAL TRENDS AND PERSPECTIVES*: AGING. Washington, DC: Bureau of the Census.

Skeet, M. (1983). *PROTECTING THE HEALTH OF THE ELDERLY*. Copenhagen: W.H.O. Regional Office for Europe.

Thomae, H., & G. L. Maddox (eds.) (1982). *NEW PERSPECTIVES ON OLD AGE*. New York: Springer Publishing Company.

United Nations (1982). *REPORT OF THE WORLD ASSEMBLY ON AGING, VIENNA, 26 JULY 6 AUGUST, 1982*. New York: United Nations Publication, Sales No.E.82.i.16.

United Nations (1983). *VIENNA INTERNATIONAL PLAN OF ACTION ON AGING*. New York: United Nations.

United Nations (1985). *REPORT OF THE WORLD CONFERENCE TO REVIEW AND APPRAISE THE ACHIEVEMENTS OF THE UNITED NATIONS DECADE FOR WOMEN*. United Nations: A/Conf/116/28.

United Nations (1986a). *WORLD POPULATION PROSPECTS; ESTIMATES AND PROJECTIONS AS ASSESSED IN 1984*. New York: United Nations Publication, Sales No.E.86.XIII.3.

United Nations (1986b). *DEVELOPMENT OF STATISTICS OF DISABLED PERSONS: CASE STUDIES*. New York: United Nations Publication, Sales No.E.86.Xvii.17.

United Nations (1987). *GLOBAL ESTIMATES AND PROJECTIONS OF POPU-LATION BY SEX AND AGE, 1984 ASSESSMENT*. New York: Litho in United Nations ST/ESA/SER.R/70.

Ware, H. (1981). *WOMEN, DEMOGRAPHY AND DEVELOPMENT*. Canberra: Australian National University.

World Bank (1987). *FINANCING HEALTH SERVICES IN DEVELOPING COUNTRIES*. Washington, DC: The World Bank.